Brad,

Happy Holidays!

AB Burch

World Event Trading

Founded in 1807, John Wiley & Sons is the oldest independent publishing company in the United States. With offices in North America, Europe, Australia, and Asia, Wiley is globally committed to developing and marketing print and electronic products and services for our customers' professional and personal knowledge and understanding.

The Wiley Trading series features books by traders who have survived the market's ever changing temperament and have prospered—some by reinventing systems, others by getting back to basics. Whether a novice trader, professional, or somewhere in-between, these books will provide the advice and strategies needed to prosper today and well into the future.

For a list of available titles, visit our Web site at www.WileyFinance.com.

World Event Trading

How to Analyze and Profit from
Today's Headlines

ANDREW BUSCH

1807
WILEY
2007

John Wiley & Sons, Inc.

Published by John Wiley & Sons, Inc., Hoboken, New Jersey.
Published simultaneously in Canada.

Wiley Bicentennial Logo: Richard J. Pacifico.

For general information on our other products and services or for technical support, please contact our Customer Care Department within the United States at (800) 762-2974, outside the United States at (317) 572-3993 or fax (317) 572-4002.

Wiley also publishes its books in a variety of electronic formats. Some content that appears in print may not be available in electronic formats. For more information about Wiley products, visit our Web site at www.wiley.com.

Library of Congress Cataloging-in-Publication Data:

Busch, Andrew, 1961-
   World event trading: how to analyze and profit from today's headlines/Andrew Busch.
      p. cm.—(Wiley trading series)
   Includes bibliographical references and index.
   ISBN 978-0-470-10677-8 (cloth)
   1. Stock exchanges and current events   2. Investments.   3. Stock exchanges.   I. Title.
   HG4551.B87 2007
   332.64′2—dc22

                                                                    2007002384

Printed in the United States of America.

10 9 8 7 6 5 4 3 2 1

For Michelle, Samantha, Andy, Albert, Jake, and Jessie

Contents

PART III   Politics

Foreword

P estilence, natural disaster, and acts of terrorism are each unpredictable in timing, location, and scope. None, however, is unpredictable in its effect on the world's financial markets.

An immense window of profit opportunity occurs when there is liquidity and price dislocation. Traders and investors in the thick of market upheaval often are not able to seize the opportunity, simply because they do not understand what is happening. Understanding the complex relationship between a global event and the collective market psychology at the time that the event occurs is crucial.

This is the essence of world event trading (WET).

Just as markets consistently shift their collective focus in determining the drivers of price action, a successful macro trader must stand ready at all times with a variety of strategies to employ. As one weapon in that arsenal, proficiency in WET is indispensable.

In-depth knowledge of past events and how their impact was manifested in the world's financial markets is not easy to come by. It is difficult to visualize the ramifications of an unusual situation or development unless you have experienced or studied many other seemingly one-off events. Associated price movements are difficult to understand and gauge for anyone other than the very experienced market professional.

Andy changes all of this by teaching you not only what to look at, but *how* to look at it. By examining global events spanning the gamut from natural disasters to country-specific policy error, he leads the way in each instance through a complete analysis of how the markets reacted and why.

Drawing upon his 20 years as a currency trader, as an analyst, and as an author, Andy takes you through many of the seminal events of the past five centuries and dissects each event and the markets' reaction to it. The result is a virtual road map, with detailed explanations of how real-world financial markets behave under duress.

What follows is a must read for traders, academics, policy makers, and students of markets everywhere.

BILL LIPSCHUTZ
Principal and Director of Portfolio Management
Hathersage Capital Management LLC

About the Author

Andrew B. Busch is a Director and Global Foreign Exchange Strategist of BMO Capital Markets in Chicago. Previously, he was the top currency trader for Northern Trust and Harris Bank. He advises the White House, the U.S. Treasury, and members of Congress on the financial markets. He writes a daily politics and money piece entitled the Busch Update. He writes a weekly column for the *Globe and Mail*, Canada's leading business newspaper. For the past two years, Busch has appeared every Friday on CNBC's *Closing Bell* with Maria Bartiromo. Also, he appears regularly on television and as a speaker at investment conferences in North America and abroad.

Acknowledgments

I've traded the currency markets since 1984 and have been writing a daily piece for BMO Financial Group since 1999. Through these years, I have learned volumes through contact with colleagues, clients, and government officials.

There are several people I'd like to thank for their advice and assistance. I'd like to thank my colleagues at BMO Capital Markets for affording me the time and space necessary to complete this endeavor. I'd like to thank Jamie Thorsen, Debbie Rechter, Tim Shroyer, and Sharla Stachurski, who supported and encouraged me to write this book. I'd like to thank John McAuliffe, Susan Senturia, Babbette Crawford, Irene Poblete, and Geethan Rayan, who provided advice and some key technical assistance.

I'd like to thank Dan Steinberg for his assistance with some of the more arcane areas of equities. I'd like to thank Scott Christiansen for his knowledge and skills in the world of media. To Boris Schlossberg and Kathy Lien for their help with getting the idea for the book in front of the right publisher and for pushing me to write it.

I'd like to thank my editors, Marty Cej and Dave Pyette, at the *Globe and Mail* for encouraging me to write a weekly column on economics, politics, and the financial markets.

I'd like to thank former U.S. Treasury Secretary John Snow, former U.S. Undersecretary Rob Nichols, former U.S. Undersecretary Pam Olsen, Undersecretary Jim Carter, U.S. Undersecretary for International Affairs Tim Adams, White House economic spokesman Tony Fratto, and Chairman of the Council of Economic Advisers Ed Lazear for educating me on how Washington works and interacts with Wall Street. As I like to say in speeches, there is something shocking about the people who run the top agencies of government: They are very, very, very smart. Also, I'd like to thank my friend Greg Valliere for his insights into D.C. and for appearing with me on CNBC.

I'd like to thank the amazing library systems in the state of Illinois, including Downers Grove, Hinsdale, and Clarendon Hills. The people who work for them are just great and ever so helpful. It's astonishing how much information can be drawn upon from these institutions. In this vein, the U.S. federal governmental agencies will surprise anyone who decides to continue to research the areas mentioned in this book. They are fountains of information and knowledge that is critical for research.

Finally, I would like to acknowledge the encouragement, patience, and inspiration from my wife Michelle and our five children as I went AWOL to research and write this book.

A. B.

Introduction

There's an old joke on Wall Street. Invest in the markets and you'll sleep like a baby: You'll wake up every two hours crying. Follow the news and you'll see why. How will a tropical depression brewing in the Caribbean affect oil refining in the Gulf Coast? Could a spike in oil prices hurt stocks? Could a change in leadership in Congress alter America's careful diplomacy with China on trade? Are currency markets anticipating legislation to slap tariffs on Chinese imported goods? A Latin American socialist strongman moves to nationalize a telecommunications company whose investors are listed on the New York Stock Exchange. Said strongman also happens to be the United States' fourth largest oil supplier. Never before have markets, geopolitics, and the news media been more closely connected. A century and a half ago, Julius Reuter used carrier pigeons to send days-old headlines to information-hungry investors in Europe. Today, we watch a killer storm develop minute by minute off the coast of Africa, and traders place bets for oil and natural gas production in the Gulf of Mexico.

Consider 2005, when lazy, quiet summer markets gave way to what would prove to be an incredibly active hurricane season. Hurricane Katrina crossed Southern Florida and, instead of weakening, picked up speed, churning through the warm waters of the Gulf of Mexico and barreling toward the oil-refining heart of America. New Orleans port warehouses were loaded with everything from bananas to frozen chicken to corn to manufactured wood panels. What started as an unnamed speck on the radar turned out to be a tragic loss of life and a stunning failure in federal emergency response: an American port city crippled, tens of thousands of people stranded, the American economy disrupted. At least 100 barges were submerged in the lower reaches of the Mississippi River, and half the world's zinc supplies were unreachable in swamped port warehouses. Nearly every industry felt the disruption, and the world's last superpower suffered a severe blow to its reputation. But a little more than a year later, U.S. stocks were again near record highs, shrugging off a costly war in Iraq, a change in leadership in Washington, and high oil prices—a testament to the resiliency of American markets.

But the fact is, future natural disasters will likely have an even greater impact on the economy and markets. Building in coastal areas continues apace, and Americans continue to live dangerously. The Census Bureau says 87 million Americans live within striking distance of an Atlantic season hurricane. That's almost 30 percent of our population. The 50,000 square coastal miles from Louisiana to the Florida Keys are three and a half times more populous today than in 1950, making evacuation more difficult and property damage more likely and more severe, with implications for every market from insurance rates to corn futures to stocks.

The great paradox of markets is that past performance is no guarantee of future results, but history tends to repeat itself. And with time, our perception of risk diminishes. Already the news cycle has moved on from hurricanes. But there will be another deadly natural disaster. Just as there will be another flu pandemic, and reporters and market analysts will scramble for comparisons to 1918, the last major worldwide flu outbreak. Mother Nature is perhaps the most unpredictable challenge for markets. But then there is perhaps the most dangerous risk to markets: human intervention. On this, I have relied on Andy Busch for expert analysis for more than a decade. He reads the tea leaves of international markets with a keen understanding that past is prologue and humans have short memories.

From Washington power politics to the war in Iraq to global trade imbalances, Andy has an extraordinary ability to instantly understand how they all are interrelated and all affect markets. I have quoted him over the years perhaps a hundred times, and his insight makes any market story better. He sees the whole picture, and, as you'll see in the pages ahead, explains complicated market phenomena with sharp insight and humor.

CHRISTINE ROMANS
CNN Correspondent

PART I

Infectious Diseases

CHAPTER 1

The Black Plague: A Paradigm for Today

We begin this book on world event trading by going back into the past and setting our time travel device for the beginning of the fourteenth century. This may appear to be a strange place to start, but we go back to show that diseases have consistency over time. The types of diseases may change, but their core characteristics and how they influence society remain consistent.

The bubonic plague, or Black Death, is going to be our base case for many of the diseases that tear through the population today. Therefore, to understand an outbreak and its impact on the world, you must know the state of civilization and the nature of the disease. Keep in mind that the basic rules of supply and demand still worked even back then and will guide us in understanding disruptions to the markets. It's these disruptions or anomalies that generate the opportunities.

By the way, we still have outbreaks of the plague today. At the end of the chapter, we review an outbreak that occurred in 1994.

IT WAS CALLED THE DARK AGES FOR A REASON

Clearly, the fourteenth century was a gloomy time for people throughout the world, especially for those unfortunate enough to be living in medieval Europe. Daily life was a struggle, and it was about to get worse. Economic conditions fluctuated wildly, with surges of inflation occurring whenever large deposits of gold or silver were found.

To counter this, governments attempted to impose price controls, but were opposed by the powerful landowners or feudal lords. As landowners raised rents to counteract the price controls, farmers were forced to increase planted acreage and farm productivity dropped as poorer land was worked and yielded less. As populations grew and more workers appeared, wages fell with the additional labor supply. From the small city-states of Italy to the large kingdoms of England and France, fiscal problems increased and bankruptcy was constantly on the horizon. David Hackett Fischer describes the situation this way in *The Great Wave*: "Great kingdoms and small city-states teetered on the edge of bankruptcy. They struggled to survive by borrowing heavily at ruinous rates of interest, and by debasing their money, thereby introducing powerful instabilities into the price system of Western Europe."

And then things really started to deteriorate. This is a common characteristic throughout disease outbreaks over time: When the area is the most stressed is usually when the outbreak can cause the most mischief and death. The medieval world would soon be severely stressed and hungry as well.

THE GREAT FAMINE OF 1314–1316

In the 1300s, farming was the most critical industry for society. The society that could successfully produce food could successfully have division of labor. Division of labor can lead to a more stable society and rapid technological progress. Unfortunately, in early 1314 in Europe it began to rain hard and it didn't seem to let up until 1317. This weather ruined the crops for three years in a row and caused widespread hunger.

This underscores the insular nature of the economies at this time. There was no world market from which to import grain or foodstuffs to offset the localized production problem. People were highly dependent on what was happening in their region. This is precisely why international trade and trade development were critical at this time and remain so today. World trade helps smooth out supply disruptions and price volatility. (Developed and fully functional international financial markets were not in existence to help hedge the underlying risks, either.) Without international trade, disasters can happen when nature intervenes.

According to Fischer, stormy weather lashed the continent for months. Dikes collapsed in England and the Low Countries. Entire fields washed away in France. Villages were destroyed by rising rivers in Germany. Once again grain and fodder crops failed. This was not merely a set of local shortages. It was, in the worlds of historian Henry Lucas, "a universal failure of crops in 1315 . . . from the Pyrenees to Slavic regions, from Scotland to Italy." The rains caused rivers to jump their banks, dams to break, and entire towns to be washed away. The rains flooded farmland and took away critical acreage for planting.

Sadly, this was occurring through most of Europe and brought about a major drop in food supply. Humans weren't the only ones impacted, as animals couldn't be fed and therefore couldn't be raised. Prices for poultry and livestock went up dramatically in addition to grain prices. Governments got involved early with precisely the wrong policy, which would make matters worse. This is another common theme in outbreaks: Governments initially do the wrong thing at the critical time to further accelerate the outbreak or compound the economic problems. The English Parliament asked King Edward II in 1314 to impose price controls to stem the rapid rise in the cost of food. As we now know, limiting the price of a commodity usually means that less of that commodity will be produced. The price controls of the 1970s in the United States are a nice modern example of this concept in action.

In 1315, the famine was in full swing as peasants struggled to survive and ate anything available, even cats, rats, reptiles, and insects. In 1316 when these ran out, they turned into cannibals. They ate the newly dead and the not so newly dead, going so far as to dig up bodies from burial grounds and cut down criminals from the gallows to eat. For a world that was already unstable, the famine proved to be devastating. It is estimated that 10 percent of the population died during this period.

BLACK DEATH

As if things weren't bad enough, wars broke out in clusters among France, England, Scotland, Germany, and other small city-states, further weakening the population and food supply. The wars wrought additional human and economic devastation.

During one war in 1346, the Genoese town of Caffa was being besieged by a Tartar army. Caffa was a walled city and the Tartars were making little headway in their attempt to take it over. Even worse for the invaders, some of them were stricken with an unusual disease that made their tongues turn white and their skin turn black.

Bubonic plague is the medical term, but it is known as the Black Death. It still exists today, and the name is somewhat of a euphemism. The following sections, taken from the Centers for Disease Control and Prevention web site (CDC, www.cdc.gov/ncidod/dvbid/plague/info.htm), describe it in greater detail. I realize this may seem odd to have a detailed description of a disease in a book on trading. However, over the years I have learned that

you can only construct a winning strategy if you fully understand the nature
of the disease.

General

Plague, caused by a bacterium called Yersinia pestis, *is transmitted
from rodent to rodent by infected fleas.*

*Plague is characterized by periodic disease outbreaks in rodent
populations, some of which have a high death rate. During these outbreaks, hungry infected fleas that have lost their normal hosts seek
other sources of blood, thus increasing the risk to humans and other
animals frequenting the area.*

*Epidemics of plague in humans usually involve house rats and
their fleas. . . . Domestic cats (and sometimes dogs) are readily infected by fleas or from eating infected wild rodents. Cats may serve
as a source of infection to persons exposed to them. Pets may also
bring plague-infected fleas into the home.*

How Is Plague Transmitted?

*Plague is transmitted from animal to animal and from animal to
human by the bites of infective fleas. Less frequently, the organism
enters through a break in the skin by direct contact with tissue or
body fluids of a plague-infected animal, for instance, in the process
of skinning a rabbit or other animal. Plague is also transmitted by
inhaling infected droplets expelled by coughing, by a person or animal, especially domestic cats, with pneumonic plague. Transmission
of plague from person to person is uncommon and has not been observed in the United States since 1924 but does occur as an important
factor in plague epidemics in some developing countries.*

Diagnosis

*The pathognomic sign of plague is a very painful, usually swollen,
and often hot-to-the-touch lymph node, called a bubo. This finding,
accompanied with fever, extreme exhaustion, and a history of possible exposure to rodents, rodent fleas, wild rabbits, or sick or dead
carnivores, should lead to suspicion of plague.*

*Onset of bubonic plague is usually two to six days after a person
is exposed. Initial manifestations include fever, headache, and general illness, followed by the development of painful, swollen regional
lymph nodes. [**My note: This is an important point, as fever can
act as an early warning indicator for bubonic plague. SARS***

has similar characteristics, and therefore the ability to quarantine people with high fever was a contributing factor toward ending the SARS outbreak. Influenza does not have this short incubation period, nor does it show itself via the high fever.] Occasionally, buboes cannot be detected for a day or so after the onset of other symptoms. The disease progresses rapidly and the bacteria can invade the bloodstream, producing severe illness, called plague septicemia.

Once a human is infected, a progressive and potentially fatal illness generally results unless specific antibiotic therapy is given. Progression leads to blood infection and, finally, to lung infection. The infection of the lung is termed plague pneumonia, and it can be transmitted to others through the expulsion of infective respiratory droplets by coughing.

The incubation period of primary pneumonic plague is one to three days and is characterized by development of an overwhelming pneumonia with high fever, cough, bloody sputum, and chills. For plague pneumonia patients, the death rate is over 50 percent.

Treatment Information

As soon as a diagnosis of suspected plague is made, the patient should be isolated, and local and state health departments should be notified. Confirmatory laboratory work should be initiated, including blood cultures and examination of lymph node specimens if possible. Drug therapy should begin as soon as possible after the laboratory specimens are taken. The drugs of choice are streptomycin or gentamycin, but a number of other antibiotics are also effective.

Those individuals closely associated with the patient, particularly in cases with pneumonia, should be traced, identified, and evaluated. Contacts of pneumonic plague patients should be placed under observation or given preventive antibiotic therapy, depending on the degree and timing of contact.

Preventive Drug Therapy

Antibiotics may be taken in the event of exposure to the bites of wild rodent fleas during an outbreak or to the tissues or fluids of a plague-infected animal.

Here are some quick comments on this description by the CDC and why it's important to include this information in the book. Note the high death incidence or mortality rate of those infected with the plague who contract pneumonia: 50 percent die today. The rate for the medieval period must have been closer to 100 percent, as there were no medicines (antibiotics) available at that time to help. The swelling of the lymph nodes around the neck and armpits were bluish-blackish in color and gave rise to the name the Black Death. As you'll see in the next chapter, pneumonia is the true killer associated with plague or influenza after the initial infection weakens the body's immune system.

One last point: Try to put yourself in the shoes of a peasant at this time. Imagine you encounter someone who is infected and has the black swellings around the neck and armpits. It must have been a terrifying sight, and the first response would be to run. Your next response would be to avoid going anywhere that you may encounter those who have the plague. This mind-set is important for understanding the impact on society and the economy.

WINNING THE BATTLE, LOSING THE WAR

Getting back to the war, the frustrated Tartars did something truly innovative. They gathered up a few of their dead, loaded them into the catapult, and tossed them over the wall into Caffa. This was one of the first recorded uses of germs as a weapon and it worked well—a little too well. As the disease spread and killed, Caffa was abandoned and the inhabitants fled in their ships. The Tartars had won battle, but the world was about to lose the war as this siege and diaspora helped begin the spread of the Black Death. This is another common development that occurs with most outbreaks: The population attempts to flee the infected area and ends up spreading the disease wherever they go.

The bubonic plague or bubo rapidly spread throughout the trading routes from Genoa. In 1347, it spread to Sicily, Sardinia, Corsica, Africa, and elsewhere in Europe. By January 1348, it had entered Venice and Marseilles. In December, it reached England. Scotland and Scandinavia were hit the following year.

The disease was remarkably efficient in its ability to spread and kill. One bite from either the infected fleas that lived on the rats or the rats themselves could prove deadly. The plague was also quite democratic as it killed children, parents, the old, the young, and animals. One of the problems was that family pets like cats and dogs were equally affected and helped bring the disease into the home. This efficient disease distribution was catastrophic to a population already under duress from famine. Population data from villages in England showed dramatic drops in numbers of men between the ages of 18 and 25.

Today, it's hard to comprehend the full psychological impact this series of events had on individuals and society at that time. The Black Death fundamentally altered the social fabric of society all the way down to the most basic components. It shredded it. When family members became infected, they were often abandoned—in the home. The other family members would flee and leave everything behind. Many of those afflicted died of starvation. Not that they were doing any good anyway, but physicians weren't readily available because most of them had died from the disease. The ones who did survive charged heavily for a visit. Therefore, even back in medieval times, a house call by a doctor was expensive. In desperation, people turned to the church for guidance, hope, and burials.

GRIM REAPER WINNERS AND LOSERS

For the financial markets, here's where things get interesting. Population numbers from back then were imprecise. However, historians estimate that Europe lost between 25 and 40 percent of its inhabitants to the disease. This depopulation created peculiar crosscurrents in prices that swirled around death. Any servants, including priests and friars, agreeing to take care of the ill saw their wages rise significantly. Obviously, the funeral business boomed as long as there were people willing to get close to the bodies. Merchants selling burial cloths and spices also did well.

Due to the worries over contracting the disease, people stopped frequenting certain public meeting places like markets, inns, and taverns. However, churches and apothecaries remained open and flourished. Hope was big business. Another oddity of the time: strictly enforced noise ordinances. Churches were discouraged from ringing bells for funerals and they were prohibited from crying out announcements of the dead. Since these were occurring frequently, the bells and town criers were a constant reminder of death and had a depressing effect on the townspeople.

Due to the Great Famine and price controls, the price of food was still rising rapidly during the early epidemic years. Then the Black Death kicked in and the massive die-off of the human race began. This was where things got weird. As the population declined, the demand for food declined, and the supply of labor declined as well. This had the simultaneous effects of prices declining for foodstuffs, but rising for services of artisans and craftsmen. To help the modern reader relate, it was like trying to find a contractor to do an addition on your home during the U.S. real estate construction boom of 2002 to 2005. If you could locate one that was available, that contractor was very expensive, was not likely to do quality work, and played golf every Wednesday.

What's interesting is that these medieval contractors pretty quickly figured out they were the only game in town. Unions weren't around at the time, but this didn't stop them from going on strike and demanding higher wages. They understood the laws of supply and demand on price. There weren't many of them left to do the work, the rest of society needed them to do the skilled labor, and therefore the price for their work had to go up. Just when things looked like they couldn't get worse, local governments attempted to limit trade and worker movements between cities. This is a perfect example of why the statement "We're the government and we're here to help" strikes terror into most free marketers. The actions were precisely the wrong policy; they hampered trade and exacerbated the wage inflation already in process.

At this time, banking systems were put under severe stress as both the king of England and the king of France defaulted on their debts. In *A History of Interest Rates*, Sidney Homer and Richard Sylla explain that this default generated new financial regulations and reforms. As an example, Venetian banks were prohibited from speculating in commodities and were required to hold their assets in safer instruments like public debt. Subsequently, interest rates for loans to princes rose, with some borrowing at 80 percent and others pawning their gold coronets for a loan of 50 percent of their value.

Personal loans saw similar high rates. The odd contradiction was that commercial loans had started the century at rates of 15 to 20 percent and declined by the end of the century to 5 percent. This may have been due to an overall drop in economic activity and therefore a drop in demand for money in commerce.

YOU CAN'T TAKE IT WITH YOU, UNLESS...

Clearly, the best trade available at this time was to stay alive. If you pulled that off, you were either very lucky or already very wealthy and could hire people to take care of you should you fall ill. Without question, the fourteenth century was limited in financial instruments to trade at that time. However, there are some broad areas of investment that would have done quite well.

Obviously, any business related to death was fantastic. From selling the cloth for shrouds, to making special clothes for mourning, to selling spices and candles for funerals, merchants who engaged in these businesses made handsome profits. Home health care providers were big winners, if they could stay alive. As the population decreased, the peasants or laborers saw their wages rise, and the selling prices of the goods and services they produced rose as well. The trick was finding enough workers to produce the goods.

Also, it was a good idea to avoid making loans or buying debt from anyone who was dependent on the population for revenue, such as kings. Why did the gilded class have problems? As the populations fell, so did the tax base for the kingdoms of France and England. Without a change in their spending habits, these kingdoms eventually defaulted on their loans and wiped out some banks in Italy. Also, loans based on real estate values were not a good investment, as demand dropped for farmland with the decline in population.

Last, trading in commodities was hot. Unfortunately, there weren't many financial products at the time to buy or sell to take advantage of the price swings. During the Great Famine, prices rose dramatically even through the initial years of the Black Death. Then they fell rather crisply as the population decreased and demand fell. During the same time frame, metals trading would have been interesting as well. Gold and silver production had reached a peak early in the century and contributed to the rise in inflation. Subsequently, production fell off with the loss of population (labor) and contributed to the drop in prices. Although coins were debased from time to time, gold and silver were essentially a nation's money supply during this time frame. If the supply of gold and siver rose, business activity rose, as did inflation. If the supply fell, the opposite occurred.

The bubonic plague pandemic was an event of truly catastrophic death and social change. In essence, the awesome killing power of the disease brought this period in history to an end and almost caused the collapse of medieval Europe. However, it is an excellent paradigm or structure by which we can learn how to view the subsequent infectious diseases that impacted our world. As you will see in subsequent chapters, there were themes back then that would remain consistent over time with disease outbreaks.

First, diseases generally break out at the worst time for a population when it is either unprepared or stressed or poor. It's usually a combination of two out of the three.

Second, the population will attempt to leave the infected area, and in the process it spreads the disease. This is why quarantines are most likely an exercise in futility at first as panic to flee sets in quickly and the disease is distributed before a quarantine can be imposed. Keep this in mind when we discuss severe acute respiratory syndrome (SARS) and bird flu.

Finally, the government pursues policies that initially make things worse from either a disease standpoint or an economic standpoint. Hurricane Katrina, the Superdome, and FEMA quickly comes to mind as a modern-day examples.

CASE STUDY: 1994 RODENT RAIN

For those of you questioning the relevancy of the plague in today's modern world, let's travel to India in August of 1994. The Surat and Beed district pneumonic plague outbreak is almost too perfect an example of how not to handle the initial outbreak of an infectious disease. It's estimated that the outbreak cost India $600 million at a time before the Indian economy could handle such a setback. The economic areas impacted were the usual suspects: tourism, international travel, and exports. It got so bad that the United Arab Emirates was reported to have cut off postal links with India out of fear that the plague would spread via mail.

It is also eerie how the conditions prior to the outbreak mimic what was occurring in the fourteenth century. According to Indian government officials at the time, only 13 percent of India's 900 million people had access to proper sanitation and only 60 percent of the garbage generated each day in India's three largest cities was picked up. The population was under duress or stress from the earthquake that had occurred in September 1993. In the Indian state of Maharashtra between 10,000 and 20,000 people died from the earthquake. The reason for the wide range in estimated loss of life is that many of those who died were very poor and the number of deaths of the poor are only estimated in India. Unfortunately, many of these dead were not buried properly, which provided an ample source of food for rats.

At that time in the neighboring state of Gujarat, many of Surat's 1.5 million inhabitants lived outside the city limits in squalid shantytowns, according to Judith B. Tysmans in her article "Plague in India 1994—Conditions, Containment, Goals":

> The conditions of these slums in August 1994 were typical of shanty-towns all over India: Open sewers, tightly clustered shelters made of cement or plastic sheets, rotting animal carcasses, heaps of garbage, and pools of stagnant water filled the alleys. Floods in early August heightened the horror as the human waste and refuse, mixed with slush and mud, were washed up and left on the riverbank, creating ideal conditions for the spread of infection. Cows, dogs, and pigs stand on top of high piles of garbage while people sell vegetables from rickety wooden carts alongside; rats thrive in such a setting.

Now, that's what I call stress.

The local authorities did get an early warning sign, but for some reason chose to ignore it. The sign goes by the wonderful name "rat fall," which is derived from rats falling from rafters and dying on the floor. Take a moment and visualize this. Okay, got it? This is what was occurring in Mamala village in Maharashtra in mid-August. In "Learning from Plague in India," T. Jacob John describes the situation:

> *There are in fact two epidemics, both in the mid-western region [of India]. The first was in the Beed district of Maharashtra State beginning in August and the second in Surat in Gujarat State in September, 500 km away. Whether the epidemics are linked epidemiologically is unknown. However, the key point is that they progressed undetected and unchecked mainly because of the lack of epidemiological alertness, skill, and interventions. For example, although the warning signs of rat fall in Mamala village, Beed district, were clearly apparent by mid-August, no investigations seem to have been conducted. . . . By mid-September, 10 percent of the village population had developed bubonic plague.*

This is something we'll see over time with infectious disease outbreaks: governments initially unable or unwilling to act to prevent the spread of the disease.

The government's inaction or inability to deal with this outbreak created fear among the population inside and outside the country. The lack of accurate information regarding the outbreak caused the population in those areas affected to panic and leave the areas. This movement ultimately spread the disease and caused a spike in the morbidity and mortality rates.

Why did this occur? According to Judith B. Tysmans,

> *A financial reason for minimizing the incidence and severity of plague was the location of factories (Surat is India's diamond-cutting and silk-production center) in the area of the slums. The "cordon sanitaire" sealing the epidemic off from the rest of the city would have prevented workers getting to the factory, cutting off their income, as well as slowing production.*
>
> *One major political reason for making efforts to deny the outbreak was the holiday season to begin only one month hence, with much visiting of family members from other countries, as well as large conferences with international guests invited to present papers and draw thousands of international tourists. Tourism is one of India's major financial businesses. India had much to lose by allowing news of a plague epidemic to reach the international press.*

As you'll see in Chapter 4 (SARS), China had a similar dilemma in 2003.

Now we get to the crux of the problem: poor information, poor sanitary conditions in the hospitals, and poor people dying of the disease. Insufficient coordination among health care officials and institutions meant that the World Health Organization guidelines for dealing with the plague were either ignored or not enacted properly. This meant specifically that a quarantine was neither set up properly nor enforced properly. Patients with the disease were not tracked, nor were the family members with whom they had contact. The disease would spread and not be contained, and once the outbreak was known to the public, the public panicked and spread the disease further. It has been estimated that 25 percent of the 1.5 million people fled the area.

And Indians weren't the only ones panicking. From Russia to the United States, tour agencies canceled their Indian itineraries. The *Washington Post* reported, "'Once Delhi and Bombay got the plague cases, then everybody reacted,' said a spokesman for the Indian Association of Tour Operators. 'The setback to tourism because of the plague could be worse than it was after Ayodhya [the communal riots] and the Bombay blasts.'"

Worse yet, several countries put restrictions on travelers from India, with Moscow imposing a six-day quarantine for all visitors from India and banning all travel to the country. Estimates for business losses for the city of Surat alone were over US$260 million. When the BBC and CNN media agencies reported on the plague situation, global depositary receipts (GDRs) fell for Indian companies. Locally, agricultural exporters saw their share prices tumble as foreign countries not only denied receiving Indian exports, but some also closed their borders. As mentioned, the plague cost the Indian economy over $600 million.

All this occurred over 56 deaths. This is the point: Fear and panic caused the bigger problems for the financial markets and economy rather than the actual disease.

All three of our disease themes are present and accounted for in this event. Also, the Surat outbreak demonstrates that major modern diseases appear to emanate from poorer areas of the world that have close, prolonged proximity between animals and humans. (Prior to Caffa, the bubonic plague's genesis has been thought by historians to have occurred somewhere in the Far East.) Therefore, along with quarantine, part of the solution to the outbreak is usually the destruction of those animals seen to be carriers of the disease. In the Surat plague, it was the killing of rats. In the China and Hong Kong SARS outbreak, it will be civet cats. In H5N1 bird flu, it will be waterfowl and chickens.

CHAPTER 2

1918 Spanish Flu

T he year began with a world that had been at war for four years and would close with the end of the hostilities. The European powers were engaged in a conflict that would shock even the most battle-hardened veterans as to its length and human devastation. American military commanders were preparing to send massive amounts of troops from the United States into battle, and these would prove to be a key determinant of the war's end. U.S. President Woodrow Wilson would start the year issuing a 14-point peace program setting out a standard for a democratic, liberal ideology for a postwar world. For the first time ever, Russia would experience democratic lawmaking and rule. It would end within 24 hours.

World War I would see the Allied forces lose more than five million men and the Central forces lose three and a half million from the conflict. The decade would be one of the most tumultuous of the twentieth century, and the political mistakes made during it would continue to influence society for another 50 years.

Yet, there were many great advances made at this time in medicine, politics, business, and finance. The medical profession in the United States took giant steps to increase the skills of physicians and to unify the study of the discipline. Prior to 1900, many medical schools only required a high school diploma for admission. The use of the microscope would greatly aid in the eventual discovery of cures for diseases that killed thousands.

In politics, the League of Nations, precursor to the United Nations, was formed, only to fail. The Federal Reserve Act of 1913 created a central bank in the United States and 12 district banks throughout the country. In business, Ford Motor Company introduced the world's first moving production line for the Model T.

In this chapter, we tackle the impact on society and the financial markets of a virus that killed four to five times more people throughout the globe than World War I. The Spanish flu (influenza strain of H1N1) had much in common with the carnage of the Great War. It killed with a lethality that resembled a bullet to the chest, with some victims literally dropping dead on the streets. It generated panic and drove many to search out God for comfort, in a way similar to what occurred during the Black Death. It also drove advances in medicine and public health. The difficulty with understanding its impact is that there were two major conflicts occurring simultaneously: a war of man against man and a war of nature against man.

INFLUENZA: PERVASIVE, PERSISTENT, AND DEADLY

There are major differences between bubonic plague, SARS, and influenza. For the purposes of this discussion, the most important one is that influenza viruses are airborne, whereas bubonic plague and SARS are droplet-borne. This means that influenza can spread more readily than SARS, which requires close contact.

SARS also has one defining characteristic for signaling when someone has contracted it: fever. Fever checkpoints in airports helped officials discern who had the disease and to isolate them. Infected influenza patients don't present with fever symptoms when they are infectious themselves. This eliminates the opportunity for quarantine before they come in contact with others.

Finally, influenza has a two-to-three-day incubation period and therefore gives authorities no time to trace contacts and set up quarantines. Airborne transmission, no symptoms when infectious, and a short incubation period mean that influenza can spread extremely rapidly when unleashed.

Most of us have had the common cold. A few of us have had the more unpleasant experience of the influenza. The flu attacks the respiratory system in the human body. Victims usually recover in 8 to 10 days. The symptoms are a cough, runny nose, sneezing, fever, headaches, and body aches. It is a virus and therefore antibiotics don't work on it. Prevention is similar to that for measles; you need to get inoculated at the beginning of every flu season with a low dose of the virus. As you'll see, there's a reason why the inoculations are a hit-or-miss strategy.

Influenza, human immunodeficiency virus (HIV), and SARS all have similar genetic structures that make them particularly difficult to deal with.

Influenza is highly efficient at infecting a victim and is amazingly reproductive. As a matter of fact, it's too productive in reproducing and does it so fast that it makes mistakes. These mistakes or mutations are a key component as to why these types of viruses are so difficult to handle and why an inoculation against one influenza may not protect from a mutant that comes along later in the season. Sometimes the mutations are weaker, which lessens the symptoms of those infected. Sometimes it's the opposite. Influenza is similar to the measles in another way: Once a victim has experienced a particular strain, the body develops immunity to it and can ward it off should it be encountered again.

One of the cruel ironies of the 1918 flu was that it didn't just occur in 1918, but had a round of attacks that extended into 1919. The first round was lethal. Unfortunately, the second round was even worse as the mutation became more viral in its ability to attack a victim and cause death. If severe enough, the virus weakens the immune system enough to allow other bacteria to enter the body and attack. This is why pneumonia accompanies influenza and can kill. The U.S. Centers for Disease Control and Prevention today estimates that over 36,000 people a year die of such complications arising from the influenza/pneumonia partnership. At the start of 1918, none of this was known.

Here is one more piece of disturbing information for the modern reader: Recent pathology tests have led scientists to believe that the 1918 strain of flu was an avian virus. This means it has a similar structure to today's H5N1 virus or bird flu.

THE SPANISH FLU: A TWENTIETH-CENTURY TRAGEDY

One of the first outbreaks of the influenza in the United States started in the small town of Haskell, Kansas. From there, several citizens traveled to Camp Funston in Kansas, which was the second largest cantonment in the country. On average, Funston contained 56,000 young troops. It was a perfect environment for the spread of influenza throughout the United States and the world. In *The Great Influenza*, John M. Barry describes the speed of the virus:

> *Only a trickle of people moved back and forth between Haskell and Funston, but a river of soldiers moved between Funston, other army bases, and France. Two weeks after the first case at Funston, on March 18, influenza surfaced at both Camps Forrest and Greenleaf in Georgia; 10 percent of the forces at both camps would report sick. Then,*

*like falling dominoes, other camps erupted with influenza. In total,
24 of the 36 largest army camps experienced an influenza outbreak
that spring. Thirty-four of the 50 largest cities in the country, most of
them adjacent to the military facilities, also suffered an April spike
in "excess mortality" from influenza, although that did not become
clear except in hindsight.*

This should remind you of what happened during the siege of the Genoese town of Caffa during the Black Death outbreak. Members of the population contracted the disease and then spread it through travel to the wider
population. This disease dispersion is common during most outbreaks and
normally occurs when the population panics and attempts to flee the areas
infected (India in 1994). In 1918, the spread was not by a disorderly flight,
but by an organized movement of soldiers across the world.

The best way to stop influenza from becoming a pandemic is to limit
exposure of those who have the disease to those who don't. The victims are
infectious for only the first five to seven days. A quarantine of that length of
time for those infected proved to be effective in stopping the transmission of
the virus. Today, this is one of the reasons that companies are encouraging
their employees to stay home should they feel the first symptoms of influenza
lest they come to work and infect others.

Sadly, the United States had just joined the war and was racing men
to Europe to head off the major 1918 German offensive. Time was of the
essence, as the British and French troops were nearly split in two and the
U.S. reinforcements were critical. The United States sent 84,000 troops in
March and another 118,000 in April. Therefore, any quarantine was almost
impossible to impose at the time and the disease spread in waves across the
country and the world. The outbreak was more acute due to the encamp-
ments of soldiers in close proximity to each other. With all the preparations
for war going on, the virus was not initially considered very important or
particularly life-threatening. It wasn't until the outbreaks at Camp Devens
near Boston that the military woke up and realized it had a major problem.

The camp was built in 1917 to house 35,000 soldiers. However, in
September 1918, it had over 46,000 in the camp and was a tinderbox ready
for the virus. On September 7, one soldier was sent to the infirmary with
symptoms diagnosed as meningitis. Within 24 hours, 12 more men would
be sent with the same diagnosis. Before the end of the month, almost 20
percent of the troops were listed on a sick report, with 1,543 in one day.
Seventy-five percent were hospitalized, according to Barry.

By the time the top U.S. medical official, Dr. William H. Welch, ar-
rived at Camp Devens on September 23, 12,604 influenza cases had been
reported and 66 men had died. By October, 17,000 would contract it and 780
would die.

Clearly, the speed and incidence of death among the healthiest members of society was troubling. Normally, influenza kills the very young or the very old. However, in this outbreak, the influenza killed in a bizarre W pattern. Starting with the deaths of the very young (0–9 years), the incidence dropped for those aged 10–19 years, spiked for those 20–29, then fell again; it rose for the age 60 and above crowd. (The graph on page 24 of *America's Forgotten Pandemic* by Alfred W. Crosby shows the strange W shape of the virus in the population.) In Louisville, Kentucky, 40 percent of those who died were between the ages of 20 and 35.

This virus had one more skill: It could kill within days of infection. Since the incubation period was two to three days, some victims contracted the flu/pneumonia and died within 48 hours. The victims' lungs would be literally torn apart from coughing and their skin color would turn blue due to the lack of oxygen—another dark reminder of the Black Death.

THINNING OF THE WORLDWIDE HERD

Just as in the Black Death, one of the major impacts on society was the change in the number of people in it. The U.S. population had increased steadily from the turn of the century as the nation drew in immigrants. World War I would cause catastrophic loss of life in Germany (1.8 million), Russia (1.7 million), France (1.4 million), and Britain (.947 million). However, the United States entered the war late and incurred losses of only 48,909 men in action. The 1918–1919 influenza outbreak killed an estimated 675,000 people in the United States or roughly 7 percent of the population. Worldwide, conservative estimates have the number of those who died at 30 million. Others have it as high as 100 million. In a world population of only 1.8 billion, these were frightening numbers.

Again, it was a major accomplishment to remain alive. Estimates of the death totals were skewed to the downside due to poor understanding of the combination of influenza and pneumonia as well as the extremely tight control of the press during wartime. However, it is now estimated that the morbidity rate (percentage of people exposed to a virus who contract the virus) was 25 percent. The mortality rate was only 2.5 to 5 percent. This lack of information and high morbidity rate helped create some of the fear that infused the public during the outbreak. It is believed that the 1918 outbreak got its name the Spanish flu because Spain was neutral during the war and the Spanish press had more freedom to report on the outbreaks. The newspapers were filled with reports on the outbreak, especially when Spanish King Alphonse XIII contracted the disease.

Fear would be a major driver of society and changes in behavior due to the outbreak. Developments similar to those during the Black Death ensued, and eliminating exposure to the virus was the key to survival. People avoided contact with other people. Public health departments issued campaigns against coughing, sneezing, and spitting. Public meetings, public gatherings, parades, schools, saloons, churches, theaters, and other places of public amusement were banned or closed in most of the cities during this time. Streets were abandoned during the hysteria. Public transportation companies were hurt as the population stayed off the streets and ridership collapsed.

SUCCESSFUL TRADES/BUSINESSES

During this time, it's pretty clear that all of these businesses lost money due to the shutdowns. The transportation, hotel, retail, travel, and entertainment sectors all suffered from lack of patrons. Clearly hospitals and health care were big winners. Hospitals were desperately looking for workers to replace those who either didn't show up or had died from the virus. There was a frantic expansion of hospital facilities during this time as the industry tried to keep up with the demand. This exacerbated the shortage of nurses, orderlies, and cooks to the point that hospitals were advertising for "any person with two hands and a willingness to work."

Entities dealing in communications did very well with the surge in demand by the public for information relating to the outbreak. However, some businesses were overwhelmed and cut back on their services. Telephone companies advised customers that they couldn't handle anything but absolutely necessary calls and would deny service. Philadelphia created a new agency called the Bureau of Information and set up a 24-hour emergency call desk for influenza.

Of course, all enterprises related to death flourished, as did businesses associated with public health and hygiene. Makers of protective masks and signs that read "Spit Means Death" did very well. The mortuary business boomed, as there was a huge upswing in demand for preparing the dead and burying them. However, this industry was overwhelmed, just like the health industry, and couldn't keep up with the surge in demand. Grave diggers, coffin manufacturers, and funeral homes all fell behind in the disposal of the dead. Similar to information technology (IT) personnel prior to Y2K, some mortuary houses raised their prices 600 percent during this time. City morgues had to be expanded, as did the number of workers in them. Without question, death was a growth industry.

Alfred W. Crosby in his book *America's Forgotten Pandemic* lists the economic costs to the city of Philadelphia:

> *The order closing public places cost the theatres, motion picture houses, and hotels 2 million dollars and the saloons $350,000. The number of passengers using streetcars dropped off so much that the transit company lost a quarter of a million dollars. . . . Estimated by the scale used by contemporary insurance companies, Spanish influenza cost the city 60 million dollars in deaths by Armistice Day (period from onset in October to November 11th), months before the final departure of the pandemic.*

Since the Spanish flu occurred during World War I, trying to single out the impact from one over the other when it comes to financial products is a Sisyphean task. How can you see if bond prices would rise during the deaths from the flu when the nation was selling war bonds? How can you see if the stock market would fall if the increased economic activity from initially being neutral to joining the war would be cranking up the industrial base? In every world event, there are crosswinds that either exacerbate or diminish its impact. In this case, the U.S. stock and bond markets showed very little reaction to the 12-to-18-month time frame around which the Spanish flu was inflicting the most destruction.

However, when we a look at the daily stock and bond prices from Dow Jones at the height of the pandemic in the United States, we can see some interesting developments. Bond prices exhibited a price direction that is consistent with how we would expect people to react amidst death and panic: buy interest-bearing instruments that are considered safe. It's the flight to quality or safety trade. It's the equivalent of the public panicking out of an area infected with a disease.

In this case, it's a flight out of perceived risky assets to a safe asset like a U.S. government bond. Bond averages put in the high for the year in mid-November. This is when the deaths for October would have been finally tabulated and released, and the public fear would have been at its highest level. Bond prices would slide from here through 1919 and never again reach the highs that November made. For the industrials, November was also the most volatile time for the year. The high to the low price spread was 8.19, a full 1.6 points above the next highest month.

Ah, but in the world of finance, things are never so clean. I would be remiss if I didn't bring up the fact that the armistice for World War I went into effect on November 11. Were the movements in the markets due to fear over Spanish flu or joy over the end of the war? We cannot separate one event's impact from the other's. It doesn't matter. It's more important to realize the direction that each would push the markets. In this case, both generated volatility (spread between high price and low price), and both provided reasons to buy bonds.

Take note that the extreme onset of the disease, its peak, and its subsequent falloff all occurred within a year's time. It wreaked havoc like no other disease had since the Black Death and impacted not only the United States, but also the entire world. The Spanish flu is our extreme case for modern diseases, showing how rapidly it can spread and how rapidly it can kill.

CHAPTER 3

Mad Cow Disease

The year 1996 would set in motion political and economic issues that the world is still dealing with in 2007. On February 25, suicide bombers killed 25 Israelis. On March 3, they killed another 19. On March 4, they killed 12 more. This also killed the peace process and the move toward Palestinian autonomy. After a summit of world leaders in Sharm el-Sheikh, Egypt, on March 13, there were two weeks of no attacks. On March 31, Hezbollah fighters in southern Lebanon began firing rockets into northern Israel and continued into the first two weeks of April. Israel responded with air strikes into southern Lebanon and on Hezbollah positions in the suburbs of Beirut.

In August, Boris Yeltsin was sworn in as the first democratically elected president of the new Russia. Yeltsin had won an extremely close race against a Communist Party candidate. Each subsequent election in Russia would be less close and less democratic.

During the elections, the mess left behind by the Russians in Afghanistan fomented into the eventual overthrow of the government by the Taliban Islamic militia. On September 27, they took control of Kabul and threw out the Communist regime under President Burhanuddin Rabbani. They quickly instituted Islamic law that forbade the education of women, mandated the growing of beards for men, and allowed for all men and women convicted of adultery to be stoned to death. The Taliban would also eventually allow Osama bin Laden to set up terrorist training camps in their country.

Finally, the United Nations World Health Organization (WHO) announced that the last remaining stocks of the smallpox virus would be destroyed in three years. This was seen as a triumph of science to rid the

world of a virus that had haunted humans for 3,500 years. The Centers for
Disease Control and Prevention (CDC) in Atlanta, Georgia, and the Russian
State Research Center for Virology and Biotechnology in Koltsovo, Siberia,
would keep the only two remaining stocks. Both the WHO and the CDC
would be called on that year to help decipher another disease that had a
mortality rate higher than smallpox.

THE DISEASE

This section contains copious information on mad cow disease. My apolo-
gies, but it's necessary so that we can understand society's reaction to the
outbreak and therefore understand the financial markets' reaction as well.
Bovine spongiform encephalopathy (BSE) is a subgroup of puzzling diseases known as transmissible spongiform encephalopathies (TSEs). TSEs
cause spongy holes to form in the brain, which destroy brain cells and neu-
rons. This makes it impossible for messages from the brain to be communi-
cated or transmitted to the body. The CDC web site (www.cdc.gov/ncidod/
dvrd/bse/) describes the disease as follows:

> *Bovine spongiform encephalopathy (BSE) is a transmissible, neu-
> rodegenerative, fatal brain disease of cattle. The disease has a long
> incubation period of four to five years, but ultimately is fatal for cattle
> within weeks to months of its onset. BSE first came to the attention
> of the scientific community in November 1986 with the appearance
> in cattle of a newly recognized form of neurological disease in the
> United Kingdom (UK).*

Unlike the bubonic plague and the Spanish flu, every case of BSE in
cattle results in death. There are several forms of TSEs in both animals and
humans.

Back to WHO, which describes the TSE associated with BSE or what
is called Creutzfeldt-Jakob disease (CJD). A newly recognized form of
CJD, variant Creutzfeldt-Jakob disease (vCJD), was first reported in March
1996 in the United Kingdom (see WHO Fact Sheet No. 180 on variant
Creutzfeldt-Jakob disease). Why is this important? The new variation is
the killer that morphed from a form that didn't cause many problems in
humans to one that did. Here are the major differences, according to WHO
(www.who.int/mediacentre/factsheets/fs113/en/):

> *In contrast to the classical forms of CJD, vCJD has affected younger
> patients (average age 29 years, as opposed to 65 years), has a*

relatively longer duration of illness (median of 14 months as op-
posed to 4.5 months), and is strongly linked to exposure, probably
through food, to BSE. Recent studies have confirmed that vCJD is dis-
tinct from sporadic and acquired CJD. From October 1996 to Novem-
ber 2002, 129 cases of vCJD have been reported in the UK, six in
France, and one each in Canada, Ireland, Italy, and the United States
of America. Insufficient information is available at present to make
any precise prediction about the future number of vCJD cases. Since
few countries have surveillance systems, the geographical distribu-
tion of the incidence of vCJD needs to be better defined. Similarities
observed between the strain of the agent responsible for vCJD and
those of BSE and closely related agents transmitted naturally and
experimentally to different animal species are consistent with the
hypothesis discussed during two 1996 WHO consultations: that the
cluster of vCJD cases is due to the same agent that caused BSE in
cattle.

Note the language here: cluster cases. These are what we look for when
we are trying to gauge whether a disease has changed from a relatively
unusual and not rapidly reoccurring one (CJD) to one that is reproducing
quickly due to exposure (vCJD).

Note that WHO says that the connection between BSE in cattle and
vCJD in humans is still a hypothesis and not officially proven. This underscores how much uncertainty still remains with mad cow disease today.
Try to imagine what was going on in the United Kingdom during the initial
discovery of BSE and the outbreak of vCJD in humans. Like BSE, vCJD is in-
variably fatal; there is no cure. If you catch it, you die. This is why there was
so much concern and panic in the United Kingdom and why the reactions
were so strong from the UK trading partners.

Let's turn to the Centers for Disease Control and Prevention (CDC)
in the United States for just a bit more information and commentary
(www.cdc.gov/ncidod/dvrd/bse/):

BSE (bovine spongiform encephalopathy) is a progressive neurologi-
cal disorder of cattle that results from infection by an unconventional
transmissible agent termed a prion. The nature of the transmissible
agent is not well understood. Currently, the most accepted theory is
that the agent is a modified form of a normal cell surface compo-
nent known as prion protein. The pathogenic form of the protein is
both less soluble and more resistant to enzyme degradation than the
normal form.

Research indicates that the first probable infections of BSE in
cows occurred during the 1970s with two cases of BSE being identified

in 1986. BSE possibly originated as a result of the feeding of scrapie-containing sheep meat-and-bone meal to cattle. There is strong evidence and general agreement that the outbreak was amplified and spread throughout the UK cattle industry by feeding rendered bovine meat-and-bone meal to young calves.

The BSE epidemic in the United Kingdom peaked in January 1993 at almost 1,000 new cases per week. Through the end of April 2005, more than 184,000 cases of BSE had been confirmed in the United Kingdom alone in more than 35,000 herds.

There has since emerged strong epidemiologic and laboratory evidence for a causal association between variant CJD in humans and the BSE outbreak in cattle. The interval between the most likely period for the initial extended exposure of the population to potentially BSE-contaminated food (1984–1986) and the onset of initial variant CJD cases (1994–1996) is consistent with known incubation periods for the human forms of the disease.

Here are the key points to think about as we attempt to understand the markets' reactions to the outbreak: (1) the uncertainty regarding the linkages between BSE and vCJD, (2) the feeding of rendered cows (bovine meat-and-bone meal) to young calves, and (3) the penetration of the disease throughout the UK herds. Think about these as they pertain to market reaction against producers and suppliers of protein products. The food chain link means that all the companies associated with that particular path will potentially be negatively impacted.

OUTBREAK IN THE UNITED KINGDOM

As the CDC points out, two cases of BSE in cattle were found in the United Kingdom in 1986. At the time, UK authorities didn't believe it posed a risk to humans. After all, scrapie (another TSE found in sheep) had been around for centuries but had never made the jump to humans, even after infected meat was consumed. Part of the problem for the British authorities with vCJD was the long incubation period from infection to showing symptoms. Scrapie showed up quickly and killed quickly, while vCJD did not. This is why in a 1989 BBC television interview, the chief veterinary officer of the British Ministry of Agriculture, Fisheries, and Food, Keith Meldrum, said, "The evidence on BSE is derived mainly from scrapie, and there is no evidence, scientific or otherwise, that scrapie does transmit from sheep or goats to man. Using this model, we are fairly confident that BSE does not transmit to man."

This view would change dramatically when an unusual group began to come down with what appeared to be common CJD: teenagers and young adults. Prior to the 1986 discovery and diagnosis of BSE, there had been only four known cases of CJD in teenagers in the world, and these were spread out over decades. Between 1990 and 1995, there were four in the United Kingdom alone. In total, there were 10 cases of BSE in teenagers and young adults in the UK. The brains of the infected humans and the brains of the infected cows displayed the same pattern: spongy holes that had a flowerlike pattern and had protein deposits or plaques surrounding the holes. On March 25, 1996, Harry Dorrell, the UK secretary of state for health, announced that BSE or mad cow disease had spread to humans. More important, the cause was most probably the consumption of infected beef.

HISTORY AIN'T WHAT IT USED TO BE

My biggest issue with most writing on the financial markets is the lack of context for a reader. Poor journalism tells you a particular stock market rose 2 percent or an economic indicator fell 5 percent without explaining what the market was expecting or the recent history of those numbers. The reader can't discern whether the announced number has any meaning for the market or whether the market was reacting in a way that was consistent with the expectations. If you are going to understand how to make money from an event, you had better understand what was going on in the world when the event was occurring. Otherwise, you are just guessing as to what will happen next. The purpose of this book is to get the reader to make better decisions on what is possible and what are the permutations of the events.

The United Kingdom had political turmoil just prior to the outbreak of vCJD. The government of Prime Minister John Major was in a precarious position and its grip on power in the House of Commons was down to just two legislators. Should a vote of no confidence arise over an issue, it would be almost a coin flip as to whether the government would lose and be forced into an immediate general election that the opposition Labour Party was sure to win. Major's party had just barely avoided this situation over Sir Richard Scott's report on arms to Iraq in the 1980s. This tenuous grip on power could be one of the explanations as to why it took the government so long to publicly announce the outbreak, which eventually contributed to the panic that ensued.

On March 8, the Bank of England (BOE) had just cut interest rates 25 basis points (a basis point is a quarter of a percentage point) for the

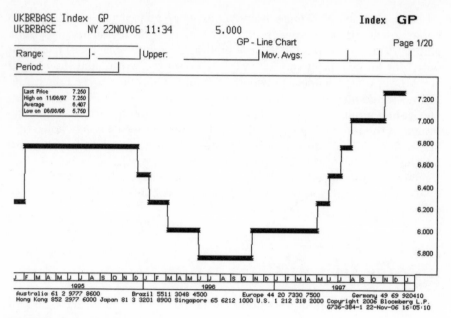

UKBRBASE Index GP
UKBRBASE   NY 22NOV06 11:34   5.000   Index GP
                                        GP - Line Chart   Page 1/20
Range: _____ - _____ | Upper: _____ | Mov. Avgs: ___ | ___ | ___ |
Period: _____

Last Price   7.250
High on 11/06/97 7.250
Average   6.407
Low on 06/06/96 5.750

Australia 61 2 9777 8600   Brazil 5511 3048 4500   Europe 44 20 7330 7500   Germany 49 69 920410
Hong Kong 852 2977 6000 Japan 81 3 3201 8900 Singapore 65 6212 1000 U.S. 1 212 318 2000 Copyright 2006 Bloomberg L.P.
                                                                    G736-384-1 22-Nov-06 16:05:10

FIGURE 3.1 UK Base Rates
Source: Used with permission from Bloomberg L.P.

second time in 1996, down to 6.00 percent (Figure 3.1). It was the third rate cut of this kind in four months. The FTSE 100 had rallied (Figure 3.2) and the 10-year UK gilt (bond) market did as well (Figure 3.3), but only briefly before the markets reacted negatively to a very strong U.S. unemployment report: Unfortunately, later in the day, the U.S. Labor Department reported that the U.S. economy had added a whopping 435,000 jobs in February (Figure 3.4), double what the markets had been anticipating. Worldwide, the markets were judging that this strong number would mean that Alan Greenspan and the Federal Open Market Committee (FOMC) would not cut rates in the United States on March 26. The FOMC had cut rates by 25 basis points in January, from 5.50 percent to 5.25 percent (Figure 3.5). The anticipated pause in rate cutting by the Federal Reserve would cause all the equity markets around the world to drop, including the FTSE 100. The yield on the 10-year gilt jumped 40 basis points, and the British pound dropped below the lows of the previous month (Figure 3.6). In the days leading up to the announcement of the outbreak, the UK equity, gilt, and currency markets had all stabilized and were attempting to regain the ground they had lost.

The interesting aspect of the timing of the outbreak is the sequence by which the markets learned of the connection to humans. Most books on mad cow disease cite the March 25 announcement in the House of Commons by

UKX ↑**6160.30 -42.30**   ---/.00   Index **GPO**
At DELAYED   Op 6202.60 Hi 6233.10 Lo 6146.30

GPO - Bar Chart   Page 1/23

| Range: | | - | | Upper: | | Mov. Avgs: | | | | Currency: | |
| Period: | | | Lower: | | Mov. Avg: | | |

Last	4118.50
High on 12/31/96	4123.20
Average	3828.82
Low on 07/16/96	3612.60

Australia 61 2 9777 8600   Brazil 5511 3048 4500   Europe 44 20 7330 7500   Germany 49 69 920410
Hong Kong 852 2977 6000 Japan 81 3 3201 8900 Singapore 65 6212 1000 U.S. 1 212 318 2000 Copyright 2006 Bloomberg L.P.
G736-384-1 22-Nov-06 16:25:08

FIGURE 3.2 UK FTSE 100 Index
Source: Used with permission from Bloomberg L.P.

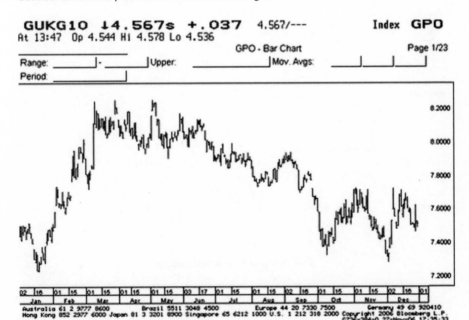

GUKG10 ↓**4.567s +.037**   4.567/---   Index **GPO**
At 13:47   Op 4.544 Hi 4.578 Lo 4.536

GPO - Bar Chart   Page 1/23

| Range: | | - | | Upper: | | Mov. Avgs: | | | |
| Period: | | |

Australia 61 2 9777 8600   Brazil 5511 3048 4500   Europe 44 20 7330 7500   Germany 49 69 920410
Hong Kong 852 2977 6000 Japan 81 3 3201 8900 Singapore 65 6212 1000 U.S. 1 212 318 2000 Copyright 2006 Bloomberg L.P.
G736-384-0 27-Nov-06 17:35:33

FIGURE 3.3 UK 10-Year Gilt Yield
Source: Used with permission from Bloomberg L.P.

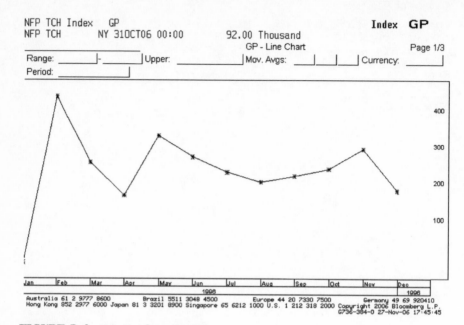

FIGURE 3.4 U.S. Nonfarm Payrolls
Source: Used with permission from Bloomberg L.P.

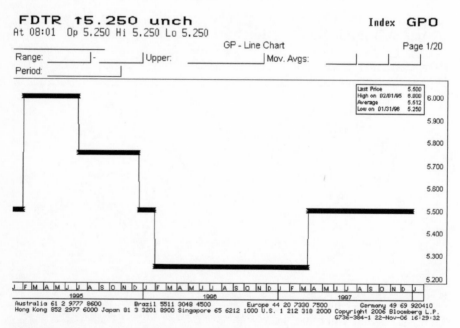

FIGURE 3.5 U.S. Federal Funds Target Rate
Source: Used with permission from Bloomberg L.P.

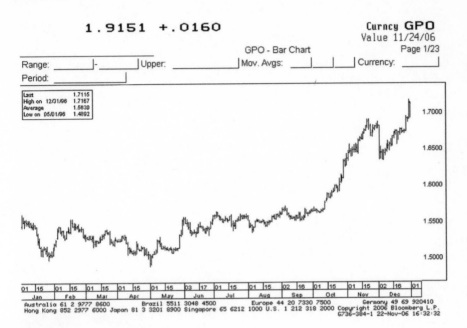

FIGURE 3.6 British Pound
Source: Used with permission from Bloomberg L.P.

Harry Dorrell, the UK secretary of state for health, as the day when the information became available. However, on March 21, Germany called for a European Union–wide ban of UK beef following the revelation of a possible link between BSE and vCJD. Scientists announced that they thought the victims might haven eaten infected beef during the first phase of the BSE outbreak between 1986 and 1989. France had already banned British beef. Essentially, this gap between the information being released and the official presentation to the House of Commons provided an amazing opportunity for taking risk for those aggressive enough to do it.

Without question, it would've been difficult to see all the permutations that would spill out from the disease. However, there were some clear connections. First, the demand for UK beef was going to drop dramatically. At one point during the initial stages of the outbreak, the price of beef dropped 50 percent. Any producers of meat and meat products were going to lose sales and profits. Initially, it was unclear as to the extent of what was needed to be done to rid the herds of the disease. Also, scientists were unsure whether vCJD could be passed through milk or milk products. This is why stock prices of UK dairy companies such as Northern Foods Plc (Figure 3.7) and Unigate Plc (now Uniq Plc) dropped quickly on March 25. The point is that you could have sold the shares on Thursday, March 21, or Friday, March 22, and made money.

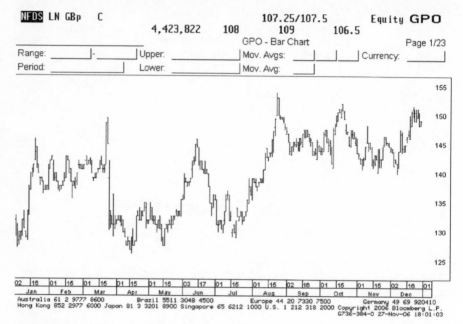

| NFDS LN GBp   C | | | | | 107.25/107.5 | | Equity **GPO** |
| 4,423,822 | 108 | | | 109 | | 106.5 |

GPO - Bar Chart   Page 1/23

| Range: | - | Upper: | Mov. Avgs: | | | Currency: |
| Period: | | Lower: | Mov. Avg: | |

Australia 61 2 9777 8600   Brazil 5511 3048 4500   Europe 44 20 7330 7500   Germany 49 69 920410
Hong Kong 852 2977 6000 Japan 81 3 3201 8900 Singapore 65 6212 1000 U.S. 1 212 318 2000 Copyright 2006 Bloomberg L.P.
G736-384-0 27-Nov-06 18:01:03

FIGURE 3.7 Northern Foods Plc Equity Price
Source: Used with permission from Bloomberg L.P.

Companies that sold the beef products in their restaurants were impacted as well. McDonald's (Figure 3.8) and other fast-food restaurants selling hamburger and beef products saw their shares drop as uncertainty over how far the disease had spread sparked concerns. It's not surprising to think that this would occur, with images of burning cows in the United Kingdom that would make anyone around the world a bit nervous about consuming a cheeseburger whose meat was of unknown origin. The odd twist to the food producer story is that shares of companies that produced chicken initially soared as the markets anticipated a pickup in demand for poultry as consumers shifted away from beef. However, the positive move in share prices for poultry producers would last only a couple of days as the market began to factor in the chance that this food product was connected to mad cow disease, too. Many of the UK food producers would see their stock prices hit lows at the end of March through mid-April before recovering.

The same reasoning applies toward the currency. On March 21, you could have had the information on UK beef and could've acted to sell the British pound. Also, you could've waited and sold on March 24 as well and still would've seen the currency go lower. On March 26, the U.S. Federal Open Market Committee (FOMC) left interest rates unchanged as expected.

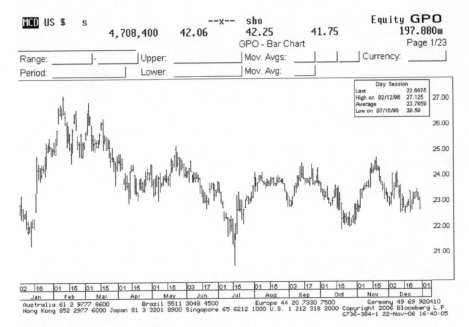

FIGURE 3.8 McDonald's Corporation Equity Price
Source: Used with permission from Bloomberg L.P.

However, the Dorrell speech coupled with a potential widening of interest rate differentials between the United Kingdom and the United States caused the British pound to lose ground until the beginning of May, when it hit bottom for the year.

The 10-year UK gilt market was impacted, but to a lesser extent. Let's run through the countervailing winds that blew so that the outbreak didn't have the same impact. The initial reaction was that this was something that overall was bad for the country and bad for the economy. You would be buying the 10-year bonds thinking that lower growth would mean lower interest rates and higher bond prices. However, the question of how many cows to slaughter arose when on March 25, UK Agriculture Minister Douglas Hogg said the government was considering slaughtering 4.5 million cows. Hogg ordering cows to be killed sounds like something from George Orwell's *Animal Farm*, but this was no allegory. The markets quickly thought that the UK producers and farmers would have to be compensated for their losses. Estimates ran between 400 million and 700 million British pounds for reimbursement of lost animals. Then, there was the concern that inflation would jump on foodstuffs as milk and beef would have to be imported until the domestic herds were rebuilt. On March 28th, the 10-year gilt yield shot up above 8.20 percent on these fears. The yields then fluctuated in a range between about 7.90 percent and 8.25 percent for three months. This is one more bizarre twist to the story. The event would cause UK meat and meat products to be shunned, thus causing a drop-off in economic activity, a net negative to the economy. Yet bond yields went up over the fear of high government payments and an increased inflation threat. It's always these add-on effects that few traders think of with world event trading that cause them to enter into losing trades.

There are several key concepts to remember for future disease outbreak situations. One, information is imperfect and not distributed evenly. This generates opportunities to take risk if you do your homework and follow the news. Two, focus on the narrow group that is impacted the most to see the bigger moves. The mind-set should be to think negatively toward what the outcomes will be and be prepared to sell the instruments that will be impacted. The converse should apply as well with industries that will see increased demand benefit (think chicken or fish in this case), and therefore these companies should be bought. A textbook hedging situation occurs where we can buy shares of a food producer that is not involved in beef and sell a food producer that mainly produces beef. Three, the broader instruments will be impacted, but to a lesser extent. As an example, an international portfolio manager might dump a UK dairy stock and then he probably needs to dump the currency as well at some point. He may just not dump all of the currency he holds and may choose to invest in another area of the country. Remember, these broader instruments (currency and bond markets) are subject to other forces that can outweigh a localized event. However, a good rule of thumb is that the smaller the country, the more likely the event will have a larger impact on its specific markets, including the broader instruments.

RATES = REWARDS

I would be failing the reader in my quest to provide context if I didn't discuss some broader perspective on this outbreak. The trades I've described are quite short-term in nature and must be viewed as such. Aggressive investors can take advantage of these if they act quickly and are willing to take on risk. However, this is not the only way to play the game. The medium-term investor can also take advantage of the situation by looking at the event and evaluating whether this is a significant change to the underlying fundamentals of the investment climate or it's a short-term blip. Granted, this is difficult to judge, as one will be pressed to evaluate the incident and what the wider implications will be.

As the saying goes, though, there is no reward without risk. This is one of the reasons I'm writing this book for investors: to give you the tools to evaluate and make better-informed decisions. For the medium-term investor, you need to look at the variables that impact the financial markets for longer periods of time, such as interest rate policy, government fiscal and tax policy, and commodity trends. Reviewing all of these factors is not my intention for this book, but let's review one key sledgehammer for any economy: interest rates.

In 1996, the Bank of England was in the process of cutting interest rates. The BOE cut rates by 25 basis points in January and in March. Simply put, lower interest rates decrease the cost of capital for companies and individuals and therefore stimulate economic growth. By extension, this should stimulate profits for businesses and consequently it should generate a rise in their stock prices. This is why equity prices can rise even in the middle of a recession when the central bank begins to cut interest rates. The reverse is true as well. The simple rule of equity investing is to buy when they cut, and pare back or sell when they hike.

Returning to the United Kingdom in March 1996, we see that the BOE cut rates at the very beginning of the month and UK equities rallied. (Some of the move occurred prior to the cut as the market was already anticipating the positive event.) Then, after a very strong U.S. employment number, equities in the United Kingdom and the rest of the world fell in March as the markets rightly predicted that the U.S. Federal Reserve would not be cutting rates. UK equities sank initially and then began to rally, with only a minor drop due to the mad cow outbreak and the banning of British beef exports.

Using our simple rule of equity investing, we would've been holding on to our UK investments. As a matter of fact, we should've been buying the sell-off in the food producers that occurred, as almost all ended the year higher than the lows that were reached in March due to the mad cow scare. The BOE rewarded equity investors by cutting rates in June by 25 basis points. The interest rate cuts all contributed to an equity rally that moved the FTSE 100 index from a low in March around 3,650 to a high in October of 4,050. For the medium-term investor, an 11 percent return in seven months is a justified reward for the risk of buying during a major negative event.

Let's see if this pattern persists during the outbreaks in Canada and the United States.

2003 OUTBREAK IN CANADA

Heading into 2003, the Canadian economy had been outgrowing those of the rest of the G7 (seven largest industrial) countries. Unlike in the United Kingdom and the United States, in Canada the central bank was in the process of raising interest rates. The Bank of Canada raised interest rates

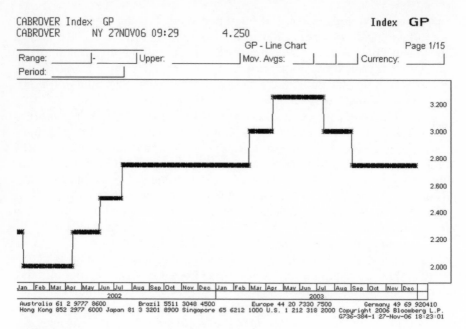

CABROVER Index GP   Index **GP**
CABROVER   NY 27NOV06 09:29   4.250
                                                GP - Line Chart   Page 1/15
Range: _____|-_____|Upper: _____|Mov. Avgs: ___|___|___|Currency: _____|
Period: _____|

FIGURE 3.9   Bank of Canada Overnight Lending Rate
Source: Used with permission from Bloomberg L.P.

25 basis points in March, from 2.75 percent to 3.00 percent and then again in April from 3.00 percent to 3.25 percent (Figure 3.9). Canadian equities put in their lows for the year in March (Figure 3.10) as the market digested the rate hike in that month, the strong possibility of a rate hike in April, and a hit to tourism in Toronto from an outbreak of severe acute respiratory syndrome (SARS). The 10-year bond yield rose from 4.80 percent in March to a peak of 5.21 percent at the beginning of April (Figure 3.11). The higher interest rates and strong growth helped propel the Canadian dollar against the U.S. dollar from a low in January of 1.5700 (.6370c) to a high in May of 1.3500 (.7407c) (Figure 3.12).

On May 20, Canada reported North America's first case of BSE in a decade. Canadian Agriculture Minister Lyle Vanclief confirmed the infection in an Alberta cow that was slaughtered on January 31 but that didn't enter into the human or livestock food chains. Canada's economy is heavily dependent upon exports, as they comprise around one-third of the gross domestic product (GDP). The United States is Canada's largest market, with 85 percent of all exports ending up in their neighbor to the south. It was devastating to the C$26 billion Canadian beef industry to have the United States suspend cattle and beef imports from their country due to the BSE finding. Japan and 32 other nations quickly followed suit and banned the Canadian beef.

FIGURE 3.10 S&P/Toronto Stock Exchange Composite Index
Source: Used with permission from Bloomberg L.P.

FIGURE 3.11 Canadian 10-Year Bond Yield
Source: Used with permission from Bloomberg L.P.

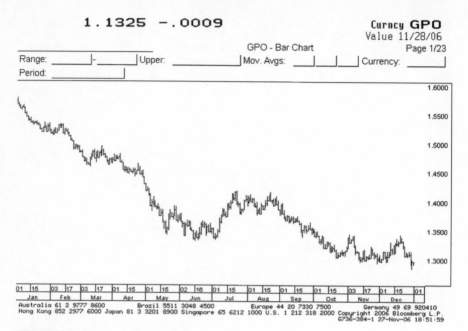

FIGURE 3.12 Canadian Dollar
Source: Used with permission from Bloomberg L.P.

The industry was worried that the Canadian authorities would require the destruction of millions of cattle just like the UK authorities did in 1996. Canada had previously had one other case of mad cow disease (in 1993), and the entire herd was destroyed as a precaution. By this time, vCJD from diseased meat had killed 125 people in the United Kingdom and at least 80 others around the world. There was also some fear at this time that Canada was holding back information on the outbreak due to the delay between when the cow died in January and when the outbreak was announced in May.

After the announcement on May 20, 2003, the financial markets showed their ability to panic first and ask questions later. Live cattle futures dropped 1.5 cents, to 72.4 cents, which was the largest drop in four months. Traders bought hogs and sold cattle on a spread trade. Stock prices of companies that produced beef, distributed the beef, and sold the beef in their restaurants dropped dramatically. McDonald's fell 6.7 percent, Wendy's fell 6.6 percent, and Tyson Foods fell 4.9 percent. The timing couldn't have been worse for the beef producers, as it was just before the prime U.S. barbeque season, with Memorial Day and the start of summer just around the corner. (Hamburger? No, I'll have the chicken, thanks.)

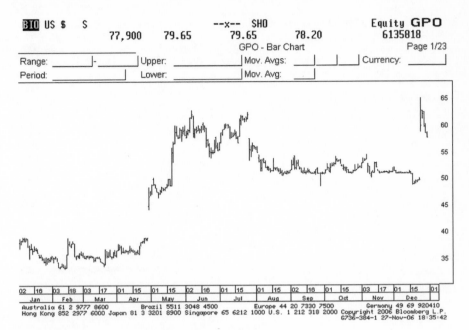

Australia 61 2 9777 8600   Brazil 5511 3048 4500   Europe 44 20 7330 7500   Germany 49 69 920410
Hong Kong 852 2977 6000 Japan 81 3 3201 8900 Singapore 65 6212 1000 U.S. 1 212 318 2000 Copyright 2006 Bloomberg L.P.
                                                                                             6736-384-1 27-Nov-06 18:35:42

FIGURE 3.13 Bio-Rad Laboratories Equity Price
Source: Used with permission from Bloomberg L.P.

In contrast, companies that produced tests for mad cow disease, like Bio-Rad Laboratories, saw their stock prices rise (Figure 3.13). In anticipation of an economic slowdown, the Canadian 10-year bond rallied and saw its yield dip from 4.60 percent to below 4.40 percent by the end of May. Amid simultaneous fears of mad cow disease and reoccurrence of SARS, its yield would eventually go as low as 4.00 percent by mid-June. Just like with the Spanish flu, we have more than one component impacting the markets. But the direction on the market is impacted in the same way. The Canadian dollar would weaken from 1.3500 (.7407c) to 1.3950 (.7168c) from May 20 to May 30. However, the Toronto Stock Exchange 100 would see only a slight drop that would last no more than a couple of days.

The fascinating development is that the pattern from the UK outbreak repeated itself in Canada. There was initial tremendous uncertainty, lack of detailed information, and sharp reaction in the financial markets. As an example, U.S. Pet Pantry recalled dog food that might have been tainted with mad cow disease although there was no scientific evidence that dogs could contract or transmit any form of the disease. Ultimately, the moves in the financial markets would be unwound as the larger influence of interest rates again would provide the stimulus for recovery. This time it would be cuts in rates from outside the country that would provide the bounce.

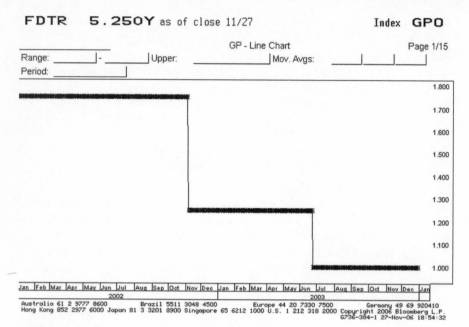

FIGURE 3.14 U.S. Federal Funds Target Rate
Source: Used with permission from Bloomberg L.P.

The FOMC was in the process of taking short-term interest rates to their lowest level since the 1950s (Figure 3.14). The FOMC cut rates to 1.00 percent in June 2003 and would eventually keep them there a year. Also, Japan was taking extraordinary measures to inject its moribund economy with liquidity as well. This monetary stimulus was exceptionally supportive for equity markets and bond markets around the world. There were serious concerns that a worldwide recession would ensue and that central banks needed to be aggressive in cutting interest rates. As an example of this extreme monetary stimulus, Ben Bernanke at this time earned his "Helicopter Ben" nickname when in a speech he said that if it was necessary the Federal Reserve could drop money from a helicopter. He would eventually go on to be the next chairman of the Federal Reserve.

After the FOMC cut in June, the Bank of Canada would follow in July and again in September, dropping overnight rates from 3.25 percent to 2.75 percent. The TSE would gain over 20 percent from the date of the announcement of BSE in Canada. The Canadian dollar would gain 7 percent. McDonald's would see a gain of over 55 percent (before the announcement of an occurrence of BSE in the United States). And here's the really fun fact: Live cattle would recover as well. This is a bit more complicated due to the fact that the markets' initial reactions were to sell cattle as they perceived there would be a drop in demand not only for Canadian beef, but also for beef from anywhere in the world. Cattle prices recovered when the markets began to price in the prospect of massive herd destructions and the taking off the market of Canadian beef exports to the United States. This situation pushed cattle prices from a low in July near 75 cents to a high in September near 107 cents: a move of over 40 percent. That's impressive.

2003 OUTBREAK IN THE UNITED STATES

The United States got to taste a bit of its own medicine at the end of the year. On December 23, the U.S. Department of Agriculture announced that a Holstein cow in the state of Washington had tested positive for BSE. Taiwan, South Korea, and Japan immediately announced suspension of U.S. beef imports. The beef industry in the United States is about $175 billion or nearly 10 times the size of Canada's. As always, context is key: The industry is only around 1.5 percent of GDP in the United States, as opposed to over 2 percent for Canada. Once again, large restaurant chains felt the immediate impact of the announcement. U.S. Agriculture Secretary Anne Veneman said at the time that the cow in question was a "downer animal" and nonambulatory. Unfortunately, only a fraction of these unable-to-walk animals were being tested for the disease. At that time I wrote in my daily client commentary (the Busch Update), "Hmm, without sounding too churlish, is it smart to eat a 'nonambulatory' cow, whether it appears healthy or not?"

Immediately, McDonald's fell 3.7 percent, Wendy's fell 2.3 percent, Outback Steakhouse fell 2 percent, and Lone Star Steakhouse & Saloon Inc. fell 7.9 percent. Producers also felt the pain, with the world's largest, Tyson Foods, falling around 10 percent. Live cattle (generic contract) had the biggest move, dropping from .90 cents to below .74 cents at the beginning of January. It was a tough break for the $27 billion a year cattle industry, which had recovered from the UK and Canadian setbacks due to the popularity of the Atkins diet plan. Also note, the bigger indexes did not react much to the news, with the Dow Jones Industrial Average and the S&P 500 reacting with a margin move down. Just to show how imperfect information was at the time, market commentary suggested that Canada would benefit from increased exports to the Far East after the U.S. beef was banned. It wasn't known until December 29 that the cow in Washington State was imported from Canada!

Here's how I summed up the situation on December 29, encapsulating the mood at the time:

The one thing you can be certain of is heavier federal regulations on the industry. As an indication, check out this flip-flop on the issue from a Texas Democrat and rancher, Rep. Charles W. Stenholm, who fought a ban on using sick or injured cows for meat by saying, "The picture the gentleman is showing, that sick animal, will never find its way into the food chain. Period." Now he says, "We need to be able to instantaneously track the history of a sick animal," and also said he was ready to work on ways to keep sick animals out of the food system, according to the New York Times *[of December 28, 2003].*

According to the article only 200,000 or so of the 104 million cattle in the U.S. are downers, suggesting that the industry may have to take a disproportionate risk in continuing to sell meat from this group. Ouch. It'll be interesting to see how the Texan President walks a fine line between angering his cattlemen friends and not doing enough quickly enough to satisfy the fears of consumers. Or of foreign markets, as Japan said it won't lift a ban on U.S. beef imports until it is satisfied the U.S. has put in place measures to ensure its meat is free of mad cow disease. Like the South Park *movie, Americans can blame Canada for their woes, but bombing the Baldwins is not going to fix the problem. Granted, at this point I don't expect the massive destruction of herds like in the U.K., but none of this is good for the industry or the (U.S.) dollar.*

Yet again, the paradigm for the outbreaks in the United Kingdom and Canada held true. The prices for live cattle, McDonald's, Tyson, and others recovered. The larger trends that were in place prior to the disease outbreak either continued or were reinforced by subsequent actions by central banks. As an example, the U.S. dollar fell more on December 24 than on December 23, the day of the BSE announcement, after an exceptionally weak durable goods number led analysts to believe the FOMC would keep interest rates unchanged.

WRAP-UP

From the three major outbreaks of BSE, we can glean some general rules to follow. First, if the outbreak is a new disease, the impact will generally be larger in terms of reactions and panic. Second, the relative size of the industry to the country is important: The larger the percentage of GDP the industry is, the larger the initial reaction will be in all the financial instruments. Third, there will be confusion and lack of information on the subject, with the potential for misunderstandings and incorrect policy.

Fourth, the time lapse between the outbreaks in the United Kingdom and Canada allowed for governments to make changes to their policies to attack the problem and lessen the potential outbreak. Elimination of ruminants into the cattle food supply for protein supplements appears to have done the job for reducing risk of BSE. In other words, the first occurrence of a disease will have the largest impact. Subsequent outbreaks will have less impact and have a shorter duration.

Lastly, the initial market reactions were panic selling of those areas in the economy that were deemed to be impacted by the outbreak. The reactions were short-lived and did present opportunities for profit. The medium-term opportunities stemmed from this activity. The larger trends for interest rates and economic activity played a stronger role influencing asset prices than did the outbreaks. This provided an opportunity to buy low and sell high later on after the panic stopped.

CHAPTER 4

Severe Acute Respiratory Syndrome (SARS)

At the beginning of 2003, I was still doing my political talk show *Politics and Money* for WebFN in Chicago. Here were the opening questions for the guests on January 8:

- Are the tax cuts just for the rich or to boost the economy?
- Do the Democrats have anything better?
- What's worse: a dictator with nuclear weapons (North Korea) or a dictator with biological weapons (Iraq)?

President Bush was proposing a stimulus plan to cut taxes and boost spending by $675 billion over 10 years. The bigger than expected plan was going to move forward tax cuts for 2004 and 2006, eliminate the double taxation of dividends, and provide incentives for companies to boost investment in equipment. Some pundits said that the dividend tax cut alone would generate a 20 percent increase in stock prices. This was going to be cheerled by a rookie administration official in the Council of Economic Advisers (R. Glenn Hubbard), in the U.S. Treasury (John Snow), and in the Senate majority leader position (Bill Frist).

At the time, Senate Minority Leader Tom Daschle said, "This plan is obscene." The debate was going to be about increasing the size of the deficit versus risking another recession. Little did they know that the U.S. economy would need this stimulus along with U.S. interest rates remaining at 1 percent for an entire year to revive a moribund economy.

At the same time, North Korea was announcing that it was pulling out of the Nuclear Non-Proliferation Treaty, to which it had been a party since 1985. "The nonproliferation treaty is being used as a tool for implanting the hostile U.S. policy toward [North Korea] aimed to disarm it and destroy its system by force," according to Pyongyang. Assistant Secretary of State James Kelly said, according to Reuters, "We are of course willing to talk. Once we get beyond nuclear weapons, there may be opportunities with the U.S., with private investors, and with other countries to help North Korea in the energy area." The U.S. response was cool and calculated, unlike its handling of the Iraq situation. However, the lack of results has continued to plague relations in the region. North Korea would shake up the world with a missile test before the end of March.

However, the key area of geopolitical focus was Iraq and UN weapon inspections led by Hans Blix and Mohamed ElBaradei. The UN and Iraq were engaged in a game of hide-and-seek with banned weapons and then Blix would report back to the UN on the progress. The two-handed reports would read like this: On the one hand, Iraq is destroying missiles; on the other hand, inspectors are not getting full cooperation. Saddam Hussein was PR crafty as ever and gave soon-to-be-demoted Dan Rather a one-on-one interview. "I am ready to conduct a direct dialogue—a debate—with your president. I will say what I want and he will say what he wants. . . . Out of my respect for the people of the United States and my respect for the people of Iraq and the people of the world. I call for this because war is no joke." Of course, he could've just done what UN resolution 1441 requested and dismantled his al-Samoud missiles and then he would've probably avoided a war.

This situation would continue to foment into the month of March, with the United States and United Kingdom losing their patience with the UN and Saddam Hussein. And then there was the whole situation with Nigerian yellowcake and. . . . Okay, we'll save that for a later chapter. On March 6, President Bush in a prime-time news conference declared that "we really don't need anybody's permission" to defend the United States. The U.S. had gone back to the UN for one more resolution that would explicitly authorize the use of force if Iraq was not in compliance with other UN resolutions on its weapons of mass destruction. However, prior to a vote, France and Russia made it very clear that they would veto this type of resolution. On March 18, President Bush gave Saddam Hussein 48 hours to comply and Homeland Security raised the terrorist alert level to orange.

After 9/11, the United States had experienced an anthrax attack as well. Homeland Security was keenly focused on the potential for a biological or nuclear attack. Some critics would eventually say that the agency stepped on civil rights in its pursuit of terrorists and protecting the United States. However, this seemed to be the right thing to do as other countries and allies were experiencing the exact trouble that the United States wanted to avoid. Raids on a London apartment found the supertoxic ricin in the midst of terrorists. In January, a British police officer was killed in a Manchester raid on suspected terrorists. UK Prime Minister Tony Blair had these sobering and foreshadowing words, according to Reuters: "We could spend billions of pounds doing it [war on terror], we could spend tens of billions of pounds . . . and we could still not identify where the attack actually is going to come. There are no limits to the potential threats which you could imagine."

This was the heightened state of geopolitics and domestic politics at the end of March. The heightened uncertainty was creating highly volatile markets in equities, bonds, currencies, and commodities. This frenzied mind-set contributed to what occurred with SARS, as markets were juiced with the impending thought of an invasion. Here's what I wrote on Monday, March 17: "For the financial markets, here's what I see: The dollar is not reacting as negatively as one would think given the immediacy of the war. Gold is now over $45 below its peak, the Dow is still 500 points above its October 2002 low, and oil is almost three bucks below its highs."

Little did the world or I know that another type of terror was lurking and already killing in the lead-up to the Iraq war. This time, the trouble would come from the Far East and an all-out medical war would ensue.

DISEASE DYNAMICS

According to the Centers for Disease Control and Prevention (CDC) fact sheet (www.cdc.gov/ncidod/sars/factsheet.htm), severe acute respiratory syndrome (SARS) is a viral respiratory illness caused by a coronavirus called SARS-associated coronavirus (SARS-CoV). SARS was first reported in Asia in February 2003. According to the World Health Organization (WHO), a total of 8,098 people worldwide became sick with SARS during the 2003 outbreak. Of these, 774 died. In the United States, only eight people had laboratory evidence of SARS-CoV infection. All of these people had traveled to other parts of the world where SARS had occurred.

The symptoms of the disease are quite similar to those of influenza. There is a high fever that is generally greater than 100.4°F. The usual discomforts of body aches and headaches are also associated with the disease. About 10 percent to 20 percent of patients have diarrhea. After two to seven days, SARS patients may develop a dry cough. The incubation period is from two to ten days. Just like patients with influenza, most SARS patients develop pneumonia, and this is what ravages their lungs and ultimately kills them. As mentioned in Chapter 2 on Spanish flu, one of the major differences between influenza and SARS is the emitting of a fever as an identifier of infection. Eventually, this characteristic allowed medical professionals to be able to identify and finally quarantine SARS patients.

Unlike influenza, which is airborne, SARS is spread by person-to-person contact or close proximity with someone infected, as in an elevator or an airplane. This underscores why quarantine was an effective tool against the disease. How ironic that a medical technique that was developed during the Black Death is still an effective tool. The CDC defines close contact as having cared for or lived with someone with SARS or having direct contact with respiratory secretions or body fluids of a patient with SARS. Examples of close contact include kissing or hugging, sharing eating or drinking utensils, talking to someone within three feet, and touching someone directly. This is why during the height of the crisis Asians were avoided by Westerners; the stigma of the disease caused fear of any contact with someone from that region.

According to the CDC, the virus that causes SARS is thought to be transmitted most readily by respiratory droplets (droplet spread) produced when an infected person coughs or sneezes. The CDC's assessment states:

Droplet spread can happen when droplets from the cough or sneeze of an infected person are propelled a short distance (generally up to 3 feet) through the air and deposited on the mucous membranes of the mouth, nose, or eyes of persons who are nearby. The virus also can spread when a person touches a surface or object contaminated with infectious droplets and then touches his or her mouth, nose, or eye(s). In addition, it is possible that the SARS virus might spread more broadly through the air (airborne spread) or by other ways that are not now known.

Of course, this is what is known now after three years of analysis by the World Health Organization, the U.S. Centers for Disease Control and Prevention, and other health agencies from around the world. In 2003, there was uncertainty and panic over a disease that was spreading rapidly and was killing the very people who sought to cure it. If the disease was similar to influenza and could spread rapidly via airborne particles, it could have tremendous killing power. It would also mean that one way to combat the disease would be quarantines and limiting travel to regions containing the disease.

Like the 1918 influenza and the recent mad cow disease, the lack of accurate and complete information relating to SARS as it spread would ultimately cause more damage than the disease itself to financial markets and the population. Try to keep in mind that people were dying, the disease was spreading, and no one understood how to stop it.

THE SARS TIME LINE

To understand the SARS phenomenon and its impact on the financial markets, you need to know the time lines involved with the spread of the disease from China to other parts of the region and world. It is also critical to understand the role that the World Health Organization (WHO) played in creating chaos and confusion by issuing something it had never done before: travel advisories.

Let's look at the sequence of SARS-related events that transpired in 2003. This list (Table 4.1) essentially comes from the WHO web site, with my modifications for emphasis. This is a fantastic learning opportunity to show how disease events unfold sequentially, how nonlinear those events can be, and how they impact the financial markets. This chapter has a slightly different feel to it than the first two chapters, as we are examining a modern disease outbreak during the age of the Internet and dramatically faster information flow. This condenses and intensifies the reactions.

SARS HINDSIGHT IS 20/20

This chronology of SARS shows that its impact was over a limited duration as the disease was quickly contained due to massive international cooperation. However, there were several lessons to take away from the outbreak.

First, fear and panic generate lots of volatility in the financial markets where the outbreaks are occurring. This means there are opportunities to take advantage of the fear factor. The bigger moves happen in the smaller markets or in the markets that are specifically impacted. This is why I focused on the Singapore dollar and companies like Shangri-La and Cathay Pacific. Singapore is a small island nation with a currency that is somewhat thinly traded. South Korea is a bigger country with a larger economy, but has similar characteristics. Japan has a large economy, but was still impacted by the region's exposure to the disease. Shangri-La was a hotel company that would've been expected to lose business as customers canceled reservations at its hotels in the region. Other major hotel chains like Starwood and Hilton experienced similar problems, but not to the extent of an entity at the epicenter of the outbreak. Cathay Pacific felt the same negative wave hit its business and its stock.

The drop in the airline's stock price was even more eye-popping as the price of oil dropped and still couldn't stem the selling that ensued due to SARS. Notice, all the major airline stock prices in the world fell as well. Air France, Lufthansa, British Airways, United Air Lines, Continental Airlines,

TABLE 4.1   The SARS Time Line

Date	Event
16 November 2002	—First known case of atypical pneumonia occurs in Foshan City, Guangdong Province, China, but is not identified until much later.
10 February 2003	—The WHO Beijing office receives an e-mail message describing a "strange contagious disease" that has "already left more than 100 people dead" in Guangdong Province in the space of one week. The message further describes "a 'panic' attitude, currently, where people are emptying pharmaceutical stocks of any medicine they think may protect them."
11 February	—WHO receives reports from the Chinese Ministry of Health of an outbreak of acute respiratory syndrome with 300 cases and 5 deaths in Guangdong Province.
12 February	—Health officials from Guangdong Province report a total of 305 cases and 5 deaths of acute respiratory syndrome. The cases and deaths occurred from 16 November 2002 to 9 February 2003. Laboratory analyses are negative for influenza viruses.
14 February	—The Chinese Ministry of Health informs WHO that the outbreak in Guangdong Province is clinically consistent with atypical pneumonia. The outbreak is said to be coming under control. **[The containment was clearly proven incorrect. This helps frame the problem of opaque communication on the disease. This was the first experience of an epidemic for many in the medical community in China and in the rest of the world. The first reaction was to deny there was a problem. This eventually led to a bigger outbreak and larger complications.]**
17 February	—A 33-year-old Hong Kong man, who had traveled with his family to Fujian Province, China, in January, dies of unknown causes in Hong Kong. His 8-year-old daughter died previously, of unknown causes, while in mainland China. His 9-year-old son is hospitalized.
19 February	—An outbreak of bird flu in Hong Kong is reported to WHO following the detection of the influenza A (H5N1) virus in the 9-year-old boy. —WHO activates its global influenza laboratory network and calls for heightened global surveillance.

TABLE 4.1	*(Continued)*
Date	**Event**
20 February	—The Department of Health in Hong Kong confirms that the boy's father was likewise infected with a strain of the influenza A (H5N1) virus. **[This was a red herring and took authorities down another blind alley that would further lengthen the time before SARS was understood.]**
21 February	—A 64-year-old medical doctor from Zhongshan University in Guangzhou (Guangdong Province) arrives in Hong Kong to attend a wedding. He checks in to the ninth floor of the Metropole Hotel (room 911). Although he had developed respiratory symptoms five days earlier, he feels well enough to sightsee and shop with his 53-year-old brother-in-law, who resides in Hong Kong. **[This turned out to be the Typhoid Mary of SARS, as other visitors staying at the hotel left and traveled to other parts of the world, spreading the disease. It also provided a link to hotels and the fear that staying there could expose someone to the disease. Companies that owned and operated hotels in the area saw their stock prices decline quickly. Shangri-La Asia Ltd is a good example, as its price would decline close to 30 percent from February through the end of April. (See Figure 4.1.)]**
22 February	—The Guangdong doctor seeks urgent care at the Kwong Wah Hospital in Hong Kong and is admitted to the intensive care unit with respiratory failure. He had previously treated patients with atypical pneumonia in Guangdong. He warns medical staff that he fears he has contracted a "very virulent disease." Health authorities in Hong Kong learn that his symptoms developed on 15 February, at which point he would have still been on the Chinese mainland.
23 February	—A 78-year-old female tourist from Toronto, Canada, checks out of the Metropole Hotel and begins her homeward journey. On arrival in Toronto she is reunited with her family.
24 February	—The Global Public Health Intelligence Network (GPHIN) picks up a report stating that over 50 hospital staff are infected with a "mysterious pneumonia" in the city of Guangzhou.
	—In Hong Kong, a 26-year-old local man develops a respiratory tract infection, but does not seek medical attention. From 15 to 23 February, he had visited an acquaintance staying on the ninth floor of the Metropole Hotel.
25 February	—The brother-in-law of the Guangdong doctor is admitted to Kwong Wah Hospital and discharged.

(continues)

TABLE 4.1	(Continued)

Date	Event
26 February	—A 48-year-old Chinese-American businessman is admitted to the French Hospital in Hanoi with a three-day history of fever and respiratory symptoms. His recent travel history includes a January trip to Shanghai, and a private trip from 8 to 10 February to Guangdong Province and Macao. He traveled to Hong Kong on 17 February, departed for Hanoi on 23 February, and fell ill there. Shortly before his departure from Hong Kong, he had stayed on the ninth floor of the Metropole Hotel in a room across the hall from the Guangdong doctor. The businessman is attended by a WHO official, Dr. Carlo Urbani, based in Vietnam.
28 February	—Dr. Urbani, alarmed by the unusual disease and concerned it might be a case of avian influenza, notifies the WHO office in Manila. WHO headquarters moves into a heightened state of alert.
1 March	—The brother-in-law of the Guangdong doctor is readmitted to Kwong Wah Hospital. —A 26-year-old woman is admitted to a hospital in Singapore with respiratory symptoms. A resident of Singapore, she was a guest on the ninth floor of the Hotel Metropole in Hong Kong from 21 to 25 February.
4 March	—The Guangdong doctor dies of atypical pneumonia at Kwong Wah Hospital.
5 March	—In Hanoi, the Chinese-American businessman, in a stable but critical condition, is air medevaced to the Princess Margaret Hospital in Hong Kong. Seven health care workers who had cared for him in Hanoi become ill. Dr. Urbani continues to help hospital staff contain further spread. —The 78-year-old Toronto woman dies at Toronto's Scarborough Grace Hospital. Five members of her family are found to be infected and are admitted to the hospital. **[The Canadian dollar broke its rally against the U.S. dollar for a two-week retracement of the trend. As we know, the U.S. Federal Reserve was in the process of cutting the federal funds target rate to the lowest levels since World War II. At the time of the outbreak, the fed funds rate was at 1.25 percent; it would be cut again to 1.00 percent in late June. (See Figure 4.2.)]**
7 March	—Health care workers at Hong Kong's Prince of Wales Hospital start to complain of respiratory tract infection, progressing to pneumonia. All have an identifiable link with Ward 8A.
8 March	—In Taiwan, a 54-year-old businessman with a travel history to Guangdong Province is hospitalized with respiratory symptoms.

TABLE 4.1	*(Continued)*

Date	Event
10 March	—At least 22 staff at the Hanoi hospital are ill with influenza-like symptoms. Twenty show signs of pneumonia, one requires breathing support, and another is in critical condition. —The Ministry of Health in China asks WHO to provide technical and laboratory support to clarify the cause of the Guangdong outbreak of atypical pneumonia.
11 March	—Dr. Urbani departs for Bangkok, on a Thai flight, where he is scheduled to give a presentation at a meeting on tropical diseases the following day. He is ill upon arrival and is immediately hospitalized.
12 March	—WHO issues a global alert about cases of severe atypical pneumonia following mounting reports of spread among staff at hospitals in Hong Kong and Hanoi. **[This alert essentially signaled to the financial markets that there was a problem. Markets reacted by selling Far Eastern currencies such as the Singapore dollar, the South Korean won, and the Japanese yen. (See Figures 4.3 to 4.5.) The U.S. dollar gained at this time as optimism over a short war kicked in as well.]**
13 March	—The Ministry of Health in Singapore reports three cases of atypical pneumonia in young women who had recently returned to Singapore after traveling to Hong Kong. All had stayed on the ninth floor of the Metropole Hotel in late February. —The 44-year-old son of Toronto's first case dies in Scarborough Grace Hospital.
14 March	—In Hong Kong, 39 staff at three hospitals undergo treatment for flulike symptoms. Twenty-four exhibit signs of pneumonia and are described as in "serious condition." —Health authorities in Ontario, Canada, take steps to alert doctors, hospitals, ambulance services, and public health units across the province that there are four cases of atypical pneumonia in Toronto that have resulted in two deaths. All occurred within a single family.
15 March	—At 2:00 A.M., Singapore health authorities notify WHO staff, by urgent telecommunication, that a 32-year-old physician, who had treated the country's first two SARS cases, had boarded a flight from New York City to Singapore, after having attended a medical conference, to return to Singapore via Frankfurt. Shortly before boarding the flight, he had reported symptoms to an alert medical colleague in Singapore, who notified health officials. WHO identifies the airline and flight, and the physician, along with his 30-year-old pregnant wife and 62-year-old mother-in-law, are removed from the flight in Frankfurt and placed in isolation. They become Germany's first SARS cases.

(continues)

TABLE 4.1	(Continued)
Date	**Event**

	—WHO issues a rare travel advisory as evidence mounts that SARS is spreading by air travel along international routes. WHO names the mysterious illness after its symptoms: severe acute respiratory syndrome (SARS), and declares it "a worldwide health threat."
	—WHO issues its first case definitions of suspect and probable cases of SARS. WHO further calls on all travelers to be aware of the signs and symptoms, and issues advice to airlines.
	—Health Canada reports eight cases of atypical pneumonia, including the two deaths.
	—Four intensive care specialists arrive in Hanoi to reinforce the Global Outbreak Alert and Response Network (GOARN) team there.
	—The Singapore Ministry of Health reports 16 cases of atypical pneumonia.
	[This highlights the role that air travel played in spreading the disease. This is why a regional airline stock price such as that of Cathay Pacific Airways Ltd was crushed at the time. It declined almost 30 percent. Note that the market was a little slow on this and you had the opportunity to sell this stock for almost two weeks before it reacted to the downside. Why did we get this window? Optimism over a speedy end to the war and a drop in the price of oil.
	Once again, it's rare that there is a trade that is solely impacted by an infectious disease outbreak. The invasion of Iraq was clearly the overriding focus and major factor impacting the markets even during the SARS crisis. This is precisely why when the outbreak peaked, the retracement of the asset price occurred and occurred rather quickly. (See Figure 4.6.)]
16 March	—Over 150 suspect and probable cases of SARS are reported from around the world.
18 March	—Cases are now being reported in Canada, Germany, Taiwan (China), Thailand, and the United Kingdom as well as in Hong Kong, Vietnam, and Singapore. The cumulative total of cases reported to WHO is 219 cases and 4 deaths.
	—Hong Kong reports 123 cases, Hanoi 57, and Singapore 23.
	—Data indicate that the overwhelming majority of cases occur in health care workers, their family members, and others having close face-to-face contact with patients, supporting the view that SARS is spread by contact with droplets when patients cough or sneeze.
	[This is why there was tremendous panic and fear: The people who were supposed to be providing health care to those who became ill were also getting sick and dying.]

TABLE 4.1 *(Continued)*	
Date	**Event**
19 March	—The brother-in-law of the Guangdong doctor dies in a Hong Kong hospital.
20 March	—The United States reports its first cases.
	—The cumulative total of cases climbs to 306, with 10 deaths.
22 March	—Thirteen countries on three continents report a cumulative total of 386 cases and 11 deaths.
23 March	—A WHO five-person GOARN team arrives in Beijing and seeks permission to travel to Guangdong Province.
24 March	—The Singapore Ministry of Health announces home quarantine measures whereby all contacts of SARS patients will be required to stay at home for 10 days. More than 300 persons are affected.
25 March	—Nine air passengers linked to a 15 March flight from Hong Kong to Beijing develop SARS after returning to Hong Kong. The flight is eventually linked to cases in 22 passengers and 2 flight attendants.
	—Scarborough Grace Hospital in Toronto is closed to new patients and visitors.
26 March	—China reports a cumulative total of 792 cases and 31 deaths in Guangdong Province from 16 November 2002 to 28 February 2003. Officials had previously reported 305 cases and 5 deaths from mid-November to 9 February.
	—With the new data from China, the world cumulative total of cases soars to 1,323, with 49 deaths.
	[Chinese intransigence over admitting it had a SARS problem created a miasma of doubt toward authorities handling the crisis in China and Hong Kong. It would cost the mayor of Beijing and the head of the Chinese health ministry their jobs. This denial would change eventually, and the Chinese would become very aggressive in pursuing the disease. This shift helped bring about the end of the outbreak as scientists would gain access to patients in the country and begin the research. However, the damage to the financial markets was already occurring.]
	—Ontario health officials warn of a possible health emergency.
27 March	—Scientists in the WHO laboratory network report major progress in the identification of the causative agent, with results from several labs consistently pointing to a new member of the coronavirus family.
	—Hong Kong announces the closure of schools until 6 April and places 1,080 people under quarantine.
	—Chinese authorities report SARS cases in other parts of China.
	—WHO issues more stringent advice to international travelers and airlines, including recommendations on screening at certain airports.
	[This helps contribute to the free fall in the airline stocks and the currencies of the Far East.]

(continues)

TABLE 4.1 *(Continued)*

Date	Event
28 March	—China joins WHO collaborative networks. —Some airlines in affected countries begin screening departing international travelers. —Financial analysts assess effects on stock markets and predict significant economic consequences if the outbreak is not controlled by June.
29 March	—Dr. Carlo Urbani, the WHO infectious disease specialist who was the first WHO officer to identify the outbreak of this new disease and treat the earliest cases in Hanoi, dies of SARS in Thailand.
30 March	—Canadian health officials close York Central Hospital to new patients and request hundreds of its employees to quarantine themselves. Thousands of Toronto residents face quarantine at home. **[Note: This was near the end of the negative impact on the Canadian dollar. It resumed its pre-SARS upward trend against the U.S. dollar.]** —Hong Kong health authorities announce that 213 residents of the Amoy Gardens housing estate have been hospitalized with SARS since reporting on the disease began. Of this total, 107 reside in a single wing of the 35-story Block E building. Most patients from Block E live in vertically interrelated flats.
31 March	—Health authorities in Hong Kong issue an unprecedented isolation order to prevent the further spread of SARS. —In Singapore, a 64-year-old vegetable hawker at a large wholesale market visits his brother in Singapore General Hospital.
1 April	—In Hong Kong, the number of cases linked to Amoy Gardens continues to grow, strongly suggesting that the disease has spread beyond its initial focus in hospitals, with tertiary as well as secondary cases almost certainly occurring. —WHO epidemiologists determine that since 19 March nine residents of Beijing, Taiwan (China), and Singapore have developed SARS following travel to Hong Kong.
2 April	—WHO recommends that persons traveling to Hong Kong and Guangdong Province consider postponing all but essential travel until further notice. This is the most stringent travel advisory issued by WHO in its 55-year history. **[This aggressive action by WHO caused a further spike in the U.S. dollar against the Singapore dollar and other Far Eastern currencies. However, this was the beginning of the end for the move. At this time, the Singapore government moved quickly to quarantine and isolate those with the disease. Ultimately, this contributed to stopping the spread of the disease.]**

TABLE 4.1 *(Continued)*

Date	Event
	Keep in mind that the announcement occurred close to the trough of the event. Perhaps the worst warnings could be taken as the all clear for the financial markets. It may be that the screaming from the mountaintop was thought to signal that authorities were finally putting all their resources to work and doing everything they could to stop the spread of the disease. It's the "darkest before the dawn" scenario.]
3 April	—The Chinese Minister of Health appears on national television to address SARS-related issues.
4 April	—China begins daily electronic reporting of cases and deaths, nationwide by province.
	—Contact tracing by Singapore health authorities traces 94 SARS cases back to the country's index case, linked to the Metropole Hotel.
7 April	—Morgan Stanley chief economist Stephen Roach estimates the global economic impact of SARS at about US$30 billion.
8 April	—A cumulative total of 2,671 cases and 103 deaths are reported from 17 countries.
9 April	—The WHO team further expresses concern about the situation in Beijing, where only a minority of hospitals make daily reports of SARS cases. Contact tracing is not carried out systematically in Beijing, and health authorities fail to investigate rumors vigorously.
10 April	—A growing number of investigative media reports suggest that cases in Beijing military hospitals are not being frankly reported.
11 April	—South Africa reports its first probable SARS case. Cases have now been reported in 19 countries on four continents.
14 April	—The WHO team in Beijing fails to secure permission to visit military hospitals.
	—The cumulative number of worldwide cases passes the 3,000 mark.
15 April	—The Beijing team is given permission to visit military hospitals. A first visit is made. No reporting of findings is authorized.
	—Hong Kong reports nine SARS deaths, the largest number of deaths for a single day reported to date.
16 April	—Exactly one month after its establishment, the WHO laboratory network announces conclusive identification of the SARS causative agent: an entirely new coronavirus, unlike any other human or animal member of the coronavirus family.
	—In Hong Kong, doctors report that SARS patients from the Amoy Gardens cluster are not responding to treatment as well as patients from other clusters.
	—The WHO team in Beijing estimates that the number of cases in the city is in the range of 100 to 200. The estimate contrasts sharply with the 37 cases officially reported two days previously. The team is granted permission to visit one military hospital.

(continues)

TABLE 4.1 *(Continued)*

Date	Event
17 April	—Economic analysts in the Far East estimate initial SARS-related damage to regional GDP growth at US$10.6–$15 billion. —China's losses, at US$2.2 billion, are the highest, but Hong Kong, where the outbreak has already cost US$1.7 billion, is the biggest SARS-related economic casualty. —In Hong Kong, retail sales have fallen by half since mid-March, tourism arrivals from mainland China have fallen 75 percent to 80 percent, and the entertainment and restaurant industries have recorded an 80 percent drop in business. **[This is about the trough for the move as the disease is just about to reach its peak infection period. The old saw about buying when there's blood in the streets is in play.]**
18 April	—The WHO team in Beijing expresses strong concern over inadequate reporting of SARS cases in military hospitals as rumors about undisclosed cases mount. —Hong Kong officials release the findings of an extensive investigation into a possible environmental cause of the Amoy Gardens cluster of cases. Attention is focused on possible transmission via the sewage system, though many other routes of exposure are also investigated. In an unusual feature, 66 percent of patients in the Amoy Gardens cluster present with diarrhea. In most other clusters of cases, diarrhea is typically seen in only 2 percent to 7 percent of cases.
19 April	—China's top leaders advise officials not to cover up cases of SARS. —Toronto authorities investigate a cluster of 31 suspect and probable SARS cases in members of a charismatic religious group, the health care workers who treated them, and close family and social contacts. Concern centers on opportunities for widespread community transmission during two large gatherings of the religious group on 28 and 29 March. —The Vietnamese government considers closing its 1,130-kilometer border with China.
20 April	—Beijing authorities announce 339 previously undisclosed cases of SARS, bringing the cumulative total of SARS cases in China to 1,959. Chinese authorities further announce that the traditional weeklong May Day holiday will be shortened. —The mayor of Beijing and the minister of health, both of whom had downplayed the SARS threat, are removed from their Communist Party posts. —Singaporean health officials close a large wholesale fruit and vegetable market following detection of a cluster of three SARS cases linked to the market. Cases are traced back to the 64-year-old vegetable hawker.

TABLE 4.1   *(Continued)*

Date	Event
22 April	—Chinese authorities report a cumulative total of 2,001 SARS cases with 92 deaths.
23 April	—Beijing officials suspend all primary and secondary schools for a two-week period.
	—Chinese authorities report a cumulative total of 2,305 probable cases of SARS and 106 deaths. The number of cases in Beijing is now 693.
	—In Singapore, 8 probable and 14 suspect SARS cases are now linked to the vegetable hawker at the wholesale market.
	—WHO advises travelers to Beijing and Shanxi Province, China, and Toronto, Canada, to consider postponing all but essential travel.
	—The cumulative number of probable SARS cases climbs to 4,288, with 251 deaths. China reports 106 of the deaths and Hong Kong reports 105.
	[This was the end of the move essentially, as WHO announced two days before they saw signs that the outbreaks had peaked. This was the last big scare for the Far East.]
25 April	—Outbreaks in Hanoi, Hong Kong, Singapore, and Toronto show signs of peaking.
28 April	—Vietnam is removed from the list of areas with recent local transmission, making it the first country to successfully contain its outbreak.
	—The cumulative total number of cases surpasses 5,000.
30 April	—WHO lifts its travel advice for Toronto.
	[The Canadian dollar didn't experience the same roller-coaster ride that the Far East did with SARS. However, individual companies in the entertainment and travel fields were hurt as tourism dropped. Canadian-based Four Seasons Hotels Inc. operates luxury hotels under the Four Seasons and Regent brand names. While the stock experienced volatility at this time, it didn't see much downside with the outbreak in Canada. The outbreak in Canada was mild compared to the Far East and therefore the stocks of travel and entertainment companies didn't experience severe reactions. (See Figure 4.7.)]
	—China, accounting for 3,460 probable cases of the global total of 5,663, now has more cases than the rest of the world combined.
2 May	—The cumulative total of cases surpasses 6,000.
3 May	—WHO sends a team to Taiwan, which is now reporting a cumulative total of 100 probable cases.
7 May	—WHO estimates that the case fatality ratio of SARS ranges from 0 percent to 50 percent depending on the age group affected, with an overall estimate of case fatality of 14 percent to 15 percent.
8 May	—Travel recommendations are extended to Tianjin and Inner Mongolia in China and to Taipei, Taiwan.

(continues)

TABLE 4.1 *(Continued)*

Date	Event
13 May	—Outbreaks at the remaining initial sites show signs of coming under control, indicating that SARS can be contained.
14 May	—Toronto is removed from the list of areas with recent local transmission.
17 May	—Travel recommendations are extended to Hebei Province, China.
21 May	—Travel recommendations are extended to all of Taiwan.
22 May	—Health authorities in Canada inform WHO of a new hospital-based cluster of five cases of acute respiratory illness in Toronto. —The cumulative global total of cases surpasses 8,000.
23 May	—Travel recommendations for Hong Kong and Guangdong Province are removed. **[Note: We did see a positive spike to Shangri-La, Cathay Pacific, and the Singapore dollar upon this announcement. Even better, you could buy these over the next couple of days and still have made money. In other words, the all clear was sounded and still there were opportunities to buy the stock. The overall positive equity environment spurred by extremely low interest rates dominated the short-term negative impact of the SARS outbreak.]** —Research teams in Hong Kong and China announce detection of a SARS-like virus in the masked palm civet and racoon-dog. These and other wild animals are traditionally consumed as delicacies and sold for human consumption in markets throughout southern China.
26 May	—Toronto returns to the list of areas with recent local transmission.
31 May	—Singapore is removed from the list of areas with recent local transmission. **[By this time, the Singapore dollar had already regained all the lost ground that occurred in March and April.]**
3 June	—The number of newly reported probable cases in China declines to a weekly average of slightly more than two.
12 June	—A team of senior WHO officials arrives in Beijing to assess the situation of SARS control in China.
13 June	—Travel recommendations for Hebei, Inner Mongolia, Shanxi and Tianjin provinces, China, are removed. Guangdong, Hebei, Hubei, Inner Mongolia, Jilin, Jiangsu, Shaanxi, Shanxi and Tianjin provinces are removed from the list of areas with recent local transmission.
17 June	—Travel alert is lifted for Taiwan.
18 June	—The global outbreak enters its 100th day as the number of new cases reported daily dwindles to a handful.
23 June	—Hong Kong is removed from the areas with recent local transmission.
24 June	—Travel recommendations are removed for Beijing, the last remaining area subject to WHO travel advice. Beijing is also removed from the list of areas with recent local transmission.

Source: World Health Organization.

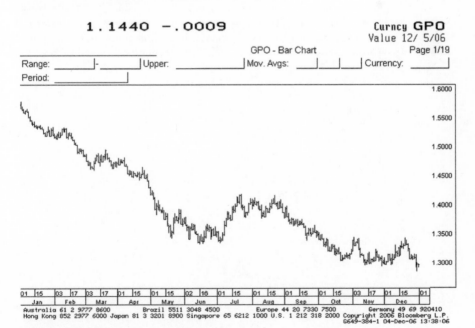

FIGURE 4.1 Shangri-La Asia Ltd
Source: Used with permission from Bloomberg L.P.

FIGURE 4.2 Canadian Dollar
Source: Used with permission from Bloomberg L.P.

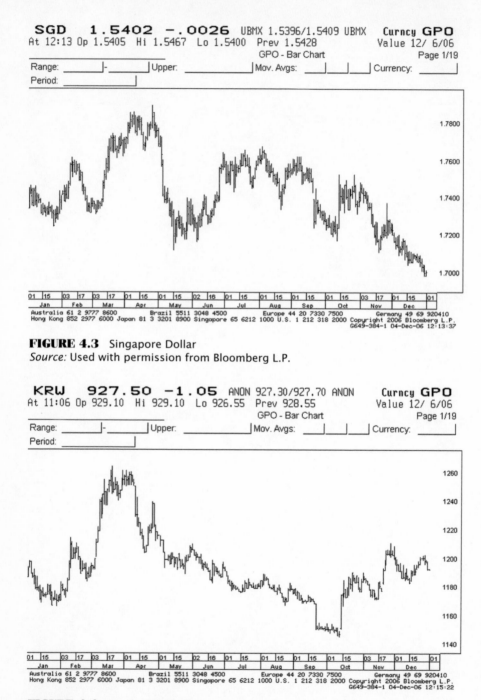

FIGURE 4.3 Singapore Dollar
Source: Used with permission from Bloomberg L.P.

FIGURE 4.4 South Korean Won
Source: Used with permission from Bloomberg L.P.

FIGURE 4.5 Japanese Yen
Source: Used with permission from Bloomberg L.P.

FIGURE 4.6 Cathay Pacific Airways Ltd
Source: Used with permission from Bloomberg L.P.

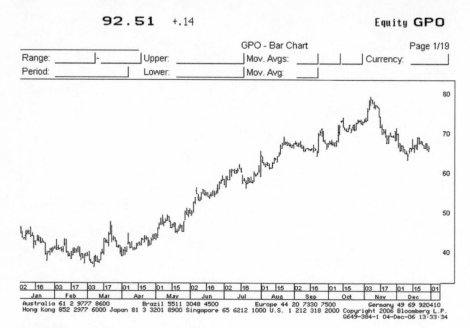

92.51 +.14   Equity **GPO**

FIGURE 4.7 Four Seasons Hotels Inc.
Source: Used with permission from Bloomberg L.P.

and American Airlines all experienced a drop of between 3 and 5 percent. Air Canada was already in a weak position and the stock price further deteriorated, dropping from C$3 to C$1 as the company flirted with bankruptcy (Figure 4.8). In contrast, drug companies that were associated with providing a cure or a test did well, and Gilead Sciences (GILD) went up as fast as the airline stocks went down (Figure 4.9).

One more general point is that disease outbreaks have sharp, short-term impacts that either exacerbate the trends in place or provide temporary pops in the other direction. As you saw in the preceding chapter, the Federal Reserve was in the process of cutting interest rates to extremely low levels when SARS broke out. This is generally U.S. dollar negative and equity positive. All of the stocks quickly recovered, as did the currencies that were negatively impacted.

Disease outbreaks offer traders and investors great opportunities to make money, *if* they can maintain composure and act. You can either go with the direction the disease is heading by selling the region impacted or you can fade the move by buying into the sell-off in expectation of a relatively quick rebound. For the fade, the risk is that the disease has a longer, more protracted effect. In that case, just like during the Black Death, the best trade will be staying alive. To reduce risk, you can buy a stock of an industry that

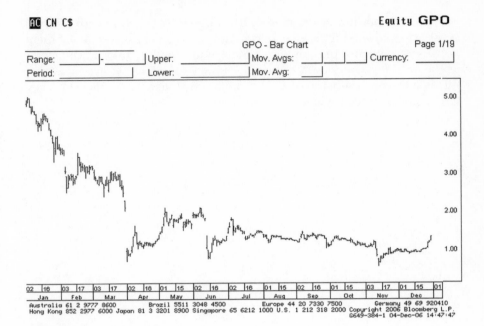

FIGURE 4.8 Air Canada
Source: Used with permission from Bloomberg L.P.

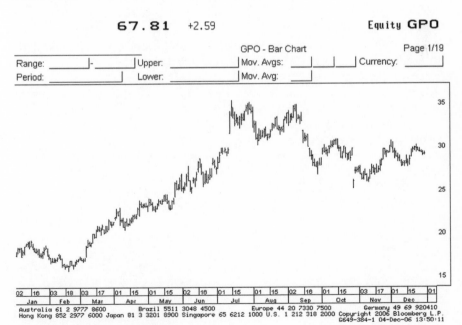

FIGURE 4.9 Gilead Sciences
Source: Used with permission from Bloomberg L.P.

is impacted, but not in the region. It's the market painting with a broad brush when it sells all the stocks in an industry just because some of them are negatively impacted. And it's a great opportunity to take advantage of as the industry leaders will rebound. Without sounding too opportunistic, this is why professional traders do well in times of social upheaval: They have a game plan for when opportunity strikes.

CHAPTER 5

Bird Flu

T he avian flu or bird flu is an unusual twist to our section on infectious diseases. Unlike the previous outbreaks, this one has already been predicted with possible cataclysmic results. It just hasn't happened yet and begs the question, will it happen? Our work from the previous chapters is the foundation for approaching this unique situation. Therefore, this chapter is going to be like the Ghost of Christmas Future, as we'll peer into the possibility of a pandemic flu outbreak that has not yet occurred, but could.

Bird flu has a long history, and the virus has been recognized as a highly lethal disease of poultry since 1901. In 1955, the United Nations Food and Agriculture Organization (FAO) identified a specific type of influenza virus as the causal agent of what was then called fowl plague. In 1997, there were outbreaks of this highly pathogenic H5N1 type virus in poultry farms and wet markets in Hong Kong. Not long after, Hong Kong reported human infections with the virus, with 18 cases and six fatalities. This is the first reported incidence of human infection with the H5N1 virus.

Since then, the reports of bird deaths have been accelerating and spreading throughout the world almost as fast as the doomsayers pushing the panic button on another 1918 Spanish flu. From Indonesia to Azerbaijan to Iraq, there have been confirmed human cases as the migratory patterns of birds have spread the disease. In fact, the H5N1 avian influenza has spread so far and so fast that it is endemic in the Far East and may become that way for Europe and Africa. It is estimated that the global fight against the disease currently needs as much as $1.3 billion to 1.5 billion to fund prevention and research over the next two years to prevent a massive outbreak. It is widely estimated that millions of people could die if bird flu mutates into a form that can be transmitted from human to human like a seasonal flu.

This chapter reviews what is currently understood about the disease, where it may be going, and how to respond should it happen.

WHAT WE KNOW ABOUT INFLUENZA

The following list is taken from the World Health Organization (WHO)'s Top Ten about a pandemic influenza (www.who.int/csr/disease/influenza/pandemic10things/en/).

1. Pandemic influenza is different from avian influenza.

Avian influenza refers to a large group of different influenza viruses that primarily affect birds. On rare occasions, these bird viruses can infect other species, including pigs and humans. The vast majority of avian influenza viruses do not infect humans. An influenza pandemic happens when a new subtype emerges that has not previously circulated in humans.

For this reason, avian H5N1 is a strain with pandemic potential, since it might ultimately adapt into a strain that is contagious among humans. Once this adaptation occurs, it will no longer be a bird virus—it will be a human influenza virus. Influenza pandemics are caused by new influenza viruses that have adapted to humans.

2. Influenza pandemics are recurring events.

An influenza pandemic is a rare but recurrent event. Three pandemics occurred in the previous century: "Spanish influenza" in 1918, "Asian influenza" in 1957, and "Hong Kong influenza" in 1968. The 1918 pandemic killed an estimated 40 to 50 million people worldwide. That pandemic, which was exceptional, is considered one of the deadliest disease events in human history. Subsequent pandemics were much milder, with an estimated 2 million deaths in 1957 and 1 million deaths in 1968.

A pandemic occurs when a new influenza virus emerges and starts spreading as easily as normal influenza—by coughing and sneezing. Because the virus is new, the human immune system will have no preexisting immunity. This makes it likely that people who contract pandemic influenza will experience more serious disease than that caused by normal influenza.

3. The world may be on the brink of another pandemic.

Health experts have been monitoring a new and extremely severe influenza virus—the H5N1 strain—for almost eight years [as of October 14, 2005]. The H5N1 strain first infected humans in Hong Kong in 1997, causing 18 cases, including six deaths. Since mid-2003, this virus has caused the largest and most severe outbreaks in poultry on record. In December 2003, infections in people exposed to sick birds were identified.

Since then, over 100 human cases have been laboratory confirmed in four Asian countries (Cambodia, Indonesia, Thailand, and Vietnam), and more than half of these people have died. Most cases have occurred in previously healthy children and young adults. Fortunately, the virus does not jump easily from birds to humans or spread readily and sustainably among humans. Should H5N1 evolve to a form as contagious as normal influenza, a pandemic could begin.

4. All countries will be affected.

Once a fully contagious virus emerges, its global spread is considered inevitable. Countries might, through measures such as border closures and travel restrictions, delay arrival of the virus, but they cannot stop it. The pandemics of the previous century encircled the globe in six to nine months, even when most international travel was by ship. Given the speed and volume of international air travel today, the virus could spread more rapidly, possibly reaching all continents in less than three months.

5. Widespread illness will occur.

Because most people will have no immunity to the pandemic virus, infection and illness rates are expected to be higher than during seasonal epidemics of normal influenza. Current projections for the next pandemic estimate that a substantial percentage of the world's population will require some form of medical care. Few countries have the staff, facilities, equipment, and hospital beds needed to cope with large numbers of people who suddenly fall ill.

6. Medical supplies will be inadequate.

Supplies of vaccines and antiviral drugs—the two most important medical interventions for reducing illness and deaths during a pandemic—will be inadequate in all countries at the start of a pandemic and for many months thereafter. Inadequate supplies of vaccines are of particular concern, as vaccines are considered the first line of defense for protecting populations. On present trends, many developing countries will have no access to vaccines throughout the duration of a pandemic.

7. Large numbers of deaths will occur.

Historically, the number of deaths during a pandemic has varied greatly. Death rates are largely determined by four factors: the number of people who become infected, the virulence of the virus, the underlying characteristics and vulnerability of affected populations, and the effectiveness of preventive measures. Accurate predictions of mortality cannot be made before the pandemic virus emerges and begins to spread. All estimates of the number of deaths are purely speculative.

WHO has used a relatively conservative estimate—from 2 million to 7.4 million deaths—because it provides a useful and plausible planning target. This estimate is based on the comparatively mild 1957 pandemic. Estimates based on a more virulent virus, closer to the one seen in 1918, have been made and are much higher. However, the 1918 pandemic was considered exceptional.

8. Economic and social disruption will be great.

High rates of illness and worker absenteeism are expected, and these will contribute to social and economic disruption. Past pandemics have spread globally in two and sometimes three waves. Not all parts of the world or of a single country are expected to be severely affected at the same time. Social and economic disruptions could be temporary, but may be amplified in today's closely interrelated and interdependent systems of trade and commerce. Social disruption may be greatest when rates of absenteeism impair essential services, such as power, transportation, and communications.

9. Every country must be prepared.

WHO has issued a series of recommended strategic actions for responding to the influenza pandemic threat. The actions are designed to provide different layers of defense that reflect the complexity of the evolving situation. Recommended actions are different for the present phase of pandemic alert, the emergence of a pandemic virus, and the declaration of a pandemic and its subsequent international spread.

10. WHO will alert the world when the pandemic threat increases.

WHO works closely with ministries of health and various public health organizations to support countries' surveillance of circulating influenza strains. A sensitive surveillance system that can detect emerging influenza strains is essential for the rapid detection of a pandemic virus.

Six distinct phases have been defined to facilitate pandemic preparedness planning, with roles defined for governments, industry, and WHO. The present situation is categorized as phase 3: A virus new to humans is causing infections, but does not spread easily from one person to another.

NOW DO I HAVE YOUR ATTENTION?

After reading this, I realize the basis instinct is to go buy masks, stock up the shelves with food and water, and hide in the basement—which I did a little myself when I first read reports on this from *Foreign Affairs* and WHO. If you really want to get spooked, read some of the U.S. government's preparation suggestions, like storing a two-week supply of water and food, at www.pandemicflu.gov.

It's important to understand that although the world is getting prepared for a pandemic, it is far from certain that one is going to occur. This virus has been around since 1901, but we've seen only three influenza outbreaks, of which only one caused massive deaths and disruption to society. Each subsequent pandemic was less lethal, as deaths declined from 40 to 50 million in 1918 according to WHO to 2 million in 1957 and to 1 million in 1968. It's this progression that leads us to various scenarios of the potential outbreak of disease.

In Chapter 2 on the 1918 H1N1 outbreak, we discussed how the virus mutates as rapid reproduction produces mistakes in the genetic code. These mutations are how the disease progresses and increases its ability to spread, along with its lethality. So far, the avian influenza has remained solely on a bird-to-human transmission schedule. This means that to contract the disease one has to come in direct contact with the birds or their droppings. Direct-contact deaths of this kind have occurred in parts of the world that have the closest and most frequent human-to-animal proximity. As we learned from Chapter 4 on SARS, the Far East gets the award for these conditions and Vietnam is the poster child for poultry-human contact.

According to the United Nations Food and Agriculture Organization (www.fao.org), approximately half of all Vietnamese households, rural and urban, keep poultry. In the eight million rural family households, three out of four typically own chickens and keep backyard flocks. Taking a step back for the entire region, the bird population for the eastern and southeastern parts of Asia is estimated to be around six billion birds. Like Vietnam, the region has a large portion of the poultry population in smaller farms. This is important for policy reasons when a government attempts to stem the spread of the disease by culling the birds. In November 2005, China had outbreaks of the disease in nine different provinces that resulted in the culling of around 20 million birds.

To recap, proximity to infected birds is the key determinant for human infection. If this is the case, then the culling would work and stop the spread of the disease. Pretty simple, right? Well, this is where the mutation component of influenza is the problem. Eventually, biologists believe the H5N1 strain will mutate and make the jump from bird-to-human to human-to-human transmission. This is when the big trouble starts and when the disease can explode into a major killer. Remember, influenza virus is airborne, unlike SARS. Its transmission is immensely facilitated by this feature. Also remember, quarantine will be useless because those who are infected with influenza and contagious can be asymptomatic and appear healthy. In other words, you wouldn't know who to stop and stick in a hospital until it's too late.

Of course, if it's like the Spanish flu, those infected could die within 48 hours of getting the disease anyway. Nice thought. The point is that, just like the Spanish flu, an avian flu pandemic would have to burn itself out or mutate itself out rather than be eradicated by any medical prevention and isolation program from a government.

BACK TO THE FUTURE: A SHORT VIEW OF A LONG TIME LINE

We're going to mention only a few points on the time line, as there has yet to be a major human avian influenza outbreak and market reaction to it. However, there are some interesting sequences for the development of the disease. This chronology comes from the World Health Organization's web site.

📖 This time line starts in 1996, and could reach as far back as 1918. Personally, I didn't take much notice of a potential pandemic until the summer of 2005 when an article by Laurie Garrett in *Foreign Affairs* called "The Next Pandemic?" came out.

The WHO's time line shows a progression of the disease as avian flu spreads in fowl first and then in humans across the globe. In three years, it has worked its way up from Vietnam into China, across to Russia, and into Europe. By the time this book is published, avian flu should be in North America and perhaps human cases will have occurred as well. Also, the virus is mutating; it's infecting not only birds, but also those lovely critters from SARS, civet cats, as well (July 15, 2005).

In November 2005, this is what the U.S. Homeland Security Council's National Strategy for Pandemic Influenza had to say:

> *The current pandemic threat stems from an unprecedented outbreak of avian influenza in Asia and Europe, caused by the H5N1 strain of the Influenza A virus. To date, the virus has infected birds in 16 countries and has resulted in the deaths, through illness and culling, of approximately 200 million birds across Asia. While traditional control measures have been attempted, the virus is now endemic in Southeast Asia, present in long-range migratory birds, and unlikely to be eradicated soon.*
>
> *A notable and worrisome feature of the H5N1 virus is its ability to infect a wide range of hosts, including birds and humans. As of the date of this document, the virus is known to have infected 121 people in four countries, resulting in 62 deaths over the past two years. Although the virus has not yet shown an ability to transmit efficiently between humans, as is seen with the annual influenza virus, there is concern that it will acquire this capability through genetic mutation or exchange of genetic material with a human influenza virus.*
>
> *It is impossible to know whether the currently circulating H5N1 virus will cause a human pandemic. The widespread nature of H5N1 in birds and the likelihood of mutations over time raise our concerns that the virus will become transmissible between humans, with potentially catastrophic consequences. If this does not happen with the current H5N1 strain, history suggests that a different influenza virus will emerge and result in the next pandemic.*

The takeaway here is that if it isn't this strain of influenza, it'll be another one sometime soon, and we had better be ready for it when it happens.

KNOWN TREATMENTS

Here's what the WHO has to say in the frequently asked questions (FAQs) section on avian influenza (www.who.int/csr/disease/avian_influenza/avian_faqs/en/index.html#drugs2):

Two drugs (in the neuraminidase inhibitors class), oseltamivir (commercially known as Tamiflu) and zanamivir (commercially known as Relenza), can reduce the severity and duration of illness caused by seasonal influenza. The efficacy of the neuraminidase inhibitors depends, among others, on their early administration (within 48 hours after symptom onset). For cases of human infection with H5N1, the drugs may improve prospects of survival, if adminis- tered early, but clinical data are limited. The H5N1 virus is expected to be susceptible to the neuraminidase inhibitors. Antiviral resis- tance to neuraminidase inhibitors has been clinically negligible so far but is likely to be detected during widespread use during a pan- demic.

An older class of antiviral drugs, the M2 inhibitors amantadine and rimantadine, could potentially be used against pandemic in- fluenza, but resistance to these drugs can develop rapidly and this could significantly limit their effectiveness against pandemic in- fluenza. Some currently circulating H5N1 strains are fully resistant to these M2 inhibitors. However, should a new virus emerge through reassortment, the M2 inhibitors might be effective.

For the neuraminidase inhibitors, the main constraints—which are substantial—involve limited production capacity and a price that is prohibitively high for many countries. At present manufactur- ing capacity, which has recently quadrupled, it will take a decade to produce enough oseltamivir to treat 20 percent of the world's pop- ulation. The manufacturing process for oseltamivir is complex and time-consuming, and is not easily transferred to other facilities.

So far, most fatal pneumonia seen in cases of H5N1 infection has resulted from the effects of the virus, and cannot be treated with antibiotics. Nonetheless, since influenza is often complicated by secondary bacterial infection of the lungs, antibiotics could be life-saving in the case of late-onset pneumonia. WHO regards it as prudent for countries to ensure adequate supplies of antibiotics in advance.

This is important, as Tamiflu and Relenza are singled out as drugs that can reduce the severity and duration of the influenza.

Countries around the world are not sitting idly by while a potential pan- demic gathers steam. The United States has a national strategy for dealing with an outbreak, which you can review at www.whitehouse.gov/homeland/ pandemic-influenza.html.

Essentially, the U.S. government is in the process of stockpiling drugs and has already ordered six million more influenza treatments from Roche Holding AG and GlaxoSmithKline Plc to increase the national stockpile to

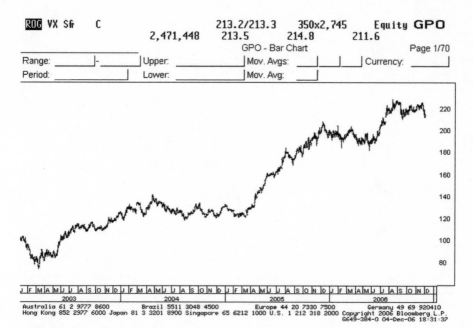

FIGURE 5.1   Roche Holding AG
Source: Used with permission from Bloomberg L.P.

26 million, according to Bloomberg: "The order includes 3.8 million courses of treatment with Roche's Tamiflu and 2.2 million of Glaxo's Relenza that would be used in case the bird virus changes into a form that's contagious in people." Therefore, we don't even need to have an outbreak occur before society reacts and drug sales are impacted. Figures 5.1 and 5.2 show the charts for both Roche Holding AG and GlaxoSmithKline Plc since 2003. The point is that the financial markets are already anticipating the outbreak with a run-up in drug company stocks. These stocks had a banner year in 2005 as the bird flu became more prevalent and the U.S. government began to stockpile their drugs.

EVALUATING THREE "KNOWN UNKNOWNS" SCENARIOS

There are several potential outcomes to the mutation pattern that influenza follows. There is a weak outbreak where only sporadic infections are occurring and the influenza never makes it past the stage of being sporadic. As I mentioned earlier, some scientists believe this is a likely outcome as

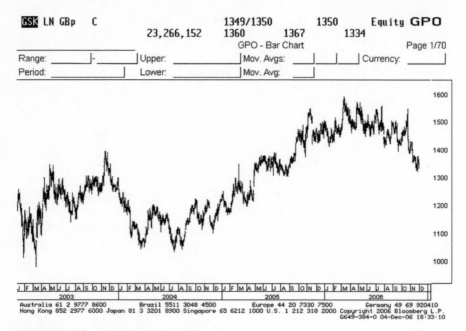

FIGURE 5.2 GlaxoSmithKline Plc
Source: Used with permission from Bloomberg L.P.

the H5N1 virus has been found in birds for a long period of time and has not made the jump from bird-to-human transmission to human-to-human transmission. A recent study in the magazine *Nature* has found that humans with H5N1 don't spread the disease easily by just coughing or sneezing, which would mean the strain is not readily transmissible through the air. This would support the theory that a pandemic is not likely to happen with the current strain of H5N1. With this scenario, we would most likely see a sell-off in drug stocks, because the market would've already owned them in anticipation of a big flu outbreak.

Next, we could have a mild outbreak that is contained to the Far East. This would potentially mimic the SARS outbreak scenario where it was a short, sharp shock to the system for the area in which the outbreak occurred, but it didn't spread further. We know from Chapter 4 that hotels, airlines, tourism, shopping malls, and entertainment industries are all on the front line for seeing their stock prices decline. Hospitals and health care providers would be early winners as their beds get filled beyond their limits. We can also anticipate weaker currencies initially in those countries where the disease spreads. However, this could be a great buying opportunity if we see a larger force at work such as a Federal Reserve easing cycle. Another aspect to this would be an overreaction to a perceived outbreak by the central banks around the world and an easing by them to avert a perceived global slowdown stemming from the disease. Investing and trading aren't easy; they're not meant to be. This is why you have to understand the larger forces at work as a mild outbreak occurs and the reactions of government agencies to the perceived risk. To state the obvious, drug companies that have a vaccine or a potential treatment for avian influenza would perform well, and have already seen their sales increase just in anticipation. However, these may not be the best plays. The entire market would benefit from lower interest rates, especially the financial sector as they would get cheap money from the central bank. This could lead to a short-term pop to the housing market as mortgage rates come down.

Let's create a 1918-style outbreak scenario. In this scenario, the outbreak can overwhelm whatever broader financial forces may be at work. It's very likely that we would see aggressive moves by G7 (the seven largest industrialized countries) central banks to ease and supply liquidity into the banking systems to ensure they stay running smoothly and calm fears. This would mean that bond prices would go higher as the European Central Bank, the Bank of Japan, and the Federal Reserve all add reserves and increased liquidity into the system.

This would be especially important should nations decide to shut borders to countries that have had outbreaks and potentially cause a liquidity squeeze for local financial institutions. Not surprisingly, the list of candidates for border closings is going to contain the poorer countries that haven't spent enough money on their health care infrastructures. It will coincide with the countries most likely to have the highest human-to-animal contact and the first major outbreak of the pandemic influenza: the Far East. The actions by the central banks should help offset the deflation that could occur should a massive outbreak happen.

The risk is that economies will shut down as workers stop showing up over fears of catching the disease. Essentially, labor-intensive industries will be negatively impacted due to this change in behavior. Pandemic emergency planners are predicting absenteeism as high as 30 percent. Consumer demand will be negatively impacted as everyone stays home and out of the malls.

In this extreme scenario, other industries come into play. Certain service industries, such as UPS and Peapod, could do extremely well. Why? Consumers reluctant to be face-to-face with large numbers of other consumers will shop online to avoid the contact, and somebody's got to deliver the goods.

Consequently, online shopping would jump tremendously. Imagine the outbreak occurring during the Christmas season. Or how about during the Super Bowl? Just like during the Black Death when people avoided social gathering places, patrons would avoid bars and stadiums for sporting events, and beer and alcohol sales would fall. Telecoms could also benefit should the massive increase in traffic necessitate a huge demand increase for the Internet and bandwidth. One more step down this path: Home entertainment providers should see demand increase for their goods. Microsoft, Nintendo, Blockbuster, and Netflix would all benefit, as well as producers of flat screen TVs and other media devices.

Those companies that have substantial business in death benefits or life insurance will feel the largest negative impact. On the opposite side, those companies that write annuity policies will see huge rewards. The ultimate hedge trade, then, is to sell companies doing life insurance and buy companies doing annuities. Unfortunately, most insurance companies do both as their own hedge.

There is one type of company under the sector of consumer discretionary that would without a doubt do *very* well. If 1918 is our paradigm, the funeral home business would not be able to keep up with the demand. Service Corporation International (SCI) is an example of a company that would be an excellent hedge against a large drop in the population. It's in the funeral business. Essentially, any company that would be engaged in the cleanup and removal of bodies would be a winner.

PART II

Natural Disasters

CHAPTER 6

Hurricanes

E ver since Hurricanes Katrina and Rita hit the U.S. Gulf Coast, the financial world has become aware of every tropical depression that forms off Africa between June 1 and November 30. The storms rocked the United States and showed that nature can eventually find and hit the weakest link in the economic armor.

Hurricanes are the monsters of the weather world. The fact that they tend to hit exactly where Americans like to live and vacation makes them especially onerous. The fact that they can also hit in an area where much of the country's domestic energy supplies come out of the ground makes hurricanes a disruptive economic force.

The name *hurricane* comes from the Arawak tribe in the Caribbean, who called the storms "evil spirit" or *hurakan*. As Paul Douglas mentions in his book, *Restless Skies*, these storms inspired so much fear and fascination that living sacrifices were offered centuries ago to appease the ruthless god Yuracan, who came from the sea, rarely showing any mercy. While I don't envision going back to that tradition, I think it would be wise to go back to that mind-set: Hurricanes are meant to be watched closely and feared.

In this chapter, we break down exactly how a storm forms, how a storm is categorized, and where storms hit in the United States. Like infectious diseases, it's important to understand the nature of the beast before we can analyze the impact it will have on the economy and the financial markets. Next, we review five major storms of the past 20 years to show the impact of the hurricanes on the areas hit and on the overall economy. Last, we examine the effects the storms had on the financial markets and on individual companies.

NOAA KNOWS BEST

According to the National Oceanic and Atmospheric Administration (NOAA, www.noaa.gov), a hurricane is actually defined as a type of tropical cyclone that is a low-pressure system that generally forms in the tropics. These large, circular storms form over warm ocean water and rotate counterclockwise in the Northern Hemisphere. The storm converts this heat into energy that feeds the beast and grows the system.

Hurricanes can form in both the Atlantic and the Pacific oceans. Hurricanes are behemoths and can grow as large as 700 miles wide. Unlike tornadoes, hurricanes can last for weeks.

- The eye at a hurricane's center is a relatively calm, clear area approximately 20 to 40 miles across.
- The eye wall surrounding the eye is composed of dense clouds that contain the highest winds in the storm.
- The storm's outer rain bands (often with hurricane-force or tropical storm–force winds) are made up of dense bands of thunderstorms ranging from a few miles to tens of miles wide and 50 to 300 miles long.
- Hurricane-force winds can extend outward about 25 miles in a small hurricane and more than 150 miles for a large one. Tropical storm–force winds can stretch out as far as 300 miles from the center of a large hurricane.
- Frequently, the right side of a hurricane is the most dangerous in terms of storm surge, winds, and tornadoes.
- A hurricane's speed and path depend on complex ocean and atmospheric interactions, including the presence or absence of other weather patterns. This complexity of the flow makes it very difficult to predict the speed and direction of a hurricane.
- Do not focus on the eye or the track—hurricanes are immense systems that can move in complex patterns that are difficult to predict. Be prepared for changes in size, intensity, speed, and direction.

The last point underscores the big problem with this weather pattern. The experts can't predict precisely where a hurricane will hit with enough time to make a difference.

Where Do Hurricane Names Come From?

According to NOAA, the National Hurricane Center has named Atlantic tropical storms since 1953. The original name lists featured only women's names. In 1979, men's names began alternating with the women's names. Currently, this list is maintained and updated by an international committee of the World Meteorological Organization. Six lists are used in rotation, which means that the 2005 list will be used again in 2011. So if you think you are experiencing déjà vu over one of these hurricanes, you probably are.

However, the nastiest and most destructive storms get their names retired—sort of a Reverse Hall of Fame, if you will. This retired list includes Andrew and Katrina.

Hurricanes are classified by wind speed, central pressure, and damage potential using something called the Saffir-Simpson Hurricane Scale. See Table 6.1.

GOOD NEWS, BAD NEWS

Let's do a little good news/bad news routine on hurricanes. The good news is that on average only five hurricanes hit the United States every three years and on average only two of those will be major (category 3 or higher). The bad news is that 2005 was not an average year as there were 28 named storms, including 15 hurricanes of which seven were major and four hit the United States (Dennis, Katrina, Rita, and Wilma). The good news is that 2006 ended without a major hurricane hitting the United States. The bad news

TABLE 6.1 Saffir-Simpson Hurricane Scale

Scale Number (Category)	Sustained Winds (MPH)	Damage	Storm Surge
1	74–95	Minimal: Unanchored mobile homes, vegetation, signs.	4–5 feet
2	96–110	Moderate: All mobile homes, roofs, small crafts, flooding.	6–8 feet
3	111–130	Extensive: Small buildings, low-lying roads cut off.	9–12 feet
4	131–155	Extreme: Roofs destroyed, trees down, roads cut off, mobile homes destroyed. Beach homes flooded.	13–18 feet
5	More than 155	Catastrophic: Most buildings destroyed. Vegetation destroyed. Major roads cut off. Homes flooded.	Greater than 18 feet

Source: Federal Emergency Management Agency (FEMA).

is that the conditions that produce major hurricanes (warmer waters) are still in existence and likely to persist.

The good news is that forecasters are getting better at predicting when and where a hurricane will hit. The bad news is that people still ignore the warnings and local, state, and federal authorities still don't coordinate their activities for the storm. The good news is that over the past century, loss of life has declined with the exception of Katrina (which resulted in approximately 1,300 deaths). The bad news is that more and more people are moving to the areas where hurricanes hit, and that means the property losses are growing with each storm.

THE WORST OF THE WORST

When you take a look at the costliest storms to hit the United States, you can view them in two ways: current dollars and normalized dollars. Table 6.2 shows an impressive list of destructive storms and their estimated costs in current dollars from 1900 to 2004. Not on the list is the no-name storm that hit southeast Florida, Mississippi, and Alabama that caused over $100 billion in 2004 dollars.

What's interesting is that the list of the top 30 storms includes seven from 2000 to 2004 and doesn't include 2005's record-breaking year of four major storms. A recalculation through 2005 would mean that over 30 percent of the worst storms in those 106 years have occurred in the last six years. Over the past 20 years, the number goes up to 40 percent.

The numbers are even worse when you look at costs unadjusted for inflation. If we include 2005, 70 percent of the most costly storms occurred in 2004 and 2005. The trend is not your friend when it comes to frequency of storms and the costliness of those storms.

Demographics have a lot to do with why the costs of these storms are going up. More and more people are drawn to the allure of living by the sea. Whereas the local Floridian Indian tribes built their villages away from the shores, modern man is doing the opposite. Florida, Alabama, North Carolina, and Georgia get the highest frequency of the costliest storms. The southern states of Texas, Louisiana, Mississippi, South Carolina, Tennessee, and Maryland round out the next group. The top six costliest storms—Andrew, Charley, Ivan, Katrina, Rita, and Wilma—all hit those areas.

With that in mind, let's examine the top five hurricanes in chronological order to see how they developed, how the impacted the country, and how they impacted the financial markets. We'll end with the most surprising twist of all: No major hurricanes hit the United States in 2006.

TABLE 6.2   The 30 Costliest Mainland U.S. Hurricanes and Tropical Storms (1900–2004)

Rank	Hurricane	Year	Category	Damage (U.S. Dollars)
1	Andrew (SE FL/SE LA)	1992	5	$26,500,000,000
2	Charley (SW FL)	2004	4	15,000,000,000
3	Ivan (AL/NW FL)	2004	3	14,200,000,000
4	Frances (FL)	2004	2	8,900,000,000
5	Hugo (SC)	1989	4	7,000,000,000
6	Jeanne (FL)	2004	3	6,900,000,000
7	Allison (N TX)	2001	TS	5,000,000,000
8	Floyd (Mid-Atlantic/NE U.S.)	1999	2	4,500,000,000
9	Isabel (Mid-Atlantic)	2003	2	3,370,000,000
10	Fran (NC)	1996	3	3,200,000,000
11	Opal (NW FL/AL)	1995	3	3,000,000,000
12	Frederic (AL/MS)	1979	3	2,300,000,000
13	Agnes (FL/NE U.S.)	1972	1	2,100,000,000
14	Alicia (N TX)	1983	3	2,000,000,000
15	Bob (NC/NE U.S.)	1991	2	1,500,000,000
15	Juan (LA)	1985	1	1,500,000,000
17	Camille (MS/SE LA/VA)	1969	5	1,420,700,000
18	Betsy (SE FL/SE LA)	1965	3	1,420,500,000
19	Elena (MS/AL/NW FL)	1985	3	1,250,000,000
20	Georges (FL Keys/MS/AL)	1998	2	1,155,000,000
21	Gloria (Eastern U.S.)	1985	3	900,000,000
22	Lili (SC/LA)	2002	1	860,000,000
23	Diane (NE U.S.)	1955	1	831,700,000
24	Bonnie (NC/VA)	1998	2	720,000,000
25	Erin (NW FL)	1998	2	700,000,000
26	Allison (N TX)	1989	TS	500,000,000
26	Alberto (NW FL/GA/AL)	1994	TS	500,000,000
26	Frances (TX)	1998	TS	500,000,000
29	Eloise (NW FL)	1975	3	490,000,000
30	Carol (NE U.S.)	1954	3	461,000,000

Source: National Oceanic and Atmospheric Administration (NOAA).

HURRICANE ANDREW (1992)

Prior to Katrina, Hurricane Andrew was the most destructive storm to hit the United States. Like most Atlantic hurricanes, it started as a tropical wave from the coast of Africa. After its birth on August 14, it then became a tropical depression and morphed into Tropical Storm Andrew three days later. Figure 6.1 shows its path through Florida and into Louisiana.

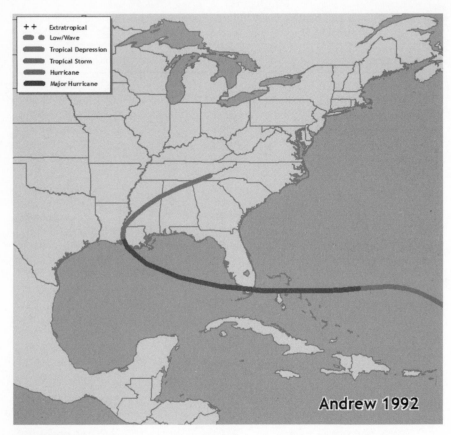

FIGURE 6.1   Path of Hurricane Andrew
Source: National Oceanic and Atmospheric Administration (NOAA).

The National Hurricane Center (NHC) describes Andrew's progression (www.nhc.noaa.gov/HAW2/english/history_printer.shtml#andrew):

Further development was slow, as the west-northwestward-moving Andrew encountered an unfavorable upper-level trough. Indeed, the storm almost dissipated on August 20 due to vertical wind shear. By August 21, Andrew was midway between Bermuda and Puerto Rico and turning westward into a more favorable environment. Rapid strengthening occurred, with Andrew reaching hurricane strength on the 22nd and Category 4 status on the 23rd. After briefly weakening over the Bahamas, Andrew regained Category 4 status as it blasted its way across south Florida on August 24. The hurricane continued westward into the Gulf of Mexico where it gradually turned northward. This motion brought Andrew to the central Louisiana coast on August 26 as a Category 3 hurricane. Andrew then turned northeastward, eventually merging with a frontal system over the Mid-Atlantic states on August 28.

Andrew caused 26 deaths and $26.5 billion in damage. Unusual for a hurricane, most of the damage was done by high winds and not flooding caused by flash flooding or storm surge. The NHC lists the four most dangerous elements of a hurricane in this order:

1. Flash flooding inland
2. Storm surge
3. High winds
4. Tornadoes

Usually, when we think of winners and losers from a hurricane we separate them into groups by who got hurt, who has to pay, and what commodity became scarce. With that in mind, let's run through the losers.

First, we have all the people in the storm's path. Next, we have the insurance companies that people have policies with that must pay out to cover the costs inflicted by the storms. Let's take a look at what happened to the NASDAQ Insurance Index in August of 1992. This is a capitalization-weighted index designed to measure the performance of all NASDAQ stocks in the insurance sector. In Figure 6.2, we can see the index tanked over the time frame that Hurricane Andrew developed and whacked Florida. The insurance industry in Florida was devastated by the incursion of $16 billion in insured losses. It forced the state legislature to create the Florida Hurricane Catastrophe Fund to help insurance companies in the event of another catastrophe and to encourage them to keep offering insurance in the state.

Home builders were not initially seen as potential beneficiaries from a hurricane, and their stock prices fell initially. After October 1992, companies like Centex (CTX, Figure 6.3) saw their stock prices rise steadily after the market realized builders would be doing big business rebuilding in Florida. The initial reaction had been to sell shares in home builders as the market believed that any homes those companies were currently building in the region would be damaged. The stock prices began to rise in late September!

Three commodities had a particularly strong run associated with Andrew: oil, natural gas, and lumber. Using the generic code for lumber (LB1) on Bloomberg, we see a big spike in lumber from mid-August through early September (Figure 6.4). But you had to be quick to take profits, as the price reversed almost as quickly.

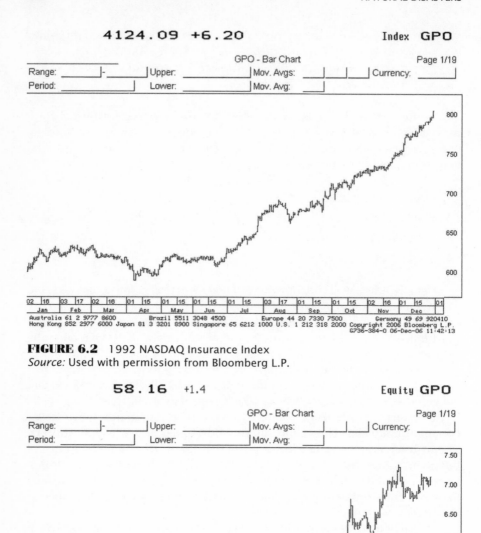

FIGURE 6.2   1992 NASDAQ Insurance Index
Source: Used with permission from Bloomberg L.P.

FIGURE 6.3   1992 Centex
Source: Used with permission from Bloomberg L.P.

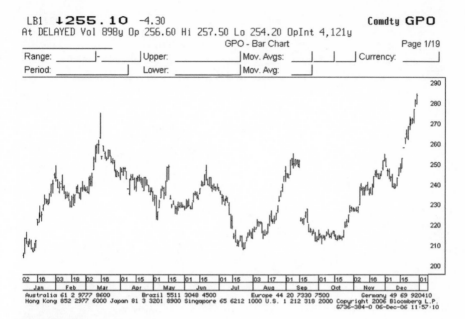

FIGURE 6.4 1992 Lumber
Source: Used with permission from Bloomberg L.P.

Oil (CL1) experienced a similar pattern with a rally that started in August, but faded in October (Figure 6.5).

Natural gas (NG1) had a similar trading pattern (Figure 6.6). All three commodities experienced short-term pops to the upside followed by reversals within two months. Lumber was the only one of the three that followed the pattern but ended the year significantly higher from August.

For the major indexes, Hurricane Andrew contributed to a new low for the Dow Jones Industrial Average (INDU INDX, Figure 6.7), a new low for the U.S. dollar index (DXY INDX, Figure 6.8), and a new low for the yield on the U.S. Treasury 10-year bond (USGG10YR INDX, Figure 6.9). As with the commodities, the price action was temporary and later unwound.

The temporary nature of the negative impact from Hurricane Andrew stems from the markets taking some time to digest a new phenomenon and what would be the implications for the economy afterward. Initially seen as a disaster, Andrew's impact was subsequently viewed as a net zero impact as the rebuilding of the areas devastated offset the devastation.

HURRICANES CHARLEY AND IVAN (2004)

Since these storms hit within a month of each other, we'll consider them in tandem as their impacts can't be separated from each other. Their unusual

FIGURE 6.5 1992 Crude
Source: Used with permission from Bloomberg L.P.

FIGURE 6.6 1992 Natural Gas
Source: Used with permission from Bloomberg L.P.

12311.49 -20.11   Index **GPO**

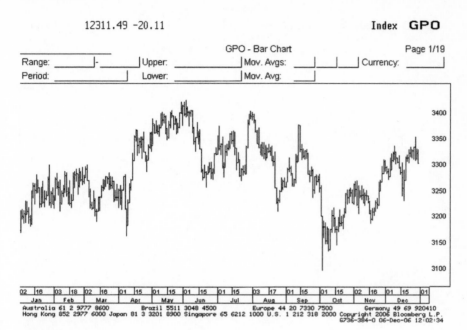

FIGURE 6.7 1992 Dow Jones Industrial Average
Source: Used with permission from Bloomberg L.P.

DXY   **82.63 +.12**   Curncy **GPO**
At DELAYED   Op 82.53 Hi 82.88 Lo 82.40

FIGURE 6.8 1992 U.S. Dollar Index
Source: Used with permission from Bloomberg L.P.

USGG10YR ↓4.468 +.027 4.471/4.468   Index **GPO**
At 12:00 Op 4.440 Hi 4.473 Lo 4.440

FIGURE 6.9 1992 U.S. 10-Year Bond Yield
Source: Used with permission from Bloomberg L.P.

behavior underscores why the serious trader must understand their nature when analyzing hurricanes. Just like my kids, they don't always do what is expected or predicted. This is why I list the entire description to show how each storm follows a unique path.

Let's start with the NHC's description and diagram of Charley. Figure 6.10 shows its path from Jamaica over Cuba, where it weakened temporarily, a familiar pattern for hurricanes as they pass over land. From the NHC web site (www.nhc.noaa.gov/HAW2/english/history_printer.shtml# charley):

> *Charley then came under the influence of an unseasonably strong mid-tropospheric trough that had dropped from the east-central United States into the eastern Gulf of Mexico. The hurricane turned north-northeastward and accelerated toward the southwest coast of Florida as it began to intensify rapidly. . . . By 10 A.M., the maximum winds had increased to near 125 m.p.h., and three hours later had increased to 145 m.p.h.—category 4 strength. Charley made landfall with maximum winds near 150 m.p.h. on the southwest coast of Florida just north of Captiva Island around 3:45 P.M. An hour later, Charley's eye passed over Punta Gorda. The hurricane then crossed*

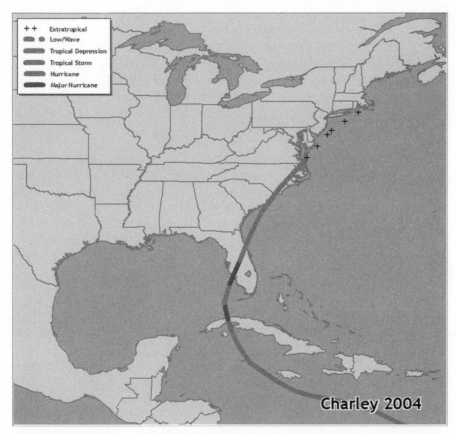

FIGURE 6.10 Path of Hurricane Charley
Source: National Oceanic and Atmospheric Administration (NOAA).

central Florida, passing near Kissimmee and Orlando. Charley was still of hurricane intensity around midnight when its center cleared the northeast coast of Florida near Daytona Beach. After moving into the Atlantic, Charley came ashore again near Cape Romain, South Carolina, near midday on the 14th as a category 1 hurricane. The center then moved just offshore before making a final landfall at North Myrtle Beach. Charley soon weakened to a tropical storm over southeastern North Carolina and became extratropical on the 15th as it moved back over water near Virginia Beach.

This was a compact storm by most standards, as the maximum winds and storm surge extended only seven miles from the eye. However, the winds crushed two cities, Punta Gorda and Port Charlotte. Hurricane Charley produced 16 tornadoes from Florida to North Carolina to Virginia. Charley also produced 15 deaths and $15 billion in damages.

Now, let's turn to Hurricane Ivan. As you'll see, this storm quickly followed on the heels of Charley, representing the worst-case scenario for a series of storms. This pattern would be followed in 2005 with a similar time frame and devastating results. To use a cliché, it's literally a one-two punch. From the National Hurricane Center (NHC) (www.nhc.noaa.gov/HAW2/english/history_printer.shtml#ivan):

> *Hurricane Ivan began developing only 16 days after Charley left the United States. Its path was similar in the Caribbean. . . . By the 5th, Ivan had become a hurricane about 1,150 miles east of the southern Windward Islands. Eighteen hours later Ivan became the southernmost storm to reach major hurricane status, at 10.2EN. Ivan was a category 3 hurricane when the center passed about 7 miles south of Grenada, a path that took the northern eyewall of Ivan directly over the island. In the Caribbean, Ivan became a category 5 hurricane, with winds of 160 m.p.h., on the 9th when it was south of the Dominican Republic, and on two occasions the minimum pressure fell to 910 mb. The center of Ivan passed within about 20 miles of Jamaica on the 11th and a similar distance from Grand Cayman on the 12th, with Grand Cayman likely experiencing sustained winds of category 4 strength. Ivan then turned to the northwest and passed through the Yucatan channel on the 14th, bringing hurricane conditions to extreme western Cuba. Ivan moved across the east-central Gulf of Mexico, making landfall as a major hurricane with sustained winds of near 120 m.p.h. on the 16th just west of Gulf Shores, Alabama.*
>
> *Ivan weakened as it moved inland, producing over 100 tornadoes and heavy rains across much of the southeastern United States, before merging with a frontal system over the Delmarva Peninsula on the 18th. While this would normally be the end of the story, the extratropical remnant low of Ivan split off from the frontal system and drifted southward in the western Atlantic for several days, crossed southern Florida, and reentered the Gulf of Mexico on the 21st. The low reacquired tropical characteristics, becoming a tropical storm for the second time on the 22nd in the central Gulf. Ivan weakened before it made its final landfall in southwestern Louisiana as a tropical depression on the 24th.*

So not only was Hurricane Ivan a category 5 storm, but it was so nasty that landfall couldn't kill it. It reformed and looped back down the Eastern Seaboard to finally end up in Louisiana. Nature can do some pretty

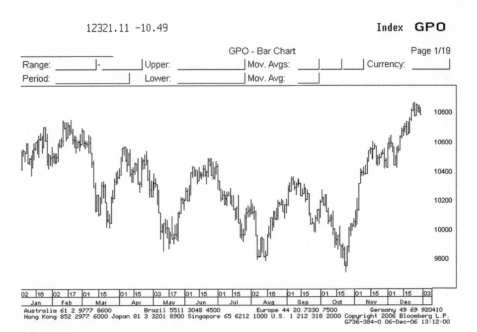

12321.11 -10.49   Index **GPO**

GPO - Bar Chart   Page 1/19

FIGURE 6.11 Dow Jones Industrial Average
Source: Used with permission from Bloomberg L.P.

weird things, and this is a perfect example of how limited science can be in predicting what can happen with weather.

Like Charley, Ivan generated damage estimated to be near $14.2 billion. However, it was far more deadly, as the death toll in the United States, Grenada, Jamaica, Dominican Republic, Venezuela, Cayman Islands, Tobago, and Barbados reached 92. NOAA said that the storm surge completely overwashed the island of Grand Cayman, where an estimated 95 percent of the buildings were damaged or destroyed. That's one nasty storm.

For the financial markets, let's look at the big indexes first. Try to keep in mind that we were in the home stretch for the 2004 presidential election during these storms. Also unusual was that Hurricanes Charley and Ivan happened just one month apart. Therefore, Ivan shortened recoil in the markets from Charley and extended the direction. Charley hit on a weekend so there was some concern heading into Friday about the storm. The Dow put in its lows for the month on Friday, August 13 (Figure 6.11). It then rallied for about a month before Ivan hit. Then it gave back all of that ground and put in new lows for the year.

The U.S. Treasury 10-year note's yield was declining prior to Charley and had a big drop just before the storm hit (Figure 6.12). The yield dropped from 4.40 percent in the beginning of August to a low of 4.00 percent after

FIGURE 6.12 U.S. Treasury 10-Year Note Yield
Source: Used with permission from Bloomberg L.P.

Ivan hit. The U.S. Dollar Index exhibited a similar trading pattern, as it was sinking when Charley hit, rebounded partially, then sank again after Ivan hit (Figure 6.13). Unlike the Dow and the 10-year Treasury note, the buck kept going south the rest of the year. The broader point to see here is that the macro trends that were in place prior to the storms were given a steroid boost by the damage, but about a month afterward their negative impact diminished for equities and bonds.

Next up, commodities. Here's where things get a little strange. First, lumber didn't have the rally that we would normally assume would happen during a rebuilding in the wake of two nasty storms like Charley and Ivan. When Charley hit, lumber rallied as we would expect (Figure 6.14). However, as Ivan was forming and hitting, lumber collapsed. This could have been caused by the U.S. Federal Reserve moving away from the 1 percent federal funds rate and raising interest rates (Figure 6.15), which would hurt housing and builders.

The energy side saw the biggest and most sustained moves. Oil rallied going into the beginning of August and backed off after Charley made landfall. Then it started a step climb from when Ivan hit that lasted almost two months (Figure 6.16). This was occurring as Nigerian rebels were hitting oil platforms and the Organization of Petroleum Exporting Countries (OPEC)

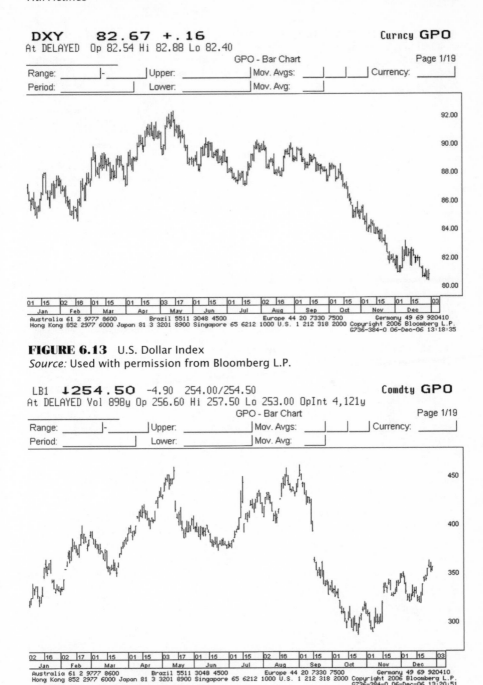

DXY   82.67 +.16   Curncy **GPO**
At DELAYED Op 82.54 Hi 82.88 Lo 82.40

GPO - Bar Chart   Page 1/19

| Range: _____|-_____ | Upper: _____ | Mov. Avgs: __|__|__ | Currency: _____ |
| Period: _____ | Lower: _____ | Mov. Avg: __ | |

```
                                                                    92.00
                                                                    90.00
                                                                    88.00
                                                                    86.00
                                                                    84.00
                                                                    82.00
                                                                    80.00
```

01 15 |02 16 |01 15 |01 15 |03 17 |01 15 |01 15 |02 16 |01 15 |01 15 |01 15 |01 15 |03
Jan   Feb   Mar   Apr   May   Jun   Jul   Aug   Sep   Oct   Nov   Dec
Australia 61 2 9777 8600   Brazil 5511 3048 4500   Europe 44 20 7330 7500   Germany 49 69 920410
Hong Kong 852 2977 6000 Japan 81 3 3201 8900 Singapore 65 6212 1000 U.S. 1 212 318 2000 Copyright 2006 Bloomberg L.P.
                                                                    G736-384-0 06-Dec-06 13:18:35

FIGURE 6.13   U.S. Dollar Index
Source: Used with permission from Bloomberg L.P.

LB1 ↓254.50 -4.90 254.00/254.50   Comdty **GPO**
At DELAYED Vol 898y Op 256.60 Hi 257.50 Lo 253.00 OpInt 4,121y

GPO - Bar Chart   Page 1/19

| Range: _____|-_____ | Upper: _____ | Mov. Avgs: __|__|__ | Currency: _____ |
| Period: _____ | Lower: _____ | Mov. Avg: __ | |

```
                                                                    450
                                                                    400
                                                                    350
                                                                    300
```

02 16 |02 17 |01 15 |01 15 |03 17 |01 15 |01 15 |02 16 |01 15 |01 15 |01 15 |01 15 |03
Jan   Feb   Mar   Apr   May   Jun   Jul   Aug   Sep   Oct   Nov   Dec
Australia 61 2 9777 8600   Brazil 5511 3048 4500   Europe 44 20 7330 7500   Germany 49 69 920410
Hong Kong 852 2977 6000 Japan 81 3 3201 8900 Singapore 65 6212 1000 U.S. 1 212 318 2000 Copyright 2006 Bloomberg L.P.
                                                                    G736-384-0 06-Dec-06 13:20:51

FIGURE 6.14   Lumber
Source: Used with permission from Bloomberg L.P.

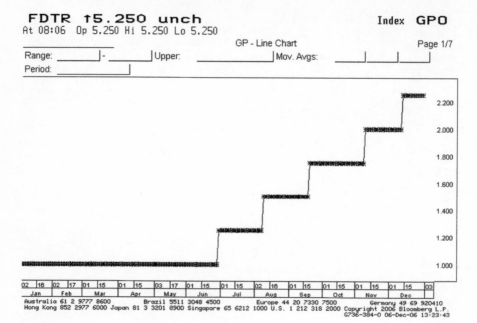

FIGURE 6.15   Federal Funds Target Rate
Source: Used with permission from Bloomberg L.P.

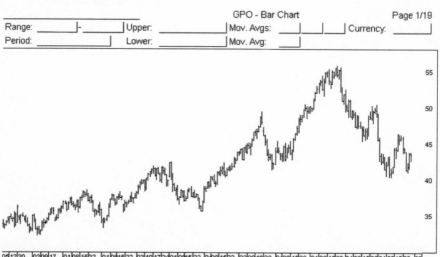

FIGURE 6.16   Crude Oil
Source: Used with permission from Bloomberg L.P.

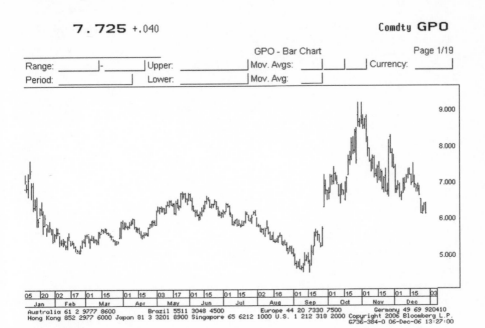

FIGURE 6.17 Natural Gas
Source: Used with permission from Bloomberg L.P.

was saying that it was essentially powerless to stop the rise in the price of crude. Oil subsequently backed off and finished the year at the levels from the beginning of the storms. Natural gas was just insane. Take a look at its price pattern in Figure 6.17. It fell from the time Charley hit until the time that Ivan hit. Then it went crazy and had rallied almost 100 percent by the end of October. It then collapsed back to the gap that was created when it exploded to the upside. To sum up, the storms created the environment for volatility to increase and for the energy commodities to rally as the paths of the storms took them through the Gulf where oil and natural gas are produced.

Last, let's take a look at more industry-specific indexes and how they reacted to the storms. The Bloomberg U.S. Homebuilders Index (BUSHBLD) is a capitalization-weighted index of the leading home builders in the United States. Looking at Figure 6.18, you can see this index was near the lows of the year in late July. It started a rally in August and took off with the landfall of Charley. It continued to rally strongly into Ivan. Then it backed away to pre-Charley levels. This is somewhat consistent with trading patterns in other indexes and commodities. Then it exploded to the upside and finished 2004 at the highest levels of the year as low interest rates and destruction from the hurricanes dramatically increased demand.

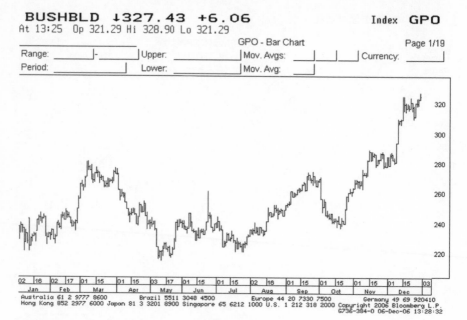

BUSHBLD ↓327.43 +6.06   Index **GPO**
At 13:25 Op 321.29 Hi 328.90 Lo 321.29

FIGURE 6.18 Bloomberg U.S. Homebuilders Index
Source: Used with permission from Bloomberg L.P.

Next up, the oil service sector. Why this group? When hurricanes run through the Gulf of Mexico, they force oil companies to shut down platforms and stop producing oil and gas. This can cause the prices of those commodities to rise and therefore cause the prices of the companies getting the oil/gas further out to sea to rise as well. The Philadelphia Oil Service Sector Index (OSX) is a price-weighted index composed of 15 companies that provide oil drilling and production services, oil field equipment, support services, and geophysical/reservoir services. Figure 6.19 shows that, unlike home builders, the OSX was selling off into Hurricane Charley. Once Charley made landfall, this index began a rally that was extended by Hurricane Ivan. It finished the year on the highest levels of the year.

Last, let's take a look at how the insurance sector did by using our NASDAQ Insurance Index (CINS, Figure 6.20) along with graphs for Allstate Corporation (ALL, Figure 6.21), Safeco Corporation (SAF, Figure 6.22), and Swiss Reinsurance (RUKN, Figure 6.23). Figures 6.20 through 6.23 show that between August and October, they all either declined or went sideways. Safeco and Allstate were hit the worst in October as they dropped to their lowest levels in several months. However, all recovered significantly and ended the year on highs (except for Swiss Re). The movement underscores the short-term nature of the impact from hurricanes, as the effect appears to last on average around two to three months.

FIGURE 6.19 Philadelphia Oil Service Sector Index
Source: Used with permission from Bloomberg L.P.

FIGURE 6.20 NASDAQ Insurance Index
Source: Used with permission from Bloomberg L.P.

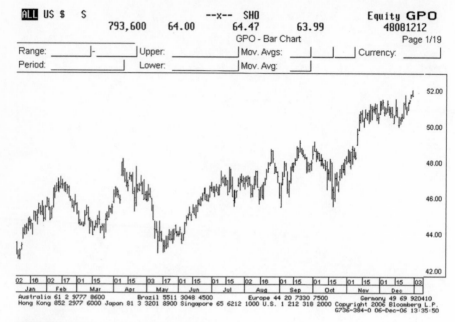

FIGURE 6.21 Allstate Corporation
Source: Used with permission from Bloomberg L.P.

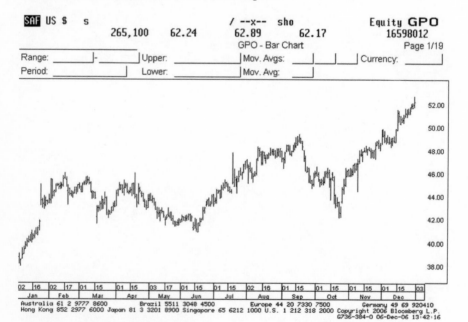

FIGURE 6.22 Safeco Corporation
Source: Used with permission from Bloomberg L.P.

FIGURE 6.23 Swiss Reinsurance
Source: Used with permission from Bloomberg L.P.

HURRICANES KATRINA AND RITA (2005)

If journalism is history's rough draft, then writing a book on an event as recent as Hurricane Katrina should be viewed as a first revision. This was a devastating event that exposed the soft underbelly of the society and the economy. Having experienced it in real time, I can say there was plenty of confusion and blame to go around from the local, state, and federal authorities as they struggled to deal with the unthinkable: a direct hit by a category 4 hurricane on New Orleans and the Gulf Coast. Less than month later, Hurricane Rita hit the Texas region as a category 3 hurricane. The twin storms' proximity created one of the worst upheavals outside of war our nation has ever seen as the combination contributed to more than 1,300 deaths and over $100 billion in damage.

Figure 6.24 shows the path of Hurricane Katrina as it made its way through the Gulf of Mexico and into the United States. Let's follow the description of Katrina by the NHC:

> *A tropical depression formed on August 23 about 200 miles south-*
> *east of Nassau in the Bahamas. Moving northwestward, it became*

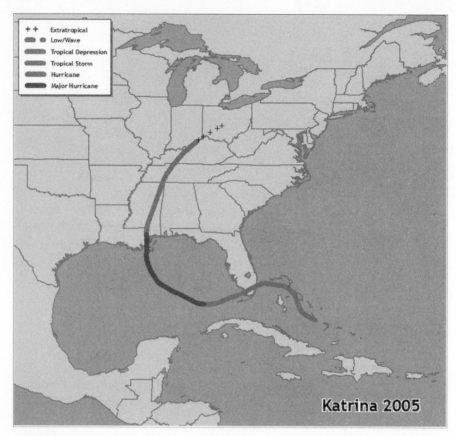

FIGURE 6.24   Path of Hurricane Katrina
Source: National Oceanic and Atmospheric Administration (NOAA).

Tropical Storm Katrina during the following day about 75 miles east-southeast of Nassau. The storm moved through the northwestern Bahamas on August 24–25, and then turned westward toward southern Florida. Katrina became a hurricane just before making landfall near the Miami-Dade/Broward county line during the evening of August 25. The hurricane moved southwestward across southern Florida into the eastern Gulf of Mexico on August 26. Katrina then strengthened significantly, reaching Category 5 intensity on August 28. Later that day, maximum sustained winds reached 175 mph with an aircraft-measured central pressure of 902 mb while centered about 195 miles southeast of the mouth of the Mississippi River. Katrina turned to the northwest and then north, with the center making landfall near Buras, Louisiana, at 1110 UTC August 29 with maximum winds estimated at 125 mph (Category 3). Continuing northward, the hurricane made a second landfall near the Louisiana/Mississippi border at 1445 UTC with maximum winds estimated at 120 mph (Category 3). Weakening occurred as Katrina moved north-northeastward over land, but it was still a hurricane near Laurel, Mississippi. The cyclone weakened to a tropical depression over the Tennessee Valley on 30 August.

Katrina caused 10 to 14 inches of rain over southern Florida, and 8 to 12 inches of rain along its track inland from the northern Gulf coast. Thirty-three tornadoes were reported from the storm.

Katrina caused catastrophic damage in southeastern Louisiana and southern Mississippi. Storm surge along the Mississippi coast caused total destruction of many structures, with the surge damage extending several miles inland. Similar damage occurred in portions of southeastern Louisiana southeast of New Orleans. The surge overtopped and breached levees in the New Orleans metropolitan area, resulting in the inundation of much of the city and its eastern suburbs. Wind damage from Katrina extended well inland into northern Mississippi and Alabama. The hurricane also caused wind and water damage in Miami-Dade and Broward counties.

I think it's important to understand three key facts about Hurricane Katrina in relation to its impact on the financial markets. First, this was a huge storm whose eyewall was large enough to hit Louisiana, Alabama, and Mississippi. Second, Katrina was a category 5 storm through most of the Gulf of Mexico, before losing strength down to category 3 before making landfall. Next, the entire region was aware that a nasty storm was coming days in advance and yet there was still massive damage inflicted and lives lost. Remember, 80 percent of New Orleans was evacuated before Katrina hit and still over 1,000 people were left dead. Last, the storm roared through a critical economic area of the country, but not critical from a gross domestic product (GDP) point of view. The three states mentioned contribute just over 4 percent of GDP and are three of the poorest states in the country. However, the region is critical for energy production, as states along the Gulf Coast produce a quarter of U.S. crude oil and house nearly half the nation's refining capacity. A hurricane hitting this region wouldn't be a big deal for energy if world oil supplies were sufficient, but they were not at the time.

Take a look at the wonderful diagram of the region that appeared in the *Wall Street Journal* on September 30, 2006 (Figure 6.25). It shows the 745 oil rigs and platforms abandoned along the Gulf of Mexico ahead of Hurricane Rita. Texas would have 16 of its 26 refineries be impacted, which process about 25 percent of U.S. oil. In Louisiana, a critical natural gas installation

FIGURE 6.25 Gulf Energy Production
Source: Reprinted by permission of the *Wall Street Journal.* Copyright © 2005
Dow Jones & Company, Inc. All Rights Reserved Worldwide. License number
1630930902466.

that channels about a third of the nation's natural gas would be damaged.
Keep this in mind as we jump to describe Hurricane Rita. From this diagram,
you can see its path through the critical oil and gas production regions.

Here's NOAA's description of Rita (www.nhc.noaa.gov/HAW2/english/
history_printer.shtml#rita):

> *A tropical wave and the remnants of an old front combined to produce
> an area of disturbed weather on 16 September. This system became
> a depression just east of the Turks and Caicos Islands late on 17
> September, which moved westward and became a tropical storm the
> following afternoon. Maximum winds increased to 70 mph as Rita
> moved through the central Bahamas on September 19. While the storm
> did not strengthen during the following night, rapid intensification
> began on September 20 as it moved through the Straits of Florida.
> Rita became a hurricane that day and reached Category 2 intensity
> as the center passed about 50 miles south of Key West, Florida.*
>
> *After entering the Gulf of Mexico, Rita intensified from Cate-
> gory 2 to Category 5 in about 24 hours. The maximum sustained
> winds reached 165 mph late on September 21, and the hurricane
> reached a peak intensity of 180 mph early on September 22. Weak-
> ening began later that day and continued until landfall around 0740
> UTC 24 September just east of the Texas/Louisiana border between
> Sabine Pass and Johnson's Bayou. At that time, maximum sustained
> winds were 115 mph (Category 3). Weakening continued after land-
> fall, but Rita remained a tropical storm until reaching northwestern
> Louisiana late on 24 September. . . . The hurricane caused storm-surge
> flooding of 10 to 15 ft above normal tide levels along the southwest-
> ern coast of Louisiana, caused a notable surge on the inland Lake*

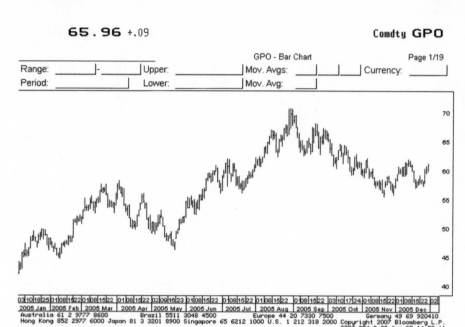

FIGURE 6.26 Crude Oil
Source: Used with permission from Bloomberg L.P.

> *Livingston, Texas, and inundated portions of the New Orleans area*
> *previously flooded by Katrina....*
>   *Rita produced rainfalls of 5 to 9 inches over large portions of*
> *Louisiana, Mississippi, and eastern Texas, with isolated amounts of*
> *10 to 15 inches. The cyclone spawned an estimated 90 tornadoes over*
> *the southern United States.*
>   *Devastating storm surge flooding and wind damage occurred in*
> *southwestern Louisiana and extreme southeastern Texas, with some*
> *surge damage occurring in the Florida Keys. Rita was responsible*
> *for seven deaths, and it caused damage estimated at $10 billion in*
> *the United States.*

As a reminder, our focus is on what was occurring in the financial markets and therefore we won't spend time on the social aspects of both storms. (There already are wonderful books on the subject, listed in the Bibliography.) Let's look at what was impacted the most when the hurricanes hit: oil and natural gas.

The dramatic move in these critical commodities caused a spasm in all of the markets. Figure 6.26 shows that oil was already rallying and at the highs for the year. It then set new all-time highs above $70 a barrel as

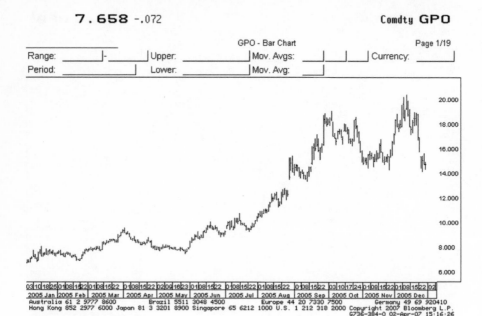

FIGURE 6.27 Natural Gas
Source: Used with permission from Bloomberg L.P.

Katrina hit. The price of crude came off and then made one more rally when Rita hit, but couldn't pierce the recent high after Katrina. In my world, this is what we call a failure, as we would expect an event like Rita to force the price of crude oil much higher, but it didn't. Therefore, we can expect the price to fall. Crude started a decline that saw the price fall about $15 from the high during Katrina.

Like after Charley/Ivan, natural gas went insane. On the open it gapped above $10 and went straight to $12 a cubic foot. Why, that's (tapping furiously on my calculator) 20 percent in one day! Since the beginning of August, it was up 50 percent. It gave back $1 prior to Rita hitting and then exploded to the upside afterward, reaching $14 by the end of September. Natural gas remained incredibly volatile for the rest of the year, setting new highs in December before falling to $11 by the end of the month (Figure 6.27). This reached across all areas of the economy, causing disruptions in disparate sectors from the home heating market to the price of fertilizer.

In commodities, lumber experienced some bizarre price action as well, but this time it seemed to make more sense than during Charley/Ivan. Figure 6.28 shows lumber in a slump as Katrina hit. Within two weeks, it did about what natural gas did: a 20 percent increase in price. It then collapsed back down to the pre-Katrina levels in September, rallied, and sold off again.

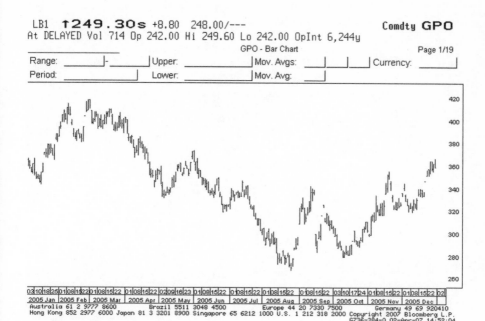

```
LB1  ↑249.30s +8.80  248.00/---                              Comdty GPO
At DELAYED Vol 714 Op 242.00 Hi 249.60 Lo 242.00 OpInt 6,244y
                              GPO - Bar Chart                     Page 1/19
```

FIGURE 6.28 Lumber
Source: Used with permission from Bloomberg L.P.

Then it steadily climbed for the rest of the year and ended 2005 above $360. Remember, this was occurring during a time frame in which the Federal Reserve was raising interest rates and beginning to put a bite into demand for home builders and therefore lumber. A key factor in the price rise was a pledge by the Bush administration to spend $110 billion to rebuild the region.

On the big indexes, the Dow dropped to its low for the month as Hurricane Katrina approached and then made landfall (see Figure 6.29). Just like the price action during Charley/Ivan, it then rallied for about a month before Rita hit. Then it gave back all of that ground and put in lows around 10,200. Unlike Charley/Ivan, the Dow rallied from there to end the year near the highs for 2005. Some of the positive mojo that the Dow felt could've been stemming from the massive rebuilding money promised to the region.

The U.S. Treasury 10-year note's yield was declining prior to Charley and had a big drop just before the storm hit. The yield dropped from 4.40 percent in the beginning of August to a low of 4.00 percent after Ivan hit. At this time, there was tremendous conjecture that the U.S. Federal Reserve policy makers would go off of their steady 25-basis-point rate-hike regime in mid-September. They did not, and raised the federal funds rate 25 basis points, from 3.50 percent to 3.75 percent just prior to Hurricane Rita. Had

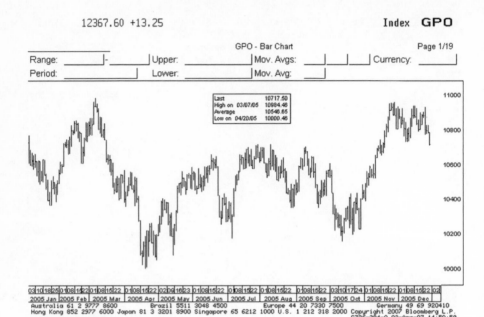

12367.60 +13.25   Index **GPO**

FIGURE 6.29 Dow Jones Industrial Average
Source: Used with permission from Bloomberg L.P.

Rita hit before the policy meeting, they may have changed their minds. See Figure 6.30.

The U.S. Dollar Index exhibited a similar trading pattern as it was sinking when Charley hit, rebounded partially, then sank again after Ivan hit. Unlike the Dow and the 10-year Treasury note, the buck kept going south the rest of the year. See Figure 6.31. Impact diminished for equities and bonds.

Finally, we look at the OSX to see how the oil service industry reacted to the destruction to the oil rigs and platforms from the twin hurricanes. With the price of crude oil and natural gas already rallying, the OSX was following along as well. However, just prior to Hurricane Katrina, the index had backed off just a bit to near $160 (Figure 6.32). When Katrina made landfall, the OSX started to move up. It put in new highs just after Rita made landfall and quickly moved lower in the month of October. Then, similar to natural gas, it rallied and finished 2005 near the highs of the year.

Let's take a look at three of the largest companies in the OSX: Halliburton Company (HAL, Figure 6.33), Baker Hughes Inc. (BHI, Figure 6.34), and Transocean Inc. (RIG, Figure 6.35). Essentially, the pattern should resemble what the OSX did, but with some wrinkles. All three were already

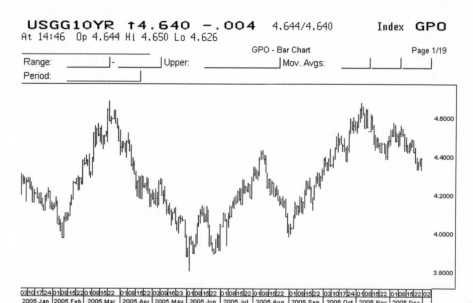

FIGURE 6.30 U.S. Treasury 10-Year Note Yield
Source: Used with permission from Bloomberg L.P.

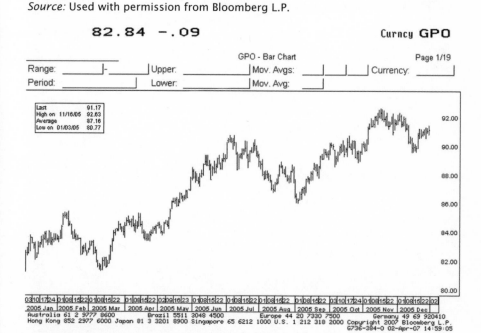

FIGURE 6.31 U.S. Dollar Index
Source: Used with permission from Bloomberg L.P.

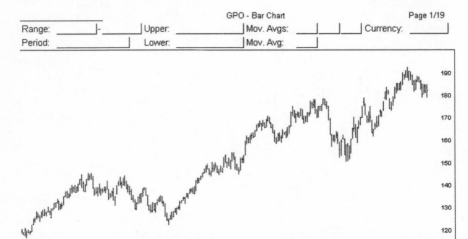

FIGURE 6.32   Philadelphia Oil Services Index
Source: Used with permission from Bloomberg L.P.

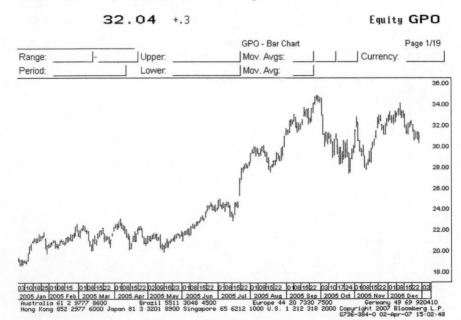

FIGURE 6.33   Halliburton Company
Source: Used with permission from Bloomberg L.P.

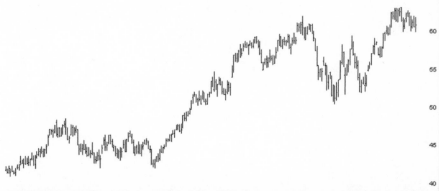

FIGURE 6.34 Baker Hughes Inc.
Source: Used with permission from Bloomberg L.P.

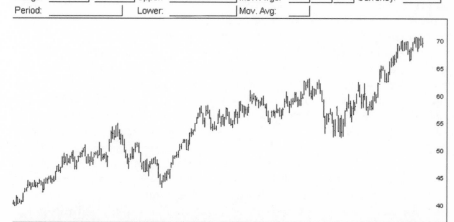

FIGURE 6.35 Transocean Inc.
Source: Used with permission from Bloomberg L.P.

FIGURE 6.36 Bloomberg U.S. Homebuilders Index
Source: Used with permission from Bloomberg L.P.

experiencing a nice pop in the stock price due to the rise in the price of oil. During Katrina, the stock prices all fell and then rebounded sharply in the interval prior to Rita. Then all three put in new highs for the year as Rita rocked Texas and Louisiana. All three dropped sharply to their levels prior to Katrina or lower. This was synchronized stock swimming at its best.

Let's take a closer look at industry-specific indexes and how they reacted to the storms. The Bloomberg U.S. Homebuilders index (BUSHBLD) is a capitalization-weighted index of the leading home builders in the United States. Looking at Figure 6.36, you can see this index was near the lows of the year in late July. It started a rally in August and took off with the landfall of Charley. It continued to rally strongly into Ivan. Then it backed away to pre-Charley levels. This is somewhat consistent with trading patterns in other indexes and commodities. Then it exploded to the upside and finished 2004 at the highest levels of the year as low interest rates and destruction from the hurricanes dramatically increased demand.

The final sector we'll look at is insurance, by using our CINS index (Figure 6.37) along with graphs for Allstate Corporation (ALL, Figure 6.38), Safeco Corporation (SAF, Figure 6.39), and Swiss Reinsurance (RUKN, Figure 6.40). The graphs show that between August and October, they all either declined or went sideways. Safeco and Allstate were hit the worst in October

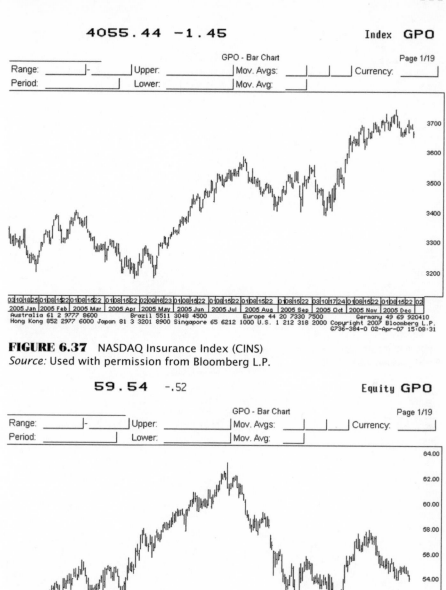

4055.44 −1.45   Index **GPO**

GPO - Bar Chart   Page 1/19

Range: _____|-_____| Upper: _____| Mov. Avgs: __|__|__| Currency: _____|
Period: _____| Lower: _____| Mov. Avg: ____|

FIGURE 6.37 NASDAQ Insurance Index (CINS)
Source: Used with permission from Bloomberg L.P.

59.54 −.52   Equity **GPO**

GPO - Bar Chart   Page 1/19

Range: _____|-_____| Upper: _____| Mov. Avgs: __|__|__| Currency: _____|
Period: _____| Lower: _____| Mov. Avg: ____|

FIGURE 6.38 Allstate Corporation (ALL)
Source: Used with permission from Bloomberg L.P.

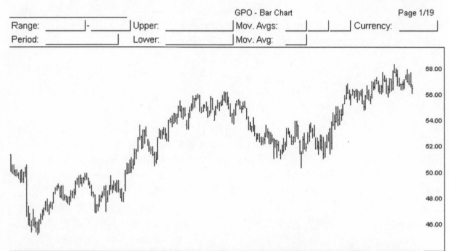

FIGURE 6.39   Safeco Corporation (SAF)
Source: Used with permission from Bloomberg L.P.

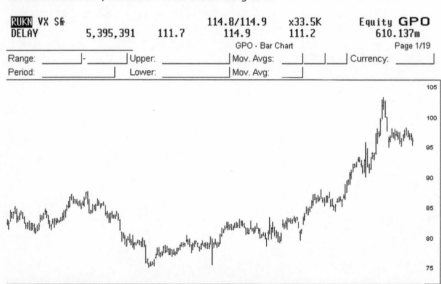

FIGURE 6.40   Swiss Reinsurance (RUKN)
Source: Used with permission from Bloomberg L.P.

as they dropped to the lows of the year. However, all recovered significantly and ended the year on highs (except for Swiss Re). The movement underscores the short-term nature of the impact from hurricanes, as the effect appears to last on average around two to three months.

2006: THE YEAR THAT WASN'T

As a follow-up to this analysis, the hurricane season for 2006 was predicted to be a terrible year, with 15 storms, three to five of them major ones. Unfortunately for the professional prognosticators, there were only five hurricanes and none hit the U.S Gulf Coast. This didn't stop crude oil, natural gas, and gasoline from rallying between April and the beginning of August. The market anticipated a bad year and supply disruptions. Then there was the Israeli invasion of Lebanon and fears of a wider Middle East war. When Israel pulled out and no hurricanes showed up, all the energy markets collapsed. This also caused the collapse of a large hedge fund that was long energy contracts.

The key takeaways on hurricanes remain that they are unpredictable, they will be anticipated, but they have a big impact on financial markets only when they hit the Gulf where energy production exists. Our next chapter deals with something even less predictable than the weather that can still have catastrophic results.

As of this writing, weather analysts are predicting a record number of major storms again for 2007.

CHAPTER 7

Earthquakes and Tsunamis

E arthquakes and tsunamis are the enigmas of the financial disaster universe. They occur with no warnings and surprise even users of the most sophisticated prediction models. For the trader, these are reaction events that force one to digest and analyze within minutes of their existence. They are paradoxical in that the largest earthquakes and tsunamis don't necessarily produce an event to trade nor do they always produce severe economic damage. It's all about when and where. These disasters are nature's way of giving the earth a heart attack. Like hurricanes, though, the usual suspects of insurance companies and construction sectors are impacted.

If it wasn't for the tsunami in southern Asia in 2004, I doubt I would've included this type of nature of disaster in this book. The financial markets rarely focus on an event that is micro short-term in its development and whose impact is primarily felt in an area of the world that usually has illiquid capital markets. This makes a tsunami particularly tricky for analyzing and developing strategies. However, when the devastation is as extreme as it was in 2004, the world sits up and takes notice. But as you'll see, the financial markets have a strange way of looking at these events and don't always react the way one would anticipate or imagine.

Following the blueprint of the previous chapters, we'll begin with what these things are and how they develop. It's important to understand their dynamics to be able to comprehend how and why the financial markets react to these events. Before you read on, take a moment to think how you would react with the knowledge that a major earthquake had just occurred in Shanghai. Think through what you have already read and project out a game plan. Now, read on. . . .

WHAT THE ?!?! WAS THAT?

Referring to the United States Geological Survey (USGS) for a description of the basics on earthquakes and tsunamis, "An earthquake is caused by a sudden slip on a fault. The tectonic plates are always slowly moving, but they get stuck at their edges due to friction. When the stress on the edge overcomes the friction, there is an earthquake that releases energy in waves that travel through the earth's crust and cause the shaking that we feel."

Here's what's really wild: The USGS estimates that several million earthquakes occur in the world *each year*. Fortunately, most earthquakes occur in remote areas or are just too small to be detected. At http://earthquake.usgs.gov/regional/world/historical_country_mag.php, the USGS shows the breakdown of magnitude and frequency of major historic earthquakes for all the countries around the world. To provide some perspective on the United States and the rest of the world, the USGS also shows how the earthquakes are distributed. In the United States, most of these occur in Alaska and California.

Why do most of the earthquakes occur around mountain ranges and volcanoes? The USGS says that the theory called plate tectonics "tells us that the Earth's rigid outer shell (lithosphere) is broken into a mosaic of oceanic and continental plates which can slide over the plastic aesthenosphere, which is the uppermost layer of the mantle. The plates are in constant motion. Where they interact, along their margins, important geological processes take place, such as the formation of mountain belts, earthquakes, and volcanoes." The USGS continues:

> *How are earthquakes connected with plate tectonics? In 1969, Muawia Barazangi and James Dorman published the locations of all earthquakes which occurred from 1961 to 1967. Most of the earthquakes are confined to narrow belts and these belts define the boundaries of the plates. The interiors of the plates themselves are largely free of large earthquakes, that is, they are aseismic.*

Figure 7.1 shows the major plates throughout the world and gives a picture of where we should look in anticipation of future earthquakes (http://earthquake.usgs.gov/learning/glossary.php?term=plate%20tectonics).

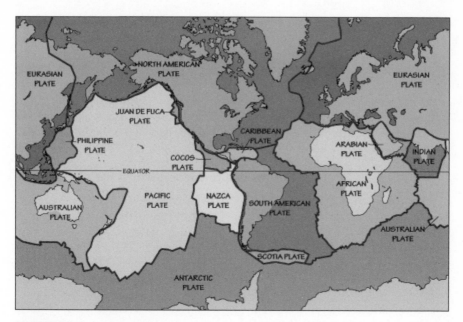

FIGURE 7.1 Tectonic Plates
Source: Courtesy of the U.S. Geological Survey (www.usgs.gov).

This map is also pretty useful for pointing out where tsunamis occur. Why? Because you can't have a tsunami without an earthquake. The Federal Emergency Management Agency (FEMA) describes them:

> *Tsunamis (pronounced soo-ná-mees), also known as seismic sea waves (mistakenly called "tidal waves"), are a series of enormous waves created by an underwater disturbance such as an earthquake, landslide, volcanic eruption, or meteorite. A tsunami can move hundreds of miles per hour in the open ocean and smash into land with waves as high as 100 feet or more.*
>
> *From the area where the tsunami originates, waves travel outward in all directions. Once the wave approaches the shore, it builds in height. The topography of the coastline and the ocean floor will influence the size of the wave. There may be more than one wave and the succeeding one may be larger than the one before. That is why a small tsunami at one beach can be a giant wave a few miles away.*
>
> *All tsunamis are potentially dangerous, even though they may not damage every coastline they strike. A tsunami can strike anywhere along most of the U.S. coastline. The most destructive tsunamis (in the U.S.) have occurred along the coasts of California, Oregon, Washington, Alaska, and Hawaii.*

Earthquake-induced movement of the ocean floor most often generates tsunamis. If a major earthquake or landslide occurs close to shore, the first wave in a series could reach the beach in a few minutes, even before a warning is issued. Areas are at greater risk if they are less than 25 feet above sea level and within a mile of the shoreline. Drowning is the most common cause of death associated with a tsunami. Tsunami waves and the receding water are very destructive to structures in the run-up zone. Other hazards include flooding, contamination of drinking water, and fires from gas lines or ruptured tanks.

It's fascinating that just like tsunamis, hurricanes inflict their severest damage not from wind or rain, but from the storm surge that brings the ocean up over the land. Tsunamis are quite different in that they offer little warning other than the registering of an earthquake in the area. This compacted time frame sets these natural disasters apart from hurricanes. There is no time to watch them develop, track them as they build, and then predict the area they will hit. Earthquakes and tsunamis come as a surprise and then a mad scramble ensues to aid the stricken and in the case of a tsunami warn others they have to run for higher ground.

Now that we have a decent understanding of how they work, let's look at some examples of earthquakes and one particular tsunami.

THE 1906 SAN FRANCISCO EARTHQUAKE

Almost everyone in the United States is familiar with the great 1906 San Francisco earthquake that registered 7.8 on the Richter scale. For geologists, it was the first major quake that was studied with scientific scrutiny similar to the new techniques used during the 1918 Spanish influenza, as professional scientific study was still in its infancy.

In their book *Earthquakes in Human History: The Far Reaching Effects of Seimic Disruptions*, Jelle Zeilinga de Boer and Donald Theodore Sanders describe the cost: "There have been earthquakes of greater magnitude, and several have cost many more lives, but few have wreaked such devastation. Throughout the affected area, property damage was inestimable. In San Francisco itself, in an area exceeding 10 square kilometers, virtually every building was destroyed or later had to be torn down, including the entire business district and well over half of the city's residential neighborhoods." Out of a population of 400,000, there were 250,000 left homeless; 28,000 buildings were eliminated over 4.7 square miles.

Photographs show the complete destruction that occurred—not just from the earthquake, but mainly from the fires that ensued. Again, the main event was the initial source of the havoc, but not the primary force of the ruination. This is analogous to the 1918 influenza in which the flu itself was not as lethal as the pneumonia that came with it. It's the same for hurricanes; it's not the wind that causes the greatest destruction usually, but the storm surge. It's like Nature is a boxer who fakes a left jab and then lands a big right hook to the jaw.

The USGS estimated property damage costs at $400,000,000 in 1906 dollars from earthquake and fire, and $80,000,000 from the earthquake alone. Remember, that's 1906 dollars. The USGS also notes that the death estimate was 3,000 (http://quake.wr.usgs.gov/info/1906/casualties.html).

Again, insurance companies were saddled with paying out hundreds of millions of dollars in claims, causing some to go bankrupt. There was political fallout as well, as the mayor and others were convicted of bribery and extortion related to the disaster. De Boer and Sanders suggest that the stock markets, too, lost heavily as a result of the disaster, helping trigger a nationwide money panic in the following months.

The scariest thing about the San Francisco quake is that it could happen again. The 1989 earthquake during the World Series at San Francisco's Candlestick Park was caused by the same fault that was activated in 1906. According to the Berkeley Seismological Laboratory, the Loma Prieta earthquake caused $5.9 billion in damages with 63 deaths and 3,757 injuries. It provides a glimpse into what can happen in the future and how unstable this region remains.

1995 EARTHQUAKE IN KOBE, JAPAN

On January 16, 1995, a 6.9 magnitude earthquake hit Kobe, Japan. This was the largest earthquake to hit Kobe since 1926. Initial reports had 600 dead, thousands injured, and 2,000 buildings destroyed. Like the 1906 San Francisco earthquake, many buildings were destroyed and lives lost not due to the immediate impact of the earthquake, but to ensuing fires that occurred. It also closed Osaka's financial markets and therefore dramatically reduced the amount of trading done in those markets.

The last time trading was shut down previously had been in 1964 due to another natural disaster event, a hurricane. Osaka at the time was the third largest city and second largest business center. Kobe was a smaller city, but was home to an important economic asset: Japan's second largest container port. It was closed after the quake. As most readers know, Japan is an island nation and a nation of exporters. Therefore, it was an economic

Australia 61 2 9777 8600   Brazil 5511 3048 4500   Europe 44 20 7330 7500   Germany 49 69 920410
Hong Kong 852 2977 6000 Japan 81 3 3201 8900 Singapore 65 6212 1000 U.S. 1 212 318 2000 Copyright 2006 Bloomberg L.P.
                                                                                                G736-384-1 07-Dec-06 15:07:27

FIGURE 7.2 The Nikkei, 1994–1996
Source: Used with permission from Bloomberg L.P.

disaster when one of the key distribution points for those exports had to be shut down.

Let's take a look at the Nikkei 225 prior to the event and see that it had been declining since June of 1994 (Figure 7.2). It had hit a low in late November and rebounded late in December. The quake unsettled a shaky market that plunged six days after the quake and would eventually lose 25 percent of its value by July. That's a big ouch and underscored the opportunity from the event. The 10-year Japanese bond yield had risen for almost all of 1994, moving up 175 basis points prior to the earthquake (Figure 7.3). The bond yield went sideways for almost a month afterward and then declined 200 basis points by July. This is not merely 20/20 hindsight trading. As in all our event trading examples, we look for situations in which the event provides an opportunity to either accelerate a trend or cause a reversal (sometimes brief) to a trend. In this case, the market was soft and the event drove it further in that direction.

Let's look a couple of harbingers of the Japanese economy. As an example, Toyota Motor Corporation at the time was receiving 34 percent of its revenues from sales abroad (Figure 7.4). It's hard to receive those revenues if you can't export your product. The same goes for electronic product maker Toshiba Corporation (Figure 7.5). Both stocks fell after the earthquake.

FIGURE 7.3 The 10-Year Japanese Bond Yield
Source: Used with permission from Bloomberg L.P.

FIGURE 7.4 Toyota Motor Corporation
Source: Used with permission from Bloomberg L.P.

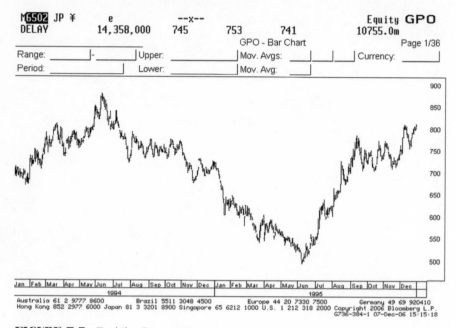

FIGURE 7.5 Toshiba Corporation
Source: Used with permission from Bloomberg L.P.

With all natural disasters, the biggest losses are borne by insurance companies, and this group saw their shares decline 6 percent. However, construction companies did very well. They bucked the trend of the general decline of the Nikkei even amidst bribery scandals in the industry at the time involving government officials. Take a look at Sumitomo Mitsui Construction Co., Ltd (Figure 7.6). It was going nowhere until the earthquake occurred and then rose 125 percent. Now, that's a nice return in a short period of time, especially after just reporting a drop in earnings of 10.36 percent for the first half of the year. The great thing is that the price in the stock jumped and then hesitated for about four days before really taking off. This gave you the opportunity to get in even if you missed the initial move.

2005 EARTHQUAKE IN PAKISTAN

The October 8, 2005, 7.6 magnitude earthquake that hit Pakistan was massive and devastating. The impact was felt in Afghanistan and India, as well. It was felt in the major cities of Islamabad and New Delhi. However, the

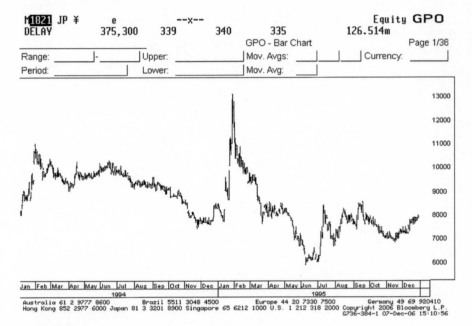

FIGURE 7.6 Sumitomo Mitsui Construction Co., Ltd
Source: Used with permission from Bloomberg L.P.

quake hit hardest in the Pakistani-controlled part of Kashmir and North-West Province, which are some of the poorest areas of an already poor country. The total fatalities that were attributed to the earthquake topped 80,000. The situation was so catastrophic that even the political tensions between India and Pakistan were set aside as India's Prime Minister Manmohan Singh called Pakistan President Pervez Musharraf and offered help, according to CNN.

Nevertheless, the impact on the financial markets was peculiar. This is an excellent example of the old real estate phrase, "Location, location, location." The quake didn't cause massive infrastructure damage to either the largest cities or key economic assets. Therefore, the fallout from the quake in the financial markets was almost nil. Granted, this is a third world country with relatively small, illiquid, opaque capital markets. But let's take a quick peek at what did happen.

The Karachi 100 index (KSE100) comprises the top company from each of the 34 sectors on the Karachi Stock Exchange in terms of market capitalization; the rest are picked on market cap ranking. Figure 7.7 shows this index over the time period in October during which the quake hit. Notice that the index went up 400 points in the 10 days following the quake, with cement companies (D. G. Kahan Cement) or refineries (National Refinery

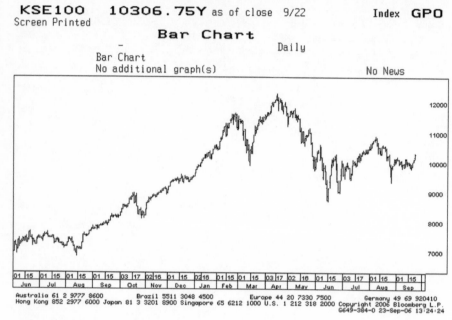

FIGURE 7.7 The Karachi 100 Index (KSE100)
Source: Used with permission from Bloomberg L.P.

Ltd) leading the way. The wild thing is that insurance companies went up, as well. This is the big disconnect: How can an insurance company that has policies in that country go up during an earthquake of that magnitude? Take a look at EFU General Insurance Ltd (EFUG PA) in Figure 7.8. It went sideways and then exploded higher in March.

Eventually, the KSE100 reversed the 400-point rally starting midway through the month of April. Some of this movement has to do with the easy money for stock purchases called "badla" financing. This is a system by which investors in Pakistan can buy shares with borrowed cash and then defer payment as long as they pay the daily loan costs.

On April 19, 2006, when the country's regulator announced a phased-out scrapping of this financing, the KSE100 started a decline that took it back to the levels of when the earthquake occurred. This is a great point to make for investors: Don't assume the structure of the U.S. financial markets extends beyond the U.S. borders. If you think our regulators are lax or not on the ball, you should take a look at other countries, including places like Japan. Even with our Enrons, WorldComs, and Refcos, the United States is still the gold standard for the rest of the world.

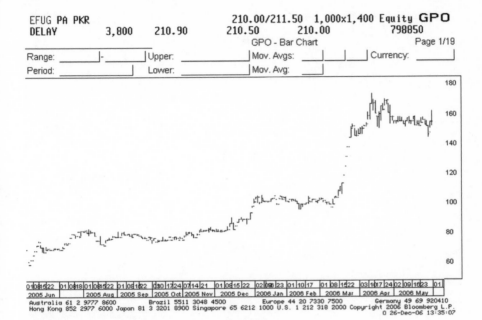

FIGURE 7.8 EFU General Insurance Ltd (EFUG PA)
Source: Used with permission from Bloomberg L.P.

2004 SOUTHEAST ASIAN TSUNAMI

The tsunami that hit Southeast Asia on December 26, 2004, was simply stunning in its speed and devastation. Off the west coast of Northern Sumatra, a 9.0 magnitude earthquake occurred. The earthquake was so large that it actually impacted the earth's rotation and made the day a few microseconds shorter than it should have been. The quake generated a tsunami that obliterated the Indonesian city of Banda Aceh, and sent a wall of water that stretched from Sumatra to Sri Lanka to India and all the way to Tanzania in Africa. It killed an estimated 283,106 people and left an estimated 5 million homeless.

For the financial markets, this is similar to what happened in Pakistan in 2005. The brunt of the tsunami hit an extremely poor area of Indonesia and no major economic asset was destroyed or impaired. Figure 7.9 shows the Jakarta Stock Price Index, which is a modified capitalization-weighted index of all stocks listed on the regular board of the Jakarta Stock Exchange. You can see the index dip in mid-December as investors were concerned over the weak currency. Strikingly, it's almost like nothing occurred on December 26

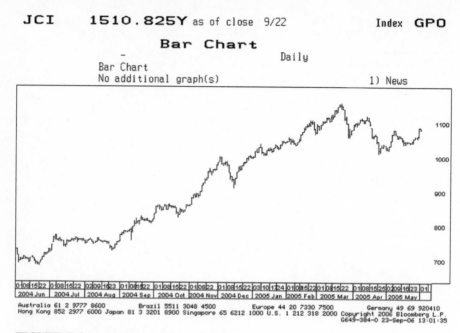

JCI   **1510.825Y** as of close 9/22   Index **GPO**

FIGURE 7.9 Jakarta Stock Price Index
Source: Used with permission from Bloomberg L.P.

and the index barely registered a move. Thailand had a bigger move in its index but it dropped only seven points (Figure 7.10). Even the normally volatile currencies of the region failed to move, with the Indonesian rupiah, the Indian rupee, and the Thai baht all going sideways. Tourism accounts for about 6 percent of gross domestic product (GDP), and initially the shares of resorts and hotels were hit, as were airline stocks serving the region. But none of it lasted more than a day.

It was a short-term event that hit a poor area and didn't dramatically change the overall trend for these markets. From a financial markets standpoint, the only thing this devastating tsunami did was provide a buying opportunity for the overall uptrend in equities.

CONCLUSION: IT'S TRICKY, BUT IT CAN BE TRADED

Earthquakes and tsunamis are amazingly powerful geological events. They seem to have an unpredictable nature, but we can predict the areas of the world where they will most likely occur. Mountain ranges and coastlines

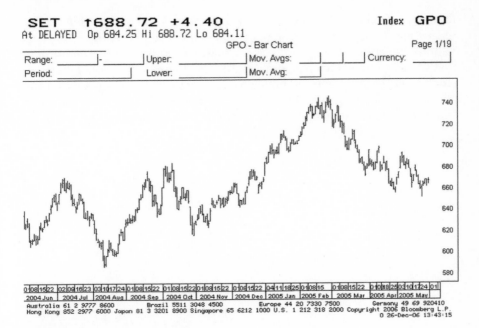

SET ↑688.72 +4.40   Index **GPO**
At DELAYED Op 684.25 Hi 688.72 Lo 684.11

FIGURE 7.10 Thailand Index
Source: Used with permission from Bloomberg L.P.

are the easiest places to pick out for potential sites. For the impact, the size of the country affected and the size of their economy have a great deal to do with whether the natural disaster makes an impact on the financial markets. Where the earthquake or tsunami occurs in the country matters a great deal. If the disaster impacts a major lever in the economy such as a port or oil and gas pipelines, the fallout will be much larger than if it hits a section of poor fishing villages. The difficult component is the time frame. Earthquakes and tsunamis happen unexpectedly and are over quickly. You must be prepared to take advantage of the event.

Referring back the question at the beginning of the chapter, what did you imagine with a major earthquake hitting Shanghai? Shanghai is the largest Chinese city. It is seen as the epicenter for important cultural, commercial, financial, industrial, and communications activity for China. Shanghai is also the world's busiest cargo port. The city contributes between 20 and 25 percent of the country's overall tax payments to Beijing. Clearly, this city is critical for the economic well-being of the country.

Therefore, a major disaster would have far-reaching effects on the country and those who are doing business there, particularly manufacturing. If we use the Kobe earthquake as a paradigm, Chinese stocks would fall, the currency would fall or be forced to fall, and Chinese bond prices would likely rally. Construction companies would do well, but multinational man-ufacturing companies would do poorly. Vietnam might be a huge winner, as Vietnamese companies could pick up some of the production and orders that Chinese companies wouldn't be able to fill. Globally, I would guess all stock markets would fall and bonds would rise with an anticipated Chinese growth slowdown. See, isn't this fun? All of this would occur quickly, and a trader would have to act promptly to take advantage of the event due to its rapid nature. This is the risk and reward.

CHAPTER 8

Global Warming

I n the early 1980s, I was having dinner with my parents and my grandfather with his new wife. She was a wonderful Southern lady who loved to tell stories. She chatted and chatted and was the polar opposite of my laconic, stern Grandpa. In the middle of one story at dinner, she was telling us about a trip she had made to a fabulous new store that sold women's clothes. Unfortunately, she couldn't remember the name of the store or where it was located. At this point, my Grandpa said, "Geez, Clarice, you didn't know where you were going when you left and when you came back you didn't know where you'd been." The same can happen to you on global warming. Let's try to know what the basic facts are, or when we're done we won't know what we have learned for investments.

This is the challenge and the opportunity with global warming: You have to take some extra time to understand the continuum of recent studies and the disparity of their findings. Some show the world is going to be under water in 100 years, while others show the polar ice caps actually growing in thickness! In 1979, some scientists speculated that we had entered into a new ice age after a series of frosty winters. So before we get into any research, we must first separate the hysteria from the normal fluctuations or variability.

What's the most basic, undisputed fact? The world's temperature is higher, but it has not changed much, about one degree Fahrenheit. The world has become a slightly warmer place over the last century or so, with most of that warming occurring in the past two decades. This may not seem like a big deal, except that scientists believe that during the last ice age, the earth's temperature was lower than it is now by only seven degrees.

So if the world's temperature is increasing, what is causing the increase, and what are the implications for a continued rise in temperature? The scientific evidence supports the theory that most of the warming that has occurred over the past 50 years comes from human behavior. The disputes come from what to do about it and whether the earth will self-correct this development.

For the markets, let's continue to play the disaster game scenario we started with earthquakes. If the world began to experience a rapid increase in temperature, who, what, and where would be impacted? What industries would benefit the most? What countries would find themselves in distress? Serious traders need to begin to develop a playbook that they can go to when this natural disaster begins to unfold. To build our playbook, we have to dissect the subject and find out where the opportunities lie.

BAD GAS, VERY BAD GAS!

Before we get into the human behavior causing the problem, let's begin with a little background on how the sun and the earth work. Let's turn to our friends at the Environmental Protection Agency (EPA) for a short explanation:

> *Energy from the sun drives the earth's weather and climate, and heats the earth's surface; in turn, the earth radiates energy back into space. Atmospheric greenhouse gases (water vapor, carbon dioxide, and other gases) trap some of the outgoing energy, retaining heat somewhat like the glass panels of a greenhouse.*

Without this natural greenhouse effect, temperatures would be much lower than they are now, and life as we know it today would not be possible. Instead, thanks to greenhouse gases (GHGs), the earth's average temperature is a more hospitable 60°F. However, problems may arise when the atmospheric concentration of greenhouse gases increases.

Since the beginning of the industrial revolution, atmospheric concentrations of carbon dioxide have increased nearly 30 percent, methane concentrations have more than doubled, and nitrous oxide concentrations have risen by about 15 percent. These increases have enhanced the heat-trapping capability of the earth's atmosphere. Sulfate aerosols, a common air pollutant, cool the atmosphere by reflecting light back into space; however, sulfates are short-lived in the atmosphere and vary regionally.

Why are greenhouse gas concentrations increasing? Scientists generally believe that the combustion of fossil fuels and other human activities are the primary reasons for the increased concentration of carbon dioxide. Animal respiration and the decomposition of organic matter release more than 10 times the CO_2 released by human activities; but these releases have generally been in balance during the centuries leading up to the industrial revolution with the carbon dioxide being absorbed by terrestrial vegetation and the oceans.

What has changed in the past few hundred years is the additional release of carbon dioxide by human activities. Fossil fuels burned to run cars and trucks, heat homes and businesses, and power factories are responsible for about 98 percent of U.S. carbon dioxide emissions, 24 percent of methane emissions, and 18 percent of nitrous oxide emissions. Increased agriculture, deforestation, landfills, industrial production, and mining also contribute a significant share of emissions. In 1997, the United States emitted about one-fifth of total global greenhouse gases.

Estimating future emissions is difficult, because the amount depends on demographic, economic, technological, policy, and institutional developments. Several emissions scenarios have been developed based on differing projections of these underlying factors. For example, by 2100, in the absence of emissions control policies, carbon dioxide concentrations are projected to be 30 to 150 percent higher than today's levels.

The EPA's web site is actually pretty awesome not only for global warming, but also for many varied environmental topics. Check it out at www.epa.gov. Yes, I realize it's the government, but you'd be surprised.

Who are the biggest emitters of GHGs? Let's focus on CO_2 emissions, as those make up the largest component of the increase of GHGs. Here's what the U.S. Department of Energy has to say:

> *Since 1751 roughly 305 billion tons of carbon have been released to the atmosphere from the consumption of fossil fuels and cement production. Half of these emissions have occurred since the mid 1970s. The 2003 global fossil-fuel CO_2 emission estimate, 7,303 million metric tons of carbon, represents an all-time high and a 4.5% increase from 2002.*
>
> *Globally, liquid and solid fuels accounted for 76.7% of the emissions from fossil-fuel burning in 2003. Combustion of gas fuels (e.g., natural gas) accounted for 19.2% (1,402 million metric tons of carbon) of the total emissions from fossil fuels in 2003 and reflects a gradually increasing global utilization of natural gas. Emissions from cement production (275 million metric tons of carbon in 2003) have more than doubled since the mid 1970s and now represent 3.8% of global CO_2 releases from fossil-fuel burning and cement production.*

Two of the biggest groups burning fossil fuels are coal-fired electricity plants and automobiles. Gases that contribute to the greenhouse effect are carbon dioxide (CO_2), methane (CH_4), hydrofluorocarbons (HFCs), perfluorocarbons (PFCs), and sulfur hexafluoride (SF_6).

These greenhouse gases (GHGs) trap the heat and warm the earth. This is known. The next important question to ask is does this matter? What are the consequences from increased air temperatures? How does the increase in temperature change the earth's environment? The simplest answer is that when you heat the air, other stuff like water heats up as well and you can melt ice. Now, it comes down to a question of how much heating will occur and over what time frames. According to the EPA, scientists estimate that if we continue at the present pace the earth's average global surface temperature could rise 1 to 4.5°F (0.6 to 2.5°C) in the next 50 years, and 2.2 to 10°F (1.4 to 5.8°C) in the next century, with significant regional variation. These predictions assume the earth doesn't autocorrect for the rise in temperatures by increased cloudiness or another method. The predictions also assume that the countries of the world won't decide to do something significant about reducing GHGs. This entire topic seems to come with disclaimers about what is actually going on and what actually can happen with the air warming.

That said, let's take a look at some of the projected outcomes of a warmer planet—albeit a more serious one than Hollywood took in the movie *The Day After Tomorrow*. Since 1979, the fact is that there has been substantial melting of the northern polar ice cap due to the warming of the earth. The recent breakup of the massive Antarctic Larsen B ice shelf is also causing great concern and is pointed to as an example of the changing ice caps due to global warming. Recently in his *Science* article "Paleoclimatic Evidence for Future Ice Sheet Instability and Rapid Sea-Level Rise," Jonathan T. Overpeck projected a massive melting of Greenland's and Antarctica's ice sheets, resulting in a sea-level rise of 12 to 18 feet by the year 2100. If true, this would have a dramatic impact on beachfront property and low-level countries like Denmark.

Then there is the potential change in worldwide weather patterns created by the El Niño effect. El Niño is the dramatic warming of the Pacific Ocean near the equator. Strong El Niño effects have created droughts and increased rainfall by disrupting the normal weather patterns via changes in the jet stream. In 1997–1998, there was a very strong El Niño that created droughts in which forest fires occurred on every continent, even in normally wet rain forests of Southeast Asia. The theory is that as greenhouse gas concentrations increase in the atmosphere, El Niño will exist in a semipermanent state and extreme weather patterns will occur on an ongoing basis.

Another example of extreme weather is what was described in Chapter 6. In 2004 and 2005, there were more frequent, more intense hurricanes hitting the United States than were ever before recorded. As we know, the fuel for a hurricane is warm water. If water temperatures are raised, especially in the Gulf of Mexico, the energy for more destructive hurricanes is possible. Studies done at the Commerce Department's Geophysical Fluid Dynamics Laboratory in Princeton, New Jersey, showed that by the year 2080 a typical hurricane could intensify by an extra half step in the Saffir-Simpson Hurricane Scale and rainfall would be nearly 20 percent more intense. All of this could be caused by higher CO_2 emissions that generate a strong greenhouse effect.

As a mild disclaimer, you have to contextualize the current temperatures and the melting of the polar ice caps. The U.S. Climatic Weather Center chart (http://yosemite.epa.gov/oar/globalwarming.nsf/content/climate.html) shows the changes in world temperatures from 1880 to 2001. The temperatures from 1880 to 1980 were at or below the average. It has only been since 1980 that temperatures have risen. As the EPA points out: "The 20th century's 10 warmest years all occurred in the last 15 years of the century. Of these, 1998 was the warmest year on record. The snow cover in the Northern Hemisphere and floating ice in the Arctic Ocean have decreased. Globally, sea level has risen 4–8 inches over the past century. Worldwide precipitation over land has increased by about 1 percent. The frequency of extreme rainfall events has increased throughout much of the United States."

Last, Patrick J. Michaels addresses some of the extreme commentary on polar ice cap melting with some fascinating information. In *Is the Sky Really Falling? A Review of Recent Global Warming Scare Stories*, Michaels takes a look at the recent accelerated Arctic (Greenland) melting. He takes umbrage at a 2005 NASA report that showed false-color satellite images comparing Arctic sea ice in 1979 and 2005. Michaels points out: "Nowhere does the press release mention that 1979 is right at the end of the second-coldest period in the Arctic in the 20th century. . . . Because temperatures in 1979 had just recovered from their lowest values since before 1920, Arctic ice was at or near its maximum extent since 1930 when the satellite became operational." Michaels points out that the world's largest ice sheets and glaciers (89.5 percent of the global total) reside in Antarctica. Of all the studies he cites that have predicted massive changes in the sea levels due to global warming, all of the available models require thousands of years to melt most of Greenland's ice and it must take even longer in Antarctica. "A run of three emissions scenarios used for the next 100 years with 18 climate models yields a mean sea-level rise from Greenland of 0.06 inch per year around 2100. As noted above, all models project that Antarctica gains ice in a warming world."

This is the dilemma of the global warming event. We know GHGs are high, we know that this contributes to the greenhouse effect, we have observed higher temperatures in the air and in the water, and we have experienced most of this in the past two decades. We don't precisely know how rapidly this will cause the earth's weather patterns to change, we don't know how rapid or consistent the melting of the polar ice caps will be, and we don't know how or even if the sea levels will change. As I've mentioned, it's very difficult to separate the over-the-top environmental hyperbole from what is the context of global warming through the last century.

So can we take the risk of assuming that no further damage will occur? Let's take this from the completely amoral, financial markets stance: Is the risk worth the return? Is our continuing to burn fossil fuels, emit emissions, generate GHGs, and heat the earth worth the potential disaster outcomes of changed climate patterns, increased cyclone/hurricane occurrence and strength, worsening droughts, and rising sea levels? Of course, when you structure the question this way the answer is always that we must act. But this issue is tremendously more complicated than that and hinges on whether you can get international agreement from big emitters to go along with reductions. We must filter these issues through a political lens to really understand what's at stake.

INTERNATIONAL AND NATIONAL NONAGREEMENTS

Believe it or not, there is broad agreement among nations that there is something going on with greenhouse gases and the world's climate. The question isn't whether we should do something about it, but rather what should we do? What is the solution and what is fair? It would be wonderful if this was exactly like the ozone layer and we could get broad agreement for an international accord (Montreal) that limited production of chlorofluorocarbons (CFCs). Sadly, it's not. The Kyoto Protocol is an international agreement that was signed in 1997 and went into effect in 2005 that set targets for industrialized countries to reduce their greenhouse gas emissions.

The goal of the treaty was to have nations limit combined emissions to 5 percent below 1990 levels by 2008–2012. It had to be ratified by a minimum of 55 nations and those nations must account for at least 55 percent of emissions from what the treaty calls "Annex 1" countries (38 industrialized countries given targets for reducing emissions, plus Belarus, Turkey, and now Kazakhstan). Australia and the United States did not ratify the agreement, but Russia did and that put the country totals over the top. Now Kyoto is legally binding for those countries that signed it.

In 2002, the world's largest emitters of CO_2, in order, were the United States, the European Union (25 countries), China, Russia, Japan, and India, according to the Organization for Economic Cooperation and Development (OECD)'s International Energy Agency (IEA). The biggest problem with Kyoto is that China and India were deemed developing countries and not required to reduce emissions. This means that they have an unfair competitive advantage in business because they are not required to bear the costs of the mandatory reduction in fossil fuel (coal-fired) burning power plants or industries. Given the current trade relationship between China and the United States, it would be almost impossible for Congress to supply the Chinese with another advantage on trade. Hence, Kyoto loses three out of the top six emitters of CO_2 from the accord.

It's interesting that this hasn't stopped individual states or groups of states within the United States from enacting their own legislation on GHGs. I think the biggest example comes from the country's largest state by population, California. In September 2006, California Governor Arnold Schwarzenegger signed legislation that calls for the state to reduce emissions of carbon dioxide and other gases by 25 percent by 2020. This puts California at the forefront of leading the United States toward reducing GHGs. By January of 2008, the law mandates that the state's Air Resources Board develop new rules requiring most industries to report their current greenhouse gas emissions. The board also must determine by that time the exact amount of GHG that needs to be reduced.

An interesting twist is that it's not just electric utilities that will be under scrutiny, but also landfills and refineries. Schwarzenegger is also considering prohibiting the state's electric utilities from buying electricity from high-polluting out-of-state power plants. The Governator's move on CO_2 emissions is a big political victory and will likely result in massive changes, but don't get too excited. California has a law on the books that requires automakers to reduce tailpipe emissions by 30 percent by 2016 beginning in 2009, but the auto industry is currently fighting it in the courts.

California is not the only state engaged in this type of activity. The Regional Greenhouse Gas Initiative (RGGI) is a cooperative effort by Northeastern and Mid-Atlantic states to reduce carbon dioxide emissions. From their web site at www.rggi.org:

> *To address this important environmental issue [of global warming], the RGGI participating states will be developing a regional strategy for controlling emissions. This strategy will more effectively control greenhouse gases, which are not bound by state or national borders. Central to this initiative is the implementation of a multi-state cap-and-trade program with a market-based emissions trading system.*

The proposed program will require electric power generators in participating states to reduce carbon dioxide emissions.

The concept is to turn emission reductions into a marketable asset that will create incentives for companies to invest in technologies that reduce GHGs, at the same time providing businesses flexibility to meet the goals at the lowest possible cost. This cap-and-trade concept is similar to the one required by federal mandate to limit emissions of sulfur dioxide that causes acid rain. Currently, 11 states are involved in the RGGI project.

IGNORE IT AT YOUR OWN RISK

The bind that companies find themselves in is knowing to what extent they have to react to the momentum that is gaining in the United States and the rest of the world toward some regulation of GHGs. According to the Council on Foreign Relations, a Pew Center on Global Climate Change report surveyed 31 large companies and found that about 85 percent thought some form of mandatory federal emissions regulations would be enacted by 2015. Judging by this survey, corporations are well aware of the direction policy is going and should be planning responses to it other than lawsuits. This means that a new sector should be in the midst of developing that is in the business of reducing emissions.

Unfortunately, since there is no single GHG regulatory program, companies will be faced with a patchwork of state and local rules restricting emissions. This lack of uniformity will make compliance tricky and expensive. The best example of this would be a utility company whose power grid extends into several states. Remember, U.S. companies don't just compete locally, and they will be forced to deal with the CO_2 regulations for those nations that are complying with Kyoto. Low-emission technologies must be developed for the auto and power sectors to compete globally, and without a federal GHG program this may not occur.

IT'S EASY, JUST BUY SOMETHING!

During the tech stock explosion in the late 1990s, it seemed that all you had to do was watch CNBC, buy one of the stocks that they mentioned, and then sell it after it went up. After the signing of the 1997 Kyoto accord, but before country ratification, the same was true for many companies whose business stands to benefit from a country's implementation of the accord. During the 2000 presidential campaign, then-candidate George W. Bush pledged to control carbon dioxide emissions from power plants. Clean air, conservation, and clean energy companies were all looking hot. Then another political event occurred; President Bush reversed course after winning and questioned the science behind the emission assessments. Then National Security Advisor Condoleezza Rice surprised European ambassadors by telling them at a private lunch at the Swedish embassy in Washington that "Kyoto is dead." Eventually, Bush announced that the accord was fatally flawed (China and India) and said that it would negatively impact the fragile U.S. economy. Stocks in this sector began to give back a lot of ground and then they really got hit after 9/11.

As you can now see with global warming, the excitement from the initial accord led to a big run-up in stocks, only to be waylaid by political expediency in the world's largest contributor of greenhouse gases. Now, it's not all a trail of tears. As I have laid out, there is acceptance of the need to do something. The environmental frisson for action is accelerating as the science improves and proves that the problems caused by GHGs are growing exponentially. This is a complex situation that is evolving quickly and is dependent on the outcome from local, state, and federal regulations. It doesn't mean there won't be big winners and losers; it just means you need to have a broad portfolio in the GHG sector to cover all the ground and reduce your risk.

A big step in this process is finding out more information as to the extent of who emits, how much they emit, and where they emit it from. Projects have been started to answer these questions by requesting companies to disclose their greenhouse gas emissions. The Rockefeller Philanthropy Advisers initiated the Carbon Disclosure Project to do just that, and the interesting angle of this is that institutional investors are signed on as well. Clearly, this signals the investment community's interest in the impact of GHGs and GHG regulations on companies and their investments. This project is analogous to what the California Air Resources Board is mandated to do. Therefore, companies that monitor emissions and report on them will be in demand. It's estimated that venture capitalists spent more than $1.6 billion in low-emission business products in 2005, a 34 percent increase from 2004. These are the leading-edge investors into this sector, and more investors will be coming to develop new industries and jobs.

To begin with, there is the pursuit of cleaner alternatives to fossil fuels like coal and oil. Water, wind, sun, and nuclear energy all contain those characteristics and they are renewable. Demand for these sources of energy and the means to produce those sources of energy will continue to be going up. Power generators, metals and mining industries, pulp and paper, and refineries are all heavy users of fossil fuels. These sectors will be the ones feeling the most pressure to change their behavior and be the ones who are most likely to develop or purchase new low-emission technologies.

GO GREEN!

Since global warming appears to be a slow-moving train of an event, there isn't the same type of analysis to be done as for hurricanes or an earthquake. Obviously, this could change with a major geological or weather event triggered by warmer temperatures. Until that occurs, I'm going to suggest a couple of interesting avenues to look at for those who want to invest in environmental/clean energy. This sector can run the entire gamut from ethanol production to manufacturers of filtration systems for emission products. As for financial products in this sector, there are individual stocks, there are mutual funds, and there are exchange-traded funds (ETFs) based on mutual funds. The problem with investing in this sector is that some firms are directly involved with environmental issues, some are indirectly involved, and some are polluters that are reducing their emissions.

Here's a great little secret for speeding up your research into these companies. Go to an "environmental" or "green" ETF or mutual fund. Then look up the companies in the fund. As you'll see, there are some interesting choices of firms for these green/clean funds. Here are two funds to get started with: Powershares Wilderhill Clean Energy Portfolio (PBW) and New Alternatives Fund Inc. (NALFX US). PBW is an exchange-traded fund that seeks to correspond to the price of the Wilderhill Clean Energy Index (ECO) by investing at least 80 percent of its assets in common stocks of companies engaged in the business of the advancement of cleaner energy and conservation. NALFX US is an open-end fund that invests 25 percent or more in companies involved in alternative energy that aims at a clean and sustainable environment.

Take a look at the graphs for both of these and you will see some serious volatility. Figure 8.1 and Figure 8.2 show the 2005–2006 prices of these funds. They are not for the faint of heart. The stocks that these funds have in them are analogous to small drug companies. They have a proprietary product, and if it wins approval or the government deems it necessary, the stock explodes. However, do your homework on the companies in the funds. They may be more attractive than the overall fund itself if you think a particular technology is more likely to be more useful in, say, reducing CO_2 emissions from autos or in filtering the emissions from smokestacks.

We've been operating under the assumption that a rapid change in temperature is not occurring. But what if it did? There are plenty of scenarios to spin from rising sea levels to increases in violent weather. Let's stick to the one that could occur the fastest and may already have: increases in violent weather. Since we've already done the heavy lifting on this subject, all we need to do is think about what companies and commodities would benefit. If we were to repeat hurricane seasons like those of 2004 and 2005, we know that oil and natural gas would likely go up as we entered the hurricane

FIGURE 8.1 Powershares Wilderhill Clean Energy Portfolio
Source: Used with permission from Bloomberg L.P.

FIGURE 8.2 New Alternatives Fund Inc.
Source: Used with permission from Bloomberg L.P.

season. We would especially be looking for a series of storms to hit on top of each other in the Gulf of Mexico. Coastal real estate values could drop and prices of warm, landlocked areas like the Southwest could increase.

If this rapid change in temperature would occur, there would potentially be major changes in behavior of countries as well. India, China, and the United States would come under severe pressure to either sign the Kyoto Protocol or enact legislation to reduce GHGs. This could lead to rapid increases in share prices of those firms that supply the technology and expertise for this change. Autos and coal-burning fuel plants would be on the front line. Companies that supply either an electric car or the scrubbers for the smokestacks (pending legislation) would most likely be the major beneficiaries. On the flip side, industries that have to meet the new regulations would see their expenses rise and likely see their profits decline. Clean-burning energy would be at a premium, and a dramatic increase in nuclear energy facilities would be likely. This would benefit companies like U.S.-based Westinghouse and French-based Areva Group. Westinghouse is already benefiting, as it has just signed a deal with China to build four nuclear power plants. However, this demand could increase dramatically should India and the United States decide to aggressively increase their nuclear energy capabilities.

From our earlier chapters, we know that bad things happen when sectors are stretched or stressed. Whether it was the famine of the early 1300s increasing the impact of the bubonic plague or hurricanes hitting the most sensitive area of the U.S. economy (oil and gas production) at the most sensitive time (tight supplies), history shows a consistent theme. With soybean inventories at record lows and demand for synfuels (synthetic or nonpetroleum fuels such as biodiesel and ethanol) at highs, any disruption to normal weather patterns will cause spikes in grain prices. Now think rapid global warming creating droughtlike conditions in the United States just as an increase in biofuel plants adds ro demand for grains. This would send grain prices soaring, it would increase the cost of food, and it might force the U.S. Federal Reserve to keep interest rates unchanged to combat this new inflation threat. This scenario might keep the Federal Reserve on hold longer than the markets want, but cause further subtrend growth for GDP in the second half of the year. With just a little imagination, the ripple effects from global warming become enormous and present interesting tertiary effects that can be traded.

The goal for this book is not to be a stock picker for the reader. The goal is to make you aware of this event and the possible ways to play it. I strongly believe that there will be continued investment into this field and therefore continued opportunities to trade environmental/green stocks. I think this field could be the equivalent of the 1990s information technology (IT) industry for stocks. Since President Bush and the Republicans have been the key opponents of Kyoto, it's logical to assume that the markets will interpret the Democrats as being supporters of the accord and the environmental field. Therefore, the market or investors will likely increase buying this sector as the Democrats come to power in the legislative branch (2006) or possibly in the executive branch (2008). The other political development to watch is whether other large states follow California's lead or the lead of a group like the RGGI. Of course, the last thing to gauge is the temperature. The faster this goes up, the faster pressure will be brought to bear on the politicians to act. The recent breaking off of a 41-square-mile ice shelf in Canada is a good example of major changes that are occurring that may spur swifter action. Of course, a drought may do that as well. Politicians will act and they will help investment into this sector.

PART III

Politics

CHAPTER 9

Terrorism

My first experience with an act of terrorism against the United States was the suicide bombing of the Marine barracks in Lebanon, but this type of attack has been going on for centuries around the world—from ancient Jewish Zealots to eleventh- and twelfth-century assassins to the Japanese kamikazes during World War II. The ability to instill fear in a population remains just as potent as it was back then. With rogue nations like North Korea developing nuclear capabilities, the possibility for an attack of epic proportions has grown, not diminished, with time. This doesn't mean we should all start building bunkers in our backyards like people did in the 1950s. However, it does mean that large population and financial centers will continue to be targets in the future.

Each type of terrorism has its own degree of impact on life, society, and the financial markets. The Irish Republican Army (IRA) attacks against the British are an excellent example of a nation becoming inured to the persist dangers of a terrorist group operating in their midst. Perhaps the lack of response to the attacks eventually contributed to the IRA coming to the bargaining table and ending its bombing campaign. Another modern example of persistent suicide bombing is the Palestinian/Israeli conflict; this has not been resolved by the Palestinians holding elections and somewhat governing their territories. A third example is the Russian/Chechen battle. Although there are great disagreements over who was ultimately responsible, the Moscow theater and the Beslan school hostage-taking events were thought by many to have been perpetrated by Chechen separatists. Neither attack changed Russian policy toward Chechnya, as it remains part of the Russian Federation.

What these quick examples point out is that there can be vastly different responses and outcomes to terrorist attacks on a nation. If the reader wants more information on suicide terrorist campaigns since 1980, Robert A. Pape's *Dying to Win: The Strategic Logic of Suicide Terrorism* has a list and is an excellent resource.

We're going to focus on the most recent attacks in the West by terrorist groups that mainly have their origins in the Middle East. There is no hidden racial, ethnic, or religious agenda on my part, but merely the recognition that these attacks had a dramatic impact on the countries and their financial markets. We'll also focus on these attacks because they are all related to the same terrorist organization, and this organization is quite active. The terrorists' impact is not solely contained to one country, nor to one region of the world. Most important, their mere presence in the Middle East means that they are in close proximity to a critical geoeconomic asset: crude oil. This alone would make them worthy of discussion. This chapter focuses on suicide bombings in particular because they represent the ultimate sacrifice, demonstrating the level of commitment terrorists have toward their cause. We also want to examine these because they are the hardest to defend against as it's almost impossible to stop someone from blowing themselves up.

SEPTEMBER 11, 2001: ATTACKS ON WORLD TRADE CENTER AND PENTAGON

The United States has never been immune to terrorist attacks or incidents on its soil. Whether it was the assassination of President Lincoln or the 1920 bombing on Wall Street, anarchists and terrorists have been active attempting to influence and change public policy. In 1983 and 1984, there were four attacks by suicide bombers on U.S. interests, and those all happened outside the country in either Beirut or Kuwait. Then on February 26, 1993, Arab Islamist terrorists blew up a rental truck filled with explosives in the parking garage below Tower One of the World Trade Center. They had hoped that the explosion would weaken the tower's structure enough to collapse the building. Foreshadowing what was to come in 2001, the terrorists were financed by the uncle of one of the members, Khalid Shaikh Mohammed, a member of al-Qaeda.

Eight years later, al-Qaeda attempted again to take down the buildings at the World Trade Center and this time they were successful. Before the opening of the U.S. equity markets on September 11, 2001, 19 terrorists hijacked four jet airliners and attempted to crash them into targets. Two of the planes hit each of the towers at the World Trade Center, and one plane hit the Pentagon. The last plane crashed into a Pennsylvania field after the passengers attempted to retake control of the plane. From the attack, 2,973 people died, with most of those in New York City due to the collapse of the twin towers. In all, there were 25 buildings damaged in Manhattan and a portion of the Pentagon as well.

The attacks initiated a profound change in the country from the way the nation viewed its role in the international community to the way Americans traveled in their own country. After sitting in the dealing room and watching the events unfold in real time, here's what I wrote to our clients:

Friends, as we sort through what has occurred today, keep these six things in mind:

1. *The United States will engage the world community in going after those that are responsible for the terrorist actions in New York and Washington.*

2. *President Bush will have broad latitude of executive powers to deal with this situation. This will be a sustained long-term effort to eradicate this element from the world society. Governments who harbor terrorists or who encourage them with propaganda will be sought out and punished.*

3. *The world central banks, including the Fed, will provide as much liquidity as necessary to lessen the deleterious effects on the world financial markets from the terrorist attack.*

4. *Obviously financial markets hate uncertainty and will go to cash. Equity markets will be dramatically hurt, and short-term U.S. government bonds will be purchased.*

5. *The U.S. dollar will be initially sold for somewhat safe haven currencies like the Swiss franc.*

6. *This is the end of a golden epoch for the United States, from the collapse of the NASDAQ to the elimination of our feeling of indestructibility. When terrorists attack the mainland of the United States, our entire society is put into question. This changes everything.*

My prayers go out to those of you in NY and to those who have friends and families in NYC or at the Pentagon or on the planes that went down.

The New York Stock Exchange (NYSE), the American Stock Exchange, and the NASDAQ did not open that day and remained closed until September 17. The collapse of the buildings did not damage the NYSE or its remote data processing sites, but it did damage an important telephone exchange facility in the area. The exchange was critical for communication for

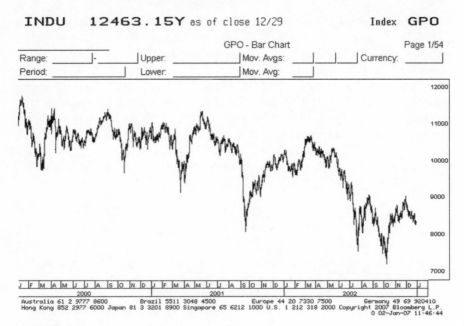

FIGURE 9.1 Dow Jones Industrial Average
Source: Used with permission from Bloomberg L.P.

member firms and clients. It was also a gateway for customers on the East Coast. I remember not being able to reset a direct line to a client in Boston for six months after the attacks. Figure 9.1 shows the Dow Jones Industrial Average from 2000 to 2002. Notice that equity prices were under pressure prior to the attacks after the U.S. Federal Reserve had raised interest rates to 6.50 percent and the U.S. economy was starting to slow from a massive investment in technology due to the millennium or Y2K scare that had occurred in 1999. The start of September had the Dow already down 1,000 points on the year and looking weak.

The U.S. 10-year bond yield was also dropping and reflected the weak economic picture. Figure 9.2 shows that the yield had gone sideways for most of the year, but was at the low of the year at the start of September. Figure 9.3 shows that the U.S. Dollar Index was above the lows of the year, but was on a downward path as well. Figure 9.4 shows the U.S. federal funds target rates. The Fed had cut rates seven times prior to the attacks, taking rates from 6.50 percent down to 3.50 percent in an aggressive easing. Clearly, Alan Greenspan was greatly concerned about the health of the U.S. economy prior to the attacks.

Now, let's take a look at what happened immediately after the attack occurred. As mentioned, all the U.S. equity markets were closed until September 17. This meant that no one could hedge their exposure or cover their

USGG10YR ↓**4.690** −**.012**   4.694/4.690   Index **GPO**
At 11:46 Op 4.702 Hi 4.706 Lo 4.666

	GPO - Bar Chart	Page 1/54
Range: _____ - _____	Upper: _____	Mov. Avgs: ___ ___ ___
Period: _____		

Australia 61 2 9777 8600   Brazil 5511 3048 4500   Europe 44 20 7330 7500   Germany 49 69 920410
Hong Kong 852 2977 6000 Japan 81 3 3201 8900 Singapore 65 6212 1000 U.S. 1 212 318 2000 Copyright 2007 Bloomberg L.P.
0 02-Jan-07 11:50:11

FIGURE 9.2 U.S. Generic 10-Year Bond Yield
Source: Used with permission from Bloomberg L.P.

DXY   **83.20** −**.45**   Curncy **GPO**
At DELAYED Op 83.29 Hi 83.31 Lo 83.15

DXY CURNCY	GPO - Bar Chart	Page 1/54
Range 01/03/00 - 01/01/03 Upper Bar Chart	Mov Avgs	Currency USD
Period Daily	Lower None	Mov Avg

Australia 61 2 9777 8600   Brazil 5511 3048 4500   Europe 44 20 7330 7500   Germany 49 69 920410
Hong Kong 852 2977 6000 Japan 81 3 3201 8900 Singapore 65 6212 1000 U.S. 1 212 318 2000 Copyright 2007 Bloomberg L.P.
0 02-Jan-07 11:53:31

FIGURE 9.3 U.S. Dollar Index
Source: Used with permission from Bloomberg L.P.

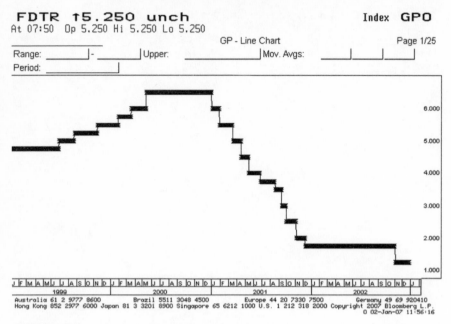

FIGURE 9.4   U.S. Federal Funds Target Rate
Source: Used with permission from Bloomberg L.P.

risks on U.S. equities. However, investors could sell on other countries' stock markets and they did. The German DAX fell 8 percent that day and opened the next day down another 4 percent.

This also meant that there would be enormous pressure on stocks when the markets did reopen. This anxiety over what would occur spilled over into currencies and bonds. The dollar was immediately sold and bonds were bought aggressively. Actually, the selling of the U.S. dollar began before the second plane even hit. As most of us stared, dumbfounded, at the TV screens, there were coolheaded and cold-blooded traders acting aggressively and selling the buck. Eventually, stock portfolio managers would join the sellers, as this was the proxy hedge for equities that traders could take advantage of and reduce the damage to their portfolios that would come when stocks reopened.

One of the first actions that the U.S. government took was to ground all air traffic. No one had any idea if there were more terrorists on their way to commandeer planes, but grounding all the planes in the country would stop them. In conjunction with this action, the airline and transportation industry would come under heavy selling pressure when equities began to trade. Airlines were already under pressure due to increased competition, high labor costs, and increased fuel costs. Figure 9.5 shows the Dow Jones

TRAN   4560.20Y as of close 12/29   Index **GPO**
        Vol n.a.

                                        GPO - Bar Chart   Page 1/54

Range: _____|-_____| Upper: _____| Mov. Avgs: __|__|__| Currency: _____|
Period: _____| Lower: _____| Mov. Avg: __|

Australia 61 2 9777 8600   Brazil 5511 3048 4500   Europe 44 20 7330 7500   Germany 49 69 920410
Hong Kong 852 2977 6000 Japan 81 3 3201 8900 Singapore 65 6212 1000 U.S. 1 212 318 2000 Copyright 2007 Bloomberg L.P.
                                                                          0 02-Jan-07 11:57:08

FIGURE 9.5 Dow Jones Transportation Average
Source: Used with permission from Bloomberg L.P.

Transportation Average, which at the start of September was in the middle of a range it had been in since the beginning of 2000. It dropped 800 points for a whopping 28.6 percent, which is more than the Dow lost during the 1987 crash.

Here's what I wrote at the end of the week, after the stock market reopened. I include this commentary because it captures the moment of what was happening and some of the psychology of the markets at the time.

> *What a week this day was in the stocks. Pre-opening, markets around the world were down on average 6.5 to 7.0 percent. Huge rally started around midmorning after GE said they expect to withstand the effects of last week's terrorist attacks and post double-digit earnings growth in 2001 and 2002. The Dow briefly went into positive territory, bringing the buck with it, only to have that reversed and back down more than 200 points. Since the September 11th attack, there have been over 110,000 announced job cuts in the United States. The DJIA has dived over 13.3 percent prior to today's close. And the dollar has fluctuated all over the map with the Swiss franc outperforming and the Australian dollar getting punished. The long bonds have followed this exceptionally volatile pattern, going down after Congress stated their*

*intention to break the lockbox on Social Security and spend like crazy.
The Treasury announced a cancellation in the bond buyback program
as well. But the bonds rallied on Friday after the Dow started the day
down more than 400 points. Everything has changed since the attacks
and it keeps changing at an increasingly rapid pace.*

*And there will be a cultural change as well. Forget about all those
boy and girl bands with their bellybuttons showing and their songs
about as deep as that body orifice. Instead of buying Britney Spears'
"Oops! I Did It Again," they'll be looking at Luciano Pavarotti's Greatest Hits containing "Ave Maria." The focus will shift to darker images
and realities of human and financial carnage that only war brings.
The thoughts turn inward during these times and become centered
on more basic needs and desires. Instead of can I get a piece of that
IPO, it's can I sell my stock at less than a 20 percent loss. Instead of
should I jump from this Internet company to another for more pay,
it's I hope I don't lose my job. Instead of we are sticking to a strong
dollar policy, it's a weaker dollar may be good for the economy. The
only constant is change.*

*And big changes are what you can expect in the economic statis-
tics once we begin to get September's numbers and how big a black
hole they make in the economy. The first one of importance will be
the Chicago Purchasing Managers on September 28th and the market
is looking for 42.5. Next week will also be the last one for September
and therefore could see the abatement of the yen repatriation. But I
have a hard time going the same way as the Bank of Japan, so I'm
not yet looking to go long dollars. Look for more details to emerge on
what the U.S. plans are in our war against terrorism. We know there
were many rumors and bomb threats this past week here and abroad.
Our allies are saying that we have asked them for their opinions on
a post-Taliban government. A post-Taliban government has a certain
ring to it, doesn't it?*

I think what's interesting in what I wrote is that the markets were beginning to look toward how bad the economy was going to be hit due to
the attacks and this would start to show up in the first batch of economic
statistics for September. These would be released in October and the unemployment rate would be the first big one. The unemployment rate remained
unchanged, but the nonfarm payroll dropped 199,000. Here's what I reported
on October 3, 2001:

*Ford and Nortel filled the air with the odor of 15,000 more job cuts
(Nortel) and a larger than expected third quarter loss (Ford and
Nortel). DaimlerChrysler's U.S. operation got into the selling act as*

well, saying that sales fell 28 percent in September and it would shut four plants for one week and one plant for three weeks. Stock markets around the world are off on the news, with the telecom and auto stocks taking the biggest hits as you would expect. But here's what I didn't expect: the euro to be gaining ground on every currency. "Euro" name it: CHF, JPY, GBP, USD all have lost ground to the mighty joint currency. Some of the EURGBP was related to Tony Blair's comments about joining the euro in this current Parliament . . . if they meet all the criteria. Don't think that was anything new there; the move probably came on the back of some Vodaphone share selling, and given what's happened to telecoms overnight that makes more sense.

Now take a look at the stock market. It had sunk to the lows immediately after all the markets reopened. It rallied into the beginning of October and then went sideways. It was a bipolar market, swinging between depressed state from the 9/11 attacks (along with fears from the new anthrax attacks) and euphoric state from the Federal Reserve cutting interest rates 100 basis points.

As we have learned throughout this book, the largest factor impacting the financial markets over the long term remains the cost of capital or interest rates. If a central bank aggressively responds to an event by pumping money into the economy, it's likely that the country's stock and bond markets will rally based off of cheaper money. In this case, there were tremendous fears that had to be overcome initially, but no more attacks came. As of the writing of this book, none have still come to U.S. soil. The problem for the Federal Reserve was that this event was unprecedented and no one could tell what medium-term impact it would have on the economy. The only thing the Fed could do was to help reopen the stock markets and begin to pump money into the system and see what would happen. Greenspan & Co., including current chairman Ben Bernanke, could only try to forestall the downshift in the economy that was already occurring prior to the attacks. This is why it's so important to have the context of what was happening beforehand to know what can happen afterward.

Humpty Dumpty comes to mind when you discuss what happened in 2002. All the Federal Reserve's efforts and all their rate cuts couldn't stop the economy from slowing. The Fed did something very crazy: It cut rates to 1.75 percent in December 2001 and then cut them to 1.25 percent in November 2002. The Fed would eventually take them all the way to 1.00 percent in 2003 and leave them there for an entire year. All of this activity sparked one of the largest, most consistent downtrends for the U.S. dollar the foreign exchange (FX) markets have ever seen. Things got so bad for the Fed that future chairman Ben Bernanke gave a speech in which he said that if things got worse, the Fed could metaphorically take a helicopter and spread money throughout the country. Hence, the development of Bernanke's nickname "Helicopter Ben."

To distill the opportunities down to a residue, here's what you could've done: sell foreign stock markets that were closely aligned to the U.S. market, sell the U.S. dollar, and buy foreign bonds and U.S. bonds. When stocks reopened, the worst thing you could've done would've been to sell U.S. stocks. You should've bought more equities and actually bought the U.S. Dollar Index. However, these would've been short-term trades (less than two quarters), as the financial markets reverted back to the direction they were headed in prior to the attacks. This is consistent with what occurs after a hurricane.

So as we head into the next examples of terrorist attacks, remember the three important factors we have learned from the other chapters:

1. The context in which the markets were previously operating.
2. The event itself and where it physically took place.
3. The response of the governing central bank to the event.

These are the key medium-term determinants of overall market direction and where it's likely the markets will return to after the shock of the event has passed.

MARCH 11, 2004: MADRID TRAIN BOMBINGS

Here's what I wrote on the day of the attacks:

> After a series of bombings in Madrid, the dollar is mixed against the major currencies with the high-yielding Australian and New Zealand dollars getting tattooed. U.S. bonds have rallied on the news, and stocks have fallen further, adding to their losses from yesterday. The bombings are a sad example of how international incidents affect us all. According to the New York Times, "Powerful explosions rocked three Madrid train stations Thursday just days before Spain's general elections, killing 170 rush-hour commuters and wounding more than 500 in what officials called the deadliest attack ever by the Basque separatist group ETA. 'This is a massacre,' government spokesman Eduardo Zaplana said." European currencies were sold at this time and their stock markets dropped. But a radical Basque nationalist leader said Thursday he did not believe ETA was behind the attack,

which could have been "an operation by sectors of the Arab resistance" (Reuters). Immediately, the financial markets moved to a safety play theme with U.S. bonds moving quickly higher; U.S. stocks were sold, and the dollar was hit hard against the Swiss franc as the markets leapt to the idea that al-Qaeda was behind the event....

However, ETA's leader may have just been playing dumb, as two ETA separatists were recently arrested with a large amount of explosives. The bombing occurs just prior to Sunday's election in Spain, which had both major parties refusing to meet with the separatists. Previously, ETA's worst attack killed 21 people in 1987. Again, NYT: "Spanish officials had said ETA was against the ropes following the arrest last year of more than 150 members or collaborators in Spain and France, including the leaders of ETA's commando network. Last year ETA killed three people, compared to 23 in 2000 and 15 in 2001." Obviously, this is a major step-up in scale for ETA (if it is them) and to some extent may point to outside assistance. And that would truly be troubling.

This encapsulates much of what was happening during the first hours after the attacks. In hindsight, we know that there were 10 explosions that went off at the height of the Madrid rush hour on four commuter trains. The attacks killed 191 people and injured more than 1,700. Since Spain had been hit in the past by Basque separatists known as ETA, the suspicion immediately fell on them. The fact that the group had recently been caught with a large amount of explosives gave the appearance that they were planning such an attack. The attacks were carried out just three days before national elections were to be held to determine the presidency.

In that time frame, it was very clear that the bombers were attempting to influence the outcome of the election and change the policies of the ruling conservative government headed by President Jose Maria Aznar. A month prior to the election, it was almost a lock for the ruling conservative party, with Aznar anointing his successor and the policies of supporting the United States in Iraq seeming to be intact. Spain's ruling party lost the election, though, and the Socialists took over with Jose Luis Rodriguez Zapatero at the helm, ending eight years of conservative rule. Zapatero immediately said he would pull Spain's troops out of Iraq in a major swing away from his predecessor's pro-American foreign policy. Spain was due to take over command of 9,000 troops in central Iraq on July 1, 2004, which was to coincide with the timetable to turn over control of the country to the Iraqis. Neither event occurred.

The election result was seen as a repudiation of Aznar's policy to support the invasion of Iraq. "If this was al-Qaeda, Aznar is responsible," according to one demonstrator from the massive protests against the bombings that occurred the weekend after the blasts. Only 48 hours after the government had claimed it was ETA, Spanish authorities found a videotape claiming that al-Qaeda carried out the Madrid terrorist attacks after three Moroccans and two Indians were arrested in connection with the bombings. The tape said the train bombings were a response to Spain's cooperation with the United States and that more blood would flow if injustices didn't stop.

Here's what I wrote on March 15:

> To say that these outcomes encourage al-Qaeda or other terrorist groups is to understate the obvious. The UK, Japan, and Poland are the next countries that would appear to be vulnerable to such activities, as all have troops in Iraq. Poland has stated that it will not pull troops out of Iraq because of terrorist attacks. "Revising our position on Iraq after terrorist attacks would be to admit that terrorists are stronger and that they are right [to pursue attacks]," said Prime Minister Leszek Miller, according to Reuters. Of course, the United States is the biggest target with a close election looming. Fueling this: Senator John Kerry's lead in the polls and his recent comments that foreign leaders were encouraging his presidential bid because of unhappiness with U.S. policy. According to the Washington Post, Kerry said the leaders were "at all different levels" of government and their support was fueled by dissatisfaction with U.S. unilateralism and an "arrogant" foreign policy. This kind of talk almost ensures we in the States will face months of rumors of domestic terrorist plots and bombs going off in the lead-up to the election in November.
>
> One attempt has already been stopped in Karachi, Pakistan. Explosive experts on Monday defused a bomb in a small van parked next to the heavily guarded U.S. consulate in this southern Pakistani city, sparing the building from "big destruction," police said, according to the New York Times. The thwarted attack came just two days ahead of a scheduled visit to Pakistan by Secretary of State Colin Powell. He was due to arrive in the country on Wednesday, but was not scheduled to visit Karachi (NYT).
>
> Again stating the obvious, things are a bit shaky around the world today. . . . And this leads to the markets jumping back into the obvious safety trades of long bonds, long CHF, and short equities.
>
> To show you how messed up the currency markets are, take a look at the price action in the Aussie dollar where it gapped open around .7400 and then fell to below .7300 and now is at .7350 because no one can quite figure out what all this uncertainty means for that country. For this country, none of this activity is good.

Clearly, the first outcome of the Madrid attack was a major change in Spain's government and its policy toward the war in Iraq.

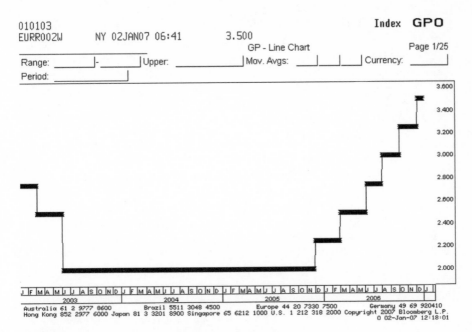

010103
EURR002W   NY 02JAN07 06:41   3.500   Index **GPO**

GP - Line Chart   Page 1/25

Range: _____ |- _____ | Upper: _____ | Mov. Avgs: ___| ___| ___| Currency: _____|
Period: _____

Australia 61 2 9777 8600   Brazil 5511 3048 4500   Europe 44 20 7330 7500   Germany 49 69 920410
Hong Kong 852 2977 6000 Japan 81 3 3201 8900 Singapore 65 6212 1000 U.S. 1 212 318 2000 Copyright 2007 Bloomberg L.P.
0 02-Jan-07 12:18:01

FIGURE 9.6 European Central Bank (ECB) Refi Rate
Source: Used with permission from Bloomberg L.P.

Let's take a look at the reactions by the financial markets to the bombings. Prior to the event, the euro was rallying against the U.S. dollar and had just put in new highs for the year. For short-term interest rates, the European Central Bank (ECB) had last cut interest rates from 2.25 percent to 2.00 percent back in June 2003 (Figure 9.6). After the bombings, the euro immediately fell 2.5 percent against the U.S. dollar and then dropped another 2.5 percent by the end of the following week (Figure 9.7).

On the equities, let's look at the IBEX 35 index for Spain (Figure 9.8). This is the official index of the Spanish Continuous Market and is comprised of the 35 most liquid stocks traded in that market. It was at the lows of the year when the event occurred and fell around 250 points in three days. However, within two weeks, the index fully recovered and was above the levels prior to the attack. Last, the generic 10-year Spanish government bond had a big sell-off, with the yields rising from around 3.80 percent to as high as 4.30 percent by the end of the next week (Figure 9.9). This is the opposite reaction that U.S. bonds initially had to the 9/11 attacks. Because Spain was a much smaller country in the midst of an election, investors dumped the bonds due to the uncertainty over the outcome of both events.

There is another major difference between the attacks of 9/11 and 3/11. The attacks in the United States were more deadly in terms of victims, more

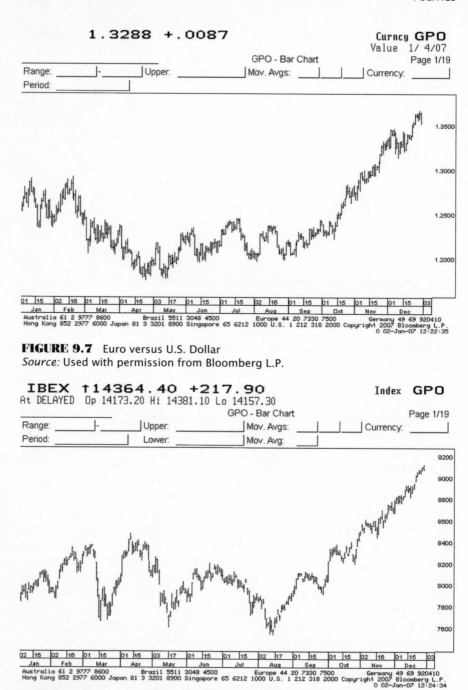

1.3288 +.0087

GPO - Bar Chart

Curncy **GPO**
Value   1/ 4/07
Page 1/19

Range: _____ |- _____ | Upper: _____ | Mov. Avgs: ___| ___| ___ | Currency: _____ |
Period: _____ |

FIGURE 9.7   Euro versus U.S. Dollar
Source: Used with permission from Bloomberg L.P.

IBEX ↑14364.40 +217.90   Index **GPO**
At DELAYED Op 14173.20 Hi 14381.10 Lo 14157.30

GPO - Bar Chart   Page 1/19

Range: _____ |- _____ | Upper: _____ | Mov. Avgs: ___| ___| | Currency: _____ |
Period: _____ | Lower: _____ | Mov. Avg: ___ |

FIGURE 9.8   IBEX 35 Index
Source: Used with permission from Bloomberg L.P.

GSPG10YR ↓**3.982** −.**025** 3.982/--- Index **GPO**
At 12:00 Op 4.004 Hi 4.004 Lo 3.968

FIGURE 9.9 Spain Generic 10-Year Bond
Source: Used with permission from Bloomberg L.P.

destructive in terms of buildings, and more disruptive in terms of shutting
the stock exchanges. There was also the shock of the 9/11 attacks as they
were the first major attacks by al-Qaeda on American soil. At that point, the
United States or the world hadn't previously experienced such an event and
due to inexperience no one was sure how to react. When 3/11 transpired, the
markets were able to contextualize the event and realize that this would not
necessarily mean that a major disruption would ensue. The airspace was
not shut down in Spain, nor was the train system. The biggest disruptions in
Spain occurred due to the protests that happened the following weekend.
The biggest indication that this was not a disastrous event for the financial system of Spain was the fact that the European Central Bank didn't
think it was necessary to lower interest rates to counteract the potential
downside effect.

The interesting play would've been to buy those Spanish bonds when
they hit 4.25 percent or so. The bond market went sideways for a month
before rallying very strongly to drop yields below where they had been
before the event. Once again, they reestablished the existing trend in the
market. The euro against the U.S. dollar had a very similar play as well. It
was rallying prior to 3/11, sold off with the event, and then resumed its trend
afterward. To a lesser extent, the IBEX was not necessarily rallying prior

to the attack, did sell off, and then began a major rally that would see the index end at the highs of the year.

JULY 7, 2005: LONDON TRAIN AND BUS BOMBINGS

On the day of the attack, here's what I wrote:

The greenback is wildly fluctuating with the news of a terrorist bomb attack in London. The U.S. dollar index is down .38 at 90.00. Globally, bonds are higher across the board as a flight to safety is occurring with the U.S. 10-year benchmark at 3.98 percent. In turn, equities are substantially lower, with markets down between 2 to 3 percent. Gold is sharply higher by $3.50 at $427.25 and oil is lower by $1.15 at $60.15. Oil at one point was down $2.60 on the news. The markets are now in the process of reversing previous moves with the exception of selling the British pound.

London was struck by a series of at least six separate and apparently coordinated explosions in its subways and buses during the morning rush hour this morning, according to the New York Times. *"The explosions ripped apart a double-decker bus and caused officials to close and evacuate the entire subway system." Reuters is now reporting seven bomb blasts. The casualties and death initially appear to be substantial, but it's still too early to tell. Prime Minister Tony Blair is leaving the G8 meeting to return to London.*

Blair made a brief statement before leaving: "It is reasonably clear that there have been a series of terrorist attacks in London. There are obviously casualties, both people who have died and people who are seriously injured, and our thoughts and prayers, of course, are with the victims and their families. . . .

"Just as it is reasonably clear that this is a terrorist attack or a series of terrorist attacks, it is also reasonably clear that it is designed and aimed to coincide with the opening of the G8. There will be time to talk later about this. It is important, however, that those engaged in terrorism realize that our determination to defend our values and our way of life is greater than their determination to cause death and destruction to innocent people in a desire impose extremism on the world. Whatever they do, it is our determination that they will never succeed in destroying what we hold dear in this country and in other civilized nations throughout the world."

I was watching Fox News on Saturday and they had on an insane number of people (seven) to discuss the housing market on Neil Cavuto's weekend show. One of the "interesting" choices to discuss that market was comedian Ben Stein. However, he was one of the few commentators to provide a cogent response to what would cause the housing market to decline. Essentially, he said there needed to be an exogenous event to disrupt employment and cause a decline in home prices. An exogenous event. The rest of Europe is on a heightened state of alert. U.S. Homeland Security has not raised the alert level here. Yet. Let's hope that exogenous event doesn't hit on our soil today.

Expect to hear stories that this is payback for participation in the war in Iraq. Spain and now the UK have been hit. Poland, Australia, and Japan will be discussed as future targets.

The market is buying back U.S. dollars as news of a freight train in Turkey that was derailed by a bomb hits the newswires. Airline and travel stocks are getting skewered early in European markets. Both the Bank of England and the European Central Bank left rates unchanged. However, this doesn't exclude action later should the situation warrant it. Obviously, the UK's economy will suffer and had been softening anyway. This will accelerate the process. And perhaps, bring forward a rate cut by the BOE as well. It would be smart for the ECB to do the same.

The coordinated attacks hit London during rush hour, blowing up three London Underground trains and one double-decker bus. The explosions killed 52 passengers, and 700 were injured (four suicide bombers were killed). It killed and injured more people than any single IRA attack and was the worst in Britain since the 1988 Pan Am Lockerbie attack, which killed 270. There were so many rumors flying after the attacks it was difficult to keep track of them—from talk of new airplane attacks in the United States to stories of UK sniper units following a dozen al-Qaeda suspects in Britain. On July 21, some of those rumors came true as another attack occurred, but the bombs failed to detonate.

From an economic standpoint, the major impact of the July 7 attack was a daylong disruption of London's transportation and mobile telecommunication infrastructure. The European Central Bank's Jean-Claude Trichet, the Bank of England's Mervyn King, and the Federal Reserve's Alan Greenspan all agreed that "the attacks will not have significant impact" on economic growth. The Bank of England didn't cut interest rates due to the event, but did cut rates a month later by 25 basis points from 4.75 percent to 4.50 percent. (Figure 9.10).

With that in mind, let's look at how the financial markets reacted. The British pound had just had a significant drop in value against the U.S. dollar

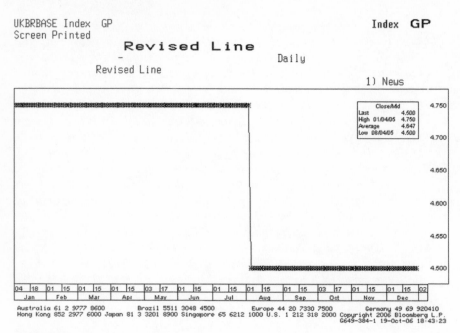

FIGURE 9.10 Bank of England Rate
Source: Used with permission from Bloomberg L.P.

in July and was making new lows for the year (Figure 9.11). After the event, it put in a new low, then rallied, then put in another new low, then rallied, and then finished the month above where it had closed on July 1. That's some confusion in a short period of three weeks. The British pound rallied from there until the beginning of September, when it renewed its sell-off and eventually closed the year below the lows established in July. This is supportive of the patterns we have seen—that an event can interrupt the trend, but doesn't kill it. The event can provide and usually does provide excellent opportunities for quick countertrend trades or even better trend trades from better levels than existed before the event. The generic 10-year UK bond's action was similar to what happened to Spanish bonds, but not nearly as dramatic (Figure 9.12). The UK bond yield fell during the event and then quickly rose in the weeks after the event. The yield would go sideways for the remainder of the year, but end the year at the lows of 4.10 percent.

For equities, we'll look at the FTSE 100 (Figure 9.13). This index had an initial drop that day of close to 200 points before recapturing almost all of its losses. It would go sideways for most of the month before resuming its upward trend. It finished the year at the highs for the year.

FIGURE 9.11 British Pound versus U.S. Dollar
Source: Used with permission from Bloomberg L.P.

FIGURE 9.12 UK Generic 10-Year Government Bond
Source: Used with permission from Bloomberg L.P.

FIGURE 9.13 FTSE 100
Source: Used with permission from Bloomberg L.P.

SUM IT UP AND MOVE ON

Terrorist attacks are like heart attacks for the financial markets. They generate tremendous initial uncertainty and discomfort as everyone attempts to assess damage and future risk, all within hours of the event. There will be rumors of additional attacks, there will be misunderstandings of who was responsible, there will be denials by some groups and other groups claiming responsibility, and there will be extremely volatile markets.

In this environment of uncertainty, there are plentiful opportunities for the coolheaded and well-prepared investor. You don't have to have tick-by-tick access to the markets to take advantage of the situations and price movements. However, you do have to be prepared with an understanding of where things have been from a trend standpoint and what the policy of the U.S. Federal Reserve has been. In this chapter, I have purposely left out references to the wars that followed from 9/11, but these will be covered in a later chapter. There were many repercussions from 9/11, 3/11, and 7/7 that will be written about for generations. My viewpoint is one of writing a rough draft of the financial history that ensued from the perspective of only a few years after the events. The longer-term social impact will be felt for decades.

CHAPTER 10

Government Change

The world of politics provides rich ground for event trading and analysis. In fact, it is so fertile that I'm devoting two chapters to this area. This chapter is devoted to change in the party in power, and how that impacts the financial markets. Like all of economics, this is an imperfect science and there are many qualifications of the event's impact on the markets. Some political change is sudden, turbulent, and easy to see like Argentina's in 2001. Other change is more subtle with longer time horizons such as the 1994 shift in the U.S. House of Representatives. As in all the chapters, our goal here is not to develop a specific model that fits all types, but rather a general paradigm that we can use to analyze most of the changes in government that occur and how to make money from them.

The three events we examine span a broad spectrum of change. We look at these chronologically as I believe each event would have been studied by political parties around the world and learned from so as to not repeat exactly the same mistakes. We look at the 1994 U.S. midterm elections, the 2001 Argentina presidential elections, and the 2005 German federal elections. The U.S. midterm elections had the Democratic Party lose control of the U.S. House of Representatives for the first time in 40 years and put in place the cast of characters who would see a U.S. president impeached. The 2001 Argentine political and economic crisis would see the head of government change three times in less than two weeks and cause the country to massively devalue its currency. Finally, the 2005 German elections were fascinating in that all of the fun and positive mojo by the victorious party would be squandered before it actually took office.

1994 U.S. MIDTERM ELECTIONS: THE RISE AND FALL OF GINGRICH

The U.S. 1994 elections for the House of Representatives and the Senate were a watershed event for numerous reasons. First and foremost, the outcome marked a change of the party in power in the House for the first time since 1954. Next, the outcome marked the first time in 40 years that Republicans controlled both houses of Congress. Last, it marked the first time that a sitting Speaker of the House (Tom Foley) would lose his seat during an election since the U.S. Civil War in 1865. The Republicans gained 54 seats and took control of the House of Representatives. In the Senate they gained 8 seats and defended all 13 of their seats that were up for election. The Republicans also gained 12 more governor seats in the states around the country. This is why it is so important to review that year and understand the changes that occurred and how those changes continue to impact U.S. politics to this day.

The outcome was the culmination of tremendous change in the Republican political leadership and ushered in a dramatic change in Congress. Congress had been a bastion of power for committees and the chairmen of those committees reigned supreme up until about the mid-1970s. Then via a series of scandals and new blood demanding change, these chairmanships were eroded until more power could be distributed to those who utilized a key new instrument in the legislative process: television. The advent of C-SPAN and the broadcasting of congressional speeches dramatically changed the way that members of Congress could get their messages or opinions out to the public. No one understood that better than Republican Newt Gingrich.

Scandal, Then a Contract

Congressman and then Speaker of the House Gingrich began laying the groundwork for taking over power in the late 1980s and early 1990s. Gingrich and the Republicans constantly attacked the Democrats and kept them on the defensive, whether it was Jim Wright's book deal or Dan Rostenkowski's felony indictment for abuse of House stamps or President Bill Clinton's investment in Whitewater. More important, the Republicans hung together and stayed united behind defeating President Bill Clinton and First Lady Hillary Clinton's health care proposal that both Clintons had staked as a key piece of legislation for the Democrats. It never even got to a vote in Congress. The Republicans did an amazing job of blocking all the attempts by the Democrats to bring any important legislation to a vote during the election year. To some extent, this continues in Congress to this day during election years. This is why all important bills must be brought up in the preceding year and why you can honestly say that members of Congress work for only half of their time in D.C.

Late in the 1994 campaign, Gingrich and 300 Republican leaders appeared on the steps of the Capitol to announce their "Contract with America" in which they pledged to carry out a 10-point platform to reform Congress and pass major pieces of conservative legislation in the first 100 days of their rule. I remember watching the event in the trading room as all the major news outlets covered the story. It was a coup for the Republicans and fueled their victory.

After the elections, a state of political gridlock ensued as the Republicans controlled both houses of Congress (legislative) and the Democrats held the presidency (executive). This has implications for the markets. From a common sense standpoint, a gridlocked government means in general one of two scenarios can exist. In scenario one, the two sides work together and compromise over what the priorities for new legislation and for spending will be. This means that neither side gets to do exactly what they want or spend exactly what they want. Therefore, government expenditures generally are contained, because no strong agenda gets favored, like health care. In scenario two, the sides don't work together, they don't compromise, and no one gets anything close to what they want. At best, this means that budget bills get passed and ongoing spending is at the same levels and same priorities as the year before. At worst, this means that the battles that flare up can escalate to a point where Congress refuses to pass budgets and debt ceilings for spending so that the government is effectively shut down.

This latter scenario is precisely the path that the Republican Congress went down with Democrat Bill Clinton. The acrimonious relationship between the Democrats and the Republicans led to partisan fighting and very little compromise. This meant that very little legislation got done without it being dragged on via extended debate. This included spending bills and meant that Congress would not overspend or increase dramatically the amount of money dedicated to new initiatives. Keep in mind, this was all happening after the fall of the Berlin Wall and the need to increase defense spending had dropped as well.

Market Reaction

Let's get to what was going on in the markets. As always, let's look at what the U.S. Federal Reserve was doing at the time. Throughout 1994, the Fed and Alan Greenspan were aggressively raising rates—they took federal funds rate from 3.00 percent at the start of the year to 5.50 percent at the end of the year (Figure 10.1). They would raise rates to a peak of 6.00 percent in

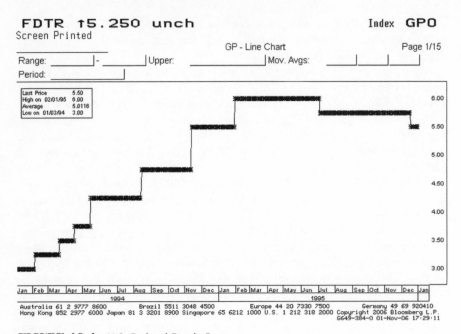

FIGURE 10.1 U.S. Federal Funds Rate
Source: Used with permission from Bloomberg L.P.

February. Look at what the generic U.S. 10-year government note was doing (Figure 10.2); it comes as no surprise that the yield was rising along with the Federal Reserve raising rates.

This set the stage for a massive rally in 1995 when the Fed began to cut rates and we had a gridlocked government. Note that the Fed cut rates only 50 basis points in 1995, but the yield on the 10-year note dropped from almost 250 basis points, from 8.00 percent to 5.50 percent. Putting it another way, the yield on the 10-year was back down to the level it had started from in 1994, but the fed funds rate at the end of 1995 was a whopping 250 basis points above where it had been at the beginning of 1994.

For stocks, clearly 1994 was not a good year, as the market was digesting the beginning of a monetary tightening cycle and uncertainty over the change in the government. In Figure 10.3, the Dow Industrials started the year at the peak and immediately went south upon the Federal Reserve raising rates. Once the Fed policy makers changed their cycle to an easing one and the gridlocked government was in place, the Dow boomed and had one of the best years on record. Interestingly enough, large-capitalization stocks outperformed the small-cap stocks in this rally, which could be interpreted to mean that no Republican Congressman could get the goodies

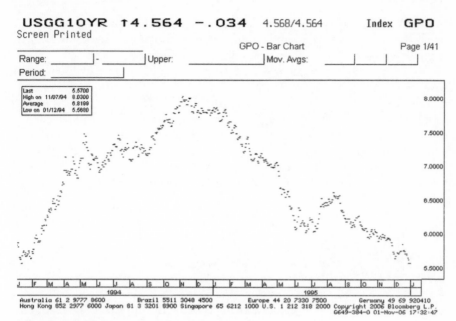

USGG1OYR ↑4.564 −.034 4.568/4.564 Index **GPO**
Screen Printed

GPO - Bar Chart Page 1/41

Range: _____ - _____ | Upper: _____ | Mov. Avgs: ___ | ___ | ___ |
Period: _____ |

Last	5.5700
High on 11/07/94	8.0300
Average	6.8199
Low on 01/12/94	5.5680

FIGURE 10.2 U.S. Generic 10-Year Government Bond
Source: Used with permission from Bloomberg L.P.

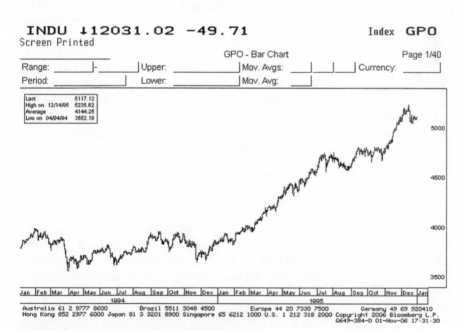

INDU ↓12031.02 −49.71 Index **GPO**
Screen Printed

GPO - Bar Chart Page 1/40

Range: _____ - _____ | Upper: _____ | Mov. Avgs: ___ | ___ | Currency: _____ |
Period: _____ | Lower: _____ | Mov. Avg: ___ |

Last	5117.12
High on 12/14/95	5235.62
Average	4144.25
Low on 04/04/94	3552.18

FIGURE 10.3 Dow Jones Industrial Average
Source: Used with permission from Bloomberg L.P.

for his district and spread them out to the smaller companies. Or it could mean that the small companies didn't have a lobbying presence in D.C. to get any meaningful spending legislation sent their way.

Extending this bickering and fighting to the ultimate showdown, 1996 saw the spending battles of President Clinton and the Gingrich-led Republicans shut down the federal government. Take a look at how the U.S. Dollar Index, the generic U.S. 10-year Treasury note, and the Dow Industrials responded. This is the ultimate example of gridlock, and all other types of gridlock should be seen as a watered-down version of this. Circling back, this is why the elections of 1994 were so important and laid the groundwork for the travails of both Gingrich and Clinton that ensued as one lost his job and one got impeached.

ARGENTINE 2001 ELECTIONS AND CRISIS

At the end of 2001, the world had a lot on its plate: the unprecedented attacks on the United States at the Pentagon and World Trade Center, a biological attack, the ensuing war in Afghanistan, and Enron, the largest corporate collapse in the history of the United States. However, the world was not distracted from the problems of a nation in the southern hemisphere that was once a proud and prosperous country that enjoyed the highest standard of living in Latin America. The events in 2001 and 2002 were triggered by a collapse in the economy in 1999 with a decrease in the gross domestic product (GDP). Of course, the seeds of this economic destruction were planted long before and had to do with trying to solve another problem that was endemic for Latin America: inflation.

In 1989, Argentina's inflation hit 200 percent per month and topped 3,000 percent on an annual basis. In an effort to deal with the problem, Argentina did something radical: It fixed the value of the currency to the U.S. dollar. Any citizen or company could go to the bank and exchange the Argentine peso in a 1:1 trade for the U.S. dollar. This meant that Argentina effectively had the same monetary policy as the United States and therefore had the same central bank deciding this policy, the Federal Reserve. This also meant that as the Federal Reserve raised and lowered interest rates that Argentina would effectively have the same thing happen regardless of whether its economy was in the same part of the business cycle as the United States. It also meant that as the U.S. dollar rose, the Argentine peso would rise as well.

Another problem associated with this arrangement was that it necessitated that there was no leakage of additional pesos being put into the system that the Argentine central bank didn't have U.S. reserves to back up. You have to essentially freeze the pesos in circulation to match your U.S. dollar reserves or you have to grow the amount of U.S. dollar reserves to match the growth of your pesos in circulation. Unfortunately for Argentina, neither of these occurred and U.S. dollars left the system due to money laundering and massive tax evasion. At the same time, currency devaluations by Argentina's major trade partners and a stronger overall U.S. dollar made Argentine exporters uncompetitive and dried up money flowing into the country from their activities.

Last, Argentina never curbed its appetite for taking on additional debt to fuel growth. It never took the difficult political medicine of raising taxes and reducing government spending to improve its finances and therefore reduce its dependency on borrowing, especially loans from the International Monetary Fund (IMF). The IMF had lent Argentina $11 billion over the previous two years in hopes of avoiding a currency collapse and default. The IMF made the loans even though it knew that the Argentine government would not make the hard choices to improve the country's finances. U.S. Treasury officials had argued that the problem was just too much debt and that the Argentine government had to borrow increasingly larger sums just to meet the debt payments. Due to the link between the peso and the U.S. dollar, Argentina could not monetize this debt by simply printing more pesos to pay it off. Of course, it didn't help when new U.S. Treasury Secretary Paul O'Neill convinced other industrialized nations to stop lending from the IMF in August of 2001. At the time, Argentina had amassed an astounding $132 billion of debt. The irony is that O'Neill eventually agreed to another $8 billion loan after Argentine Economic Minister Domingo Cavallo pleaded for two weeks for more time to carry out doomed reform.

While this was occurring in 2001, fears of currency devaluation caused tremendous flight of capital out of the country and further stressed the currency peg system. When a November swap of Argentine debt essentially signaled a default, the government froze all bank accounts for 12 months. The people started protesting, and political instability ensued. Government after government resigned amidst the turmoil while five different presidents came and went—not exactly a process that would instill confidence in anyone who might be dumb enough to lend money to Argentina at the time.

This is why I wrote this note to clients on January 4, 2002:

And on to Argentina, the slowest train wreck in the history of financial disasters. It officially devalued its currency by 29 percent and ended a 10-year-old peg to the U.S. dollar. The new peso will be "fixed" at 1.4 per dollar and the government will let the peso trade freely within a few months. "We are in a collapse. We are broke. That means we

*have to be very prudent," said Economic Minister Remes. Most debt
holders to this country took a hit a long time ago, so there is little
excitement or fear of dislocation occurring in the financial markets.
The only people who have been hurt are those who didn't have the
political or criminal influence to have gotten their money out of the
banks when accounts were frozen. Argentines need to understand that
capitalism didn't fail, but their leaders did. The new programs that
are being talked about to help that country remind me of a sitcom:
That '70s Show. Because that's the time period they are coming from.
And anyone who believes protectionism during a time of recession is
a good idea hasn't studied the great U.S. depression of the 1930s. A
mountain of debt ($132 billion), a recession, and higher taxes have
all led a very wealthy nation to be humiliated.*

Let's do the numbers, then, on what happened. The currency was taken
off the peg of 1:1 and devalued in 2002 to about 4:1 (Figure 10.4). Eventually, the currency was allowed to float and inflation went nuts, rising to
80 percent. The Argentine Merval stock index went down in anticipation
of the devaluation and then rose after it (Figure 10.5). This is pretty as-
tounding that the panic that was caused leading up to the devaluation

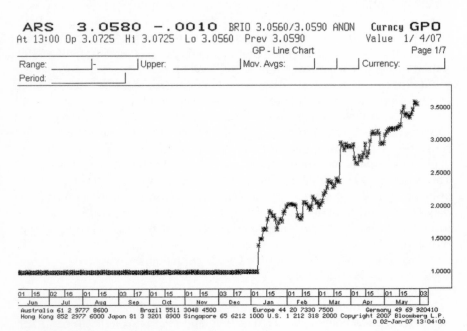

FIGURE 10.4 U.S. Dollar versus Argentine Peso
Source: Used with permission from Bloomberg L.P.

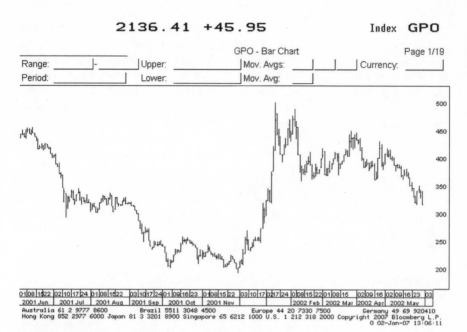

2136.41 +45.95   Index **GPO**

FIGURE 10.5 Argentine Merval Stock Index
Source: Used with permission from Bloomberg L.P.

provided an amazing opportunity to buy Argentine stocks very cheaply. The key would've been to wait until the devaluation occurred and then buy the stocks when they dipped back below 300, as this would've reduced the currency risk. Today, there are exchange-traded funds (ETFs) that allow you to invest in this area of the world without having to buy the currency.

The government's next ploy for stemming the flood of money out of the country: "pesofication." If there ever was something that sounded like an incurable financial disease, pesofication was it. All bank accounts would be converted from U.S. dollars into Argentine pesos at the official rate of 1.4 pesos to the U.S. dollar. Consumer spending collapsed, importers of foreign goods went bankrupt, the national airline had to stop all international flights at times, and the U.S. government put restrictions on food and drugs coming from Argentina due to fears that they were inferior. Finally, the government defaulted on its debt, which caused tremendous angst in Europe, where pensioners in Italy, France, and Germany had owned the paper and now were experiencing tremendous losses.

As a follow-up to this story, the Argentines did pay down some of their debts and bondholders received somewhere between 25 and 35 cents on the dollar for their bonds. In January 2006, the government of Argentina made a payment to the IMF to cover its debts. The government still owes approximately $123 billion in debt that was restructured at much lower terms and tied to the overall economic performance of the economy. Most of the financial markets could see this coming back in 1997–1998 during the Asian currency crisis and adjusted their portfolios accordingly. Unfortunately, the biggest losers of this crisis were the citizens of Argentina who were not so connected that they could get their money out of country before the massive devaluation occurred.

2005 GERMAN FEDERAL ELECTIONS

Like the Argentine elections and crisis, the party on this event started well before the election took place. Although there was no extreme economic crisis, the economy's poor performance was central to the election process as it continued to experience double-digit unemployment and low GDP. At the time, Germany was ruled by a governing coalition of the Socialist Democratic Party (SPD) and the Green Party. Chancellor Gerhard Schröder had been at the head of the coalition from 1998 and had recently remained in power by opposing the invasion of Iraq during a 2002 election. Unfortunately for his coalition, the voters perceived him to be ineffectual in bringing significant change to the moribund German economy and to bringing positive change to the welfare state in the country. Schröder had been very successful in bringing changes into energy policy by funding Green Party initiatives for renewable energy and reducing nuclear energy. In 2003, he pledged to reform the welfare state, cut taxes, and bring Germany back to world prominence. (I think he included a cure for cancer, but I'm not sure.) The point is that his coalition delivered very little on this "Agenda 2010" and his poll ratings began to drop.

At this time, he decided to make a calculated risk in forcing a fall election after a motion of no confidence passed on July 1, 2005. The ruling German was not alone in his problems. Here's what I wrote to clients on May 25:

And sagging is exactly what's happening to the fortunes of most ruling European politicians. Germany's Chancellor Schröder has called for early elections in September in an attempt to catch the opposition wrong-footed with an unpopular leader. But with his party 17 points behind at this point, I kinda don't think it matters. Italy's Berlusconi had to form a new government (shocker) last month with his country in a full-blown recession. And last but certainly not least and a country that is near and dear to most Americans, France is struggling with the referendum on an EU constitution that it helped write. Underscoring the fact that most Frenchmen are unhappy with current

President Jacques Chirac, the opinion polls are showing between a 3 and 8 percent no vote against the 448-article text that has almost nothing controversial in it. On May 20, European Commissioner Jose Barroso said that a defeat would be perceived outside of Europe as a failure for Europe. He added that there is no plan B if it fails. Adding insult to injury, the UK is preparing for a vote on the constitution next year. However, newly reelected Tony Blair astutely put it this way: You "can't have a vote on nothing."

At the time, the German and Italian business executives seemed to be having a contest over who could be the most pessimistic. German business confidence fell to the lowest level in 21 months, with the Ifo Institute reporting that its survey showed a drop to 92.9 in May from 93.3 in April. Not to be outdone, Italian confidence dropped from 84.8 to 84.2, according to the Institute for Studies and Economic Analyses (ISAE). Also, the Organization for Economic Cooperation and Development (OECD) reduced its growth forecast for the Eurozone to 1.2 percent and said Europe was dragging down the global economy.

The German opposition parties of the Christian Democratic Union (CDU) and the Christian Social Union (CSU), with their junior partner the Free Democratic Party (FDP), had to win over 50 percent of the vote to govern in an outright majority position. The leader of the CDU was Angela Merkel. She was campaigning on personal and business tax cuts along with reforming the government to cut social spending. In July, Merkel and the CDU/CSU/FDP coalition had a 21-point lead. There was great hope in the financial markets that Germany would have a leader and a mandate to change the structure of the economy and promote growth by reducing tax burdens and decreasing regulations on German businesses.

From May through August, the German DAX (Figure 10.6) rallied on these hopes. Also helping, the European Central Bank had cut interest rates to a new low of 2.0 percent (Figure 10.7) and kept them there for almost two years. Even the beleaguered euro seemed to take some comfort from the direction of Germany and stabilized in the low 1.20s against the U.S. dollar (Figure 10.8).

Ah, but all was not to be so simple. Schröder had not survived seven years at the helm of Germany without being able to resurrect himself and his coalition. It also helped that Merkel made a series of missteps, from confusing the difference between net and gross income figures to seriously bad hair. The worst mistake Merkel made was having a debate with the telegenic and ready-for-prime-time Schröder. She appeared awkward, and voters didn't like her flat tax proposal. By midweek, the SPD coalition came within a couple of percentage points of the CDU coalition. The key was that neither showed an ability to be able to garner an outright majority with any

DAX ↑6284.19 +19.27 .00/.00   Index **GPO**
Screen Printed
                                              GPO - Bar Chart   Page 1/37
Range: _____|_____| Upper: _____| Mov. Avgs: ___|___|___| Currency: _____
Period: _____| Lower: _____| Mov. Avg: ___|

Jan Feb Mar Apr May Jun Jul Aug Sep Oct Nov Dec Jan Feb Mar Apr May Jun Jul Aug Sep Oct
                          2005   2006
Australia 61 2 9777 8600   Brazil 5511 3048 4500   Europe 44 20 7330 7500   Germany 49 69 920410
Hong Kong 852 2977 6000 Japan 81 3 3201 8900 Singapore 65 6212 1000 U.S. 1 212 318 2000 Copyright 2006 Bloomberg L.P.
                                                                                          G736-384-0 26-Oct-06 17:05:09

FIGURE 10.6 German DAX Stock Index
Source: Used with permission from Bloomberg L.P.

EURR002W Index GPO   Index **GPO**
EURR002W   NY 02JAN07 06:41   3.500
                                              GP - Line Chart   Page 1/19
Range: _____|_____| Upper: _____| Mov. Avgs: ___|___|___| Currency: _____
Period: _____|

J F M A M J J A S O N D J F M A M J J A S O N D J F M A M J J A S O N D J
         2004   2005   2006
Australia 61 2 9777 8600   Brazil 5511 3048 4500   Europe 44 20 7330 7500   Germany 49 69 920410
Hong Kong 852 2977 6000 Japan 81 3 3201 8900 Singapore 65 6212 1000 U.S. 1 212 318 2000 Copyright 2007 Bloomberg L.P.
                                                                                          0 02-Jan-07 13:23:40

FIGURE 10.7 European Central Bank Refi Rate
Source: Used with permission from Bloomberg L.P.

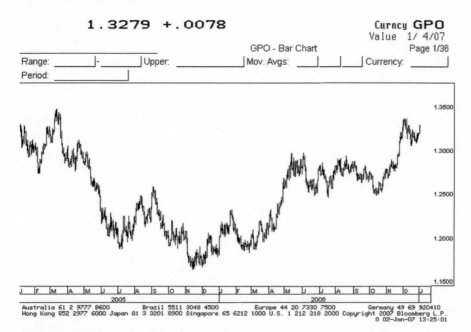

1.3279 +.0078

Curncy **GPO**
Value 1/ 4/07

GPO - Bar Chart

Page 1/36

Range: _____ |- _____ | Upper: _____ | Mov. Avgs: ___|___|___ | Currency: _____ |
Period: _____ |

Australia 61 2 9777 8600   Brazil 5511 3048 4500   Europe 44 20 7330 7500   Germany 49 69 920410
Hong Kong 852 2977 6000 Japan 81 3 3201 8900 Singapore 65 6212 1000 U.S. 1 212 318 2000 Copyright 2007 Bloomberg L.P.
0 02-Jan-07 13:25:01

FIGURE 10.8 Euro versus U.S. Dollar
Source: Used with permission from Bloomberg L.P.

of their coalitions. On September 18, exit polls showed that the CDU had won, but with a razor-thin margin of victory over the SPD of 35 percent to 34 percent. Both sides claimed victory, as neither side could form a ruling majority outright within their coalitions.

Here's what I wrote on September 19:

> *There were actually two close elections over the weekend with very similar results for their currencies: negative. It's strange and ironic that the markets wanted both incumbents out and were disappointed when that didn't happen and that the final outcome may not be known for weeks. The elusive "worst of both worlds" phrase is appropriate for New Zealand and Germany. But let's keep this in perspective: The GDP of Germany is 2.7 trillion and the GDP of New Zealand is 96 billion.*
>
> *Therefore, let's focus on our friends in Germany. In the 613-member lower house of parliament, Angela Merkel's opposition conservative party won 225 seats and incumbent Chancellor Gerhard Schröder's Social Democrats won 222. Neither has a clear majority and they must partner with junior parties to form a government. They have a month to do it before the lower chamber by law has to meet and elect a chancellor. Schröder's party and its junior partner*

won 42.4 percent, but Merkel's party along with its junior partner FDP won only 45 percent of the seats. Neither can form a government without help from each other or the new Left Party (East German Communists and a splinter SPD) that got 8.7 percent of the votes. Already the head of the FDP has ruled out a "traffic-light" coalition of Schröder's Social Democrats, the Green Party, and the FDP.

This is ugly. A "grand coalition" of both parties is going to be very difficult to form and almost impossible to administer. As I wrote in the Globe and Mail *(my newspaper column) on Friday, "the groups that are going to get zapped are the investors. Unfortunately, they will continue to feel the impact of a failed domestic program that is unable to cope with an anemic economy, heavy outsourcing, and an aging population that will cause serious strain on their social safety net system. After Sunday, I'm guessing they will slide out of that country to an alternative country like Japan."*

The euro currency sank, as did the DAX, for the month of October as the two sides attempted to hammer out a compromise. This indecision on the election was eerily similar to what had occurred during the U.S. 2000 election. In this case, the opposition parties had to agree to a coalition that included representation from both groups. On October 10, a compromise was reached with Angela Merkel as the new chancellor and an even split of the 16 cabinet seats between the CDU/CSU and the SPD. With the uncertainty removed, the stock market powered higher as the coalition promised to cut public spending and to cut employment protection during the first two years on the job.

Here's what I wrote after the coalition was formed:

Of course, it helps the buck when Europe has self-inflicted political wounds like what's going on in Germany. The Christian Democrats' (CDU) Angela Merkel has finally been named the new German chancellor in a power-sharing deal with the opposition Social Democrats (SPD). The deal has the CDU controlling the chancellorship, the cabinet-level chief of staff post, and six cabinet seats while the SPD gets eight cabinet posts. This almost ensures that Merkel's pledges of tax cuts and labor reform will at best be seriously watered down and at worst not happen at all. This should translate into years more of double-digit unemployment and sideways GDP.

Merkel herself wasn't too excited at the prospects. At a news conference, Merkel announced the terms of the coalition, but almost neglected to mention the fact that she would become chancellor. While she read the four-minute statement, she didn't smile once. It's like the old joke about the prizes of contest no one wants to win. First prize is a week in Cleveland, and second prize is two weeks. Merkel won the election, but really got two weeks in Cleveland.

The impact from this event covered the time from when the election was called for until when the election was finally settled. In these forms of government, the campaigning is relatively short compared to the United States primary system. In this German event, the impact on the financial markets was primarily seen in the stock market as the election evolved around changes to the tax and social payment structure of the government. The German bond market suffered from anticipation of faster German growth along with the European Central Bank raising rates. The generic German 10-year government bond (Figure 10.9) saw the yields hit their lows over the uncertainty of the outcome of the election in late September. Then, the yields went up from there and reached a peak in mid-2006.

This somewhat flies in the face of the theory that bonds should perform better during a coalition or gridlock government than during a unified one. In this case, the Germans had a unique situation in which both parties campaigned on similar reform issues and reducing social spending. In other words, it didn't matter who won as both were going to attempt to enact legislation that was bond market friendly. This was really going to be a question

FIGURE 10.9 German Generic 10-Year Government Bond
Source: Used with permission from Bloomberg L.P.

of who won with how large a mandate. Mandates from the electorate are critical for providing the impetus for pushing change through the system. Refer back to the 1994 U.S. midterm elections. I seriously doubt that the Republicans would've been able to enact their 10 points in 100 days without the backing of a major victory in the midterm elections, especially with a Democratic president.

As of this writing, Merkel's grand coalition honeymoon is over, and not much has been accomplished. As I've written, the markets had hope that there would be positive change and that the government would lift the Eurozone's largest economy out of the ditch. Unfortunately, they made no strides in reforming social security or in reforming the rigidity of the labor market. The biggest step they have taken is to raise the retirement age to 67—eventually. This is the mouse in the snake routine. For the longer term (2050), the Eurozone population will gray dramatically as low fertility rates and longer life expectancy will eventually drive the dependency ratio of those who work (ages 16–63) to those who don't (below 16 and above 63) from 50 percent to 80 percent. The point is that the current government hasn't had the will or the mandate from the voters to change the system to address these long-term issues. No one wants to have their taxes raised, nor does anyone want to limit the social safety net to protect them during periods of unemployment. To use a cliché, this is a slow-burning fuse on a bomb that will explode eventually with massive costs the longer the day of reckoning is put off.

CPWT: CHAMPIONSHIP POLITICAL WRESTLING AND TRADING!

Government change is a tricky world event in terms of trading. Since politics is a social science and involves the study of human beings, then understanding politics is an inexact science by definition. Human beings are difficult to gauge when it comes to their reasons for voting and supporting specific candidates. More important, the time frames involved in elections are a moving target, especially when it comes to parliamentary elections, as those are predicated upon the ruling party's ability to maintain a functioning majority. If they can't either control their members or maintain their coalition, they will be forced to call elections and dissolve the government.

In the United States, a ruling president can still be president long after he has lost the ability to influence the legislative process and agenda. This happens so frequently that we have a name for it: lame-duck president. Normally, this refers to the last two years of almost every presidency that has gone for two consecutive terms. It can also refer to when a president loses both Houses of Congress at the midpoint of his term. The broader point to take away is that we watch the opinion polls in the United States for elections, but we have a set time to do this for as the elections are every four years for the president and then every two years for the midterms. This is a much different animal than a parliament that can change should the ruling party lose a vote on a key piece of legislation like a budget or defense policy.

How does this loss of control happen? This has as many permutations as there are prejudices on what voters consider their hot-button topics. The usual list of suspects contains the economy, poor management of budgets, war, and scandals. To some extent, all of these can get bound up in what I like to call my Political Rule of 12. Once a party has ruled for over 12 years, it generally starts losing its grip on the majority and eventually loses the government to the opposition. This happened with the 2006 U.S. midterm elections with Republican control of the U.S. House, it happened with the 2006 Swedish elections, and it happened with the 2006 Canadian elections. The Rule of 12 is a simple time gauge of knowing that after 12 years, the party in power has done enough bad things to upset the voters and warrant the mood of "throw the bums out."

For trading, what we learn is that there are opportunities that arise from understanding the overall direction of why the government is changing and understanding the time frames involved. If a government is changing because of a desire by the voters to bring change to policy that is positive like cutting taxes or reducing government spending on social welfare to boost the economy, then this is going to be anticipated, as a positive move and the markets will generally like the idea. Investors will react favorably to this perceived change and buy equities and the currency of the nation in advance of the actual election taking place. This is precisely what happened in Germany. If the party that wants to do this then loses its lead or shows that party leaders are incompetent or that they will not will in an outright majority, thus necessitating that their policies will get watered down, then this expectation of a favorable event is taken away and investors sell their holdings.

However, if the government is changing because of bad behaviors like scandal or a prolonged war, then the markets will not necessarily have a clear direction to go and the expectations will merely be positive to get rid of the incumbents, but not much more. Let's take a look at these in the next chapter.

CHAPTER 11

Government Scandals

The United States has a rich and varied history of scandals, which makes it difficult to narrow the list down as there are so many worthy examples of skulduggery and bad behavior. The more outrageous scandals seem to correlate strongly with the smaller offices and backwaters where there is less oversight of the officeholders' activity. In other words, mold doesn't grow where there's sunlight. Local officials seem to have special proclivity for using influence and muscle to get what they want. The graft/corruption/sex scandals are more numerous at the local level, but not as important for shifting power for a broader group. The continuum looks like this: numerous/frequent scandals on the left side with small impact geographically to less numerous/frequent with large impact geographically on the right side as we move from local to state to federal government. Remember, scandals don't always mean that the people involved get booted out of office. However, those government officials usually lose their respect and power.

Growing up in the Chicago area, I've been exposed to more political scandals than I can ever put down in one chapter. There's a nice range of gubernatorial misdeeds to choose from, with one governor getting caught taking bribes from racetrack owners just to get additional highway exits to their tracks to a recent governor being involved in the sale of government licenses and contracts while he was secretary of state. Then there was a secretary of state who died and they found shoeboxes full of cash in his closet. There are so many aldermanic examples that it is impossible to choose, but just think about the nicknames like Bathhouse John or Hinky Dink and you get the idea. The best way to sum up the Chicago experience comes from Al Capone as he was encouraging people to go to the polls: "Vote early and often." It has been our motto ever since.

It's with this in mind that we begin our investigation of the impacts that scandals have had on governments and the reactions in the financial markets to these contretemps. The events we review are major scandals, although they may have started with seemingly minor offenses.

2000 U.S. PRESIDENTIAL ELECTION

Like so much of politics, the origins of the outcome of the 2000 presidential election started several years earlier. U.S. President Bill Clinton had been plagued throughout his presidency by accusations of sexual harassment, but on January 17, 1998, things got crazy. A story broke that U.S. Attorney General Janet Reno had granted independent counsel Kenneth Starr the authority to investigate Clinton's relationship with Monica Lewinsky. Clinton denied that he had had an affair with Lewinsky; he denied it to his wife, to his Democratic colleagues, and to the American people. On January 26, I watched Clinton turn red-faced on national television when he stated, "I want to say one thing to the American people. I want you to listen to me.... I did not have sexual relations with that woman, Miss Lewinsky." By August 17, Clinton had a different approach as he apologized to the nation for his "inappropriate relationship" with Ms. Lewinsky.

The president wasn't the only one having problems in 1998. The U.S. midterm elections didn't go as planned for the Republicans, as they had anticipated a significant addition to their majority in the aftermath of the Clinton/Lewinsky situation. Unfortunately, the Republicans made history, the wrong kind of history. For the first time since 1822, the party not in control of the White House (Republicans) had failed to gain seats in the midterm election of a president's second term. That's pretty ugly. It cost U.S. Speaker of the House Newt Gingrich the support of his party and his job as Speaker. (It didn't help that Gingrich was the first House Speaker to be sanctioned for ethics violations and had to pay a fine of $300,000.)

However, the Republicans in the House didn't have to turn over the reins until January. This meant they could proceed with the impeachment hearings that they had approved on October 8. During the lame-duck session of Congress, they tried Clinton on charges of perjury and obstruction of justice that emanated from Starr's investigation of Clinton's relationship with Monica Lewinsky. By definition, this scandal hits on all cylinders, as you have a barely legal White House intern, the president, sex, and lies all in the same sentence. Perhaps we should have seen something like this coming when Clinton's 1996 campaign strategist, Dick Morris, resigned after reports surfaced about his relationship with a prostitute came out during the Democratic National Convention in Chicago.

House Republicans ultimately impeached Bill Clinton on December 19, 1998. They did this with the knowledge that it was highly unlikely that the U.S. Senate would convict him of the charges. On February 12, by a vote of 55 "not guilty" to 45 "guilty" in the Senate, Clinton missed the ignominy of being tossed out of the White House for lying about an extramarital affair.

Nevertheless, the event served its purpose for the Republicans.

The Ensuing Election

William Jefferson Clinton was a very popular president, and his vice president absorbed some of that popularity from Clinton's coattails. This made Al Gore a formidable candidate for the 2000 presidential elections. However, the impeachment forever stained both men in the eyes of American voters.

The scandal prevented Gore from using Clinton extensively in the campaign. Without the scandal, Gore could have run on the theme of four more years of economic good times and prosperity and might have handily won. Due to the scandal, though, morality was the central theme of the 2000 election. Gore chose to run on a theme of "a new morality" and distanced himself from Clinton. But problems at a Democratic fund-raiser at a California Buddhist Temple for Clinton's 1996 presidential campaign sabotaged this message. This was where Gore raised funds during a luncheon at the Hsi Lai Temple. The fund-raiser luncheon was attended by Gore and was organized by Democratic National Committee fund-raisers John Huang and Maria Hsia. According to U.S. law at the time, it was illegal for religious organizations to donate money to politicians or political groups due to their tax-free status. Gore denied any wrongdoing, but his "no controlling legal authority" legal position gave the appearance of using a technicality to get away with it.

To shore up his theme and image, Gore picked Joe Lieberman to be his running mate. Senator Lieberman was one of the first members of the Democratic Party to denounce Clinton's affair with Lewinsky and was seen as a straight shooter. He was also the first Jewish American to run on a major presidential ticket.

The Republicans ran George W. Bush, son of former president George H. W. Bush. Bush was not as polished as Gore or Lieberman, but his folksy way of talking and his ability to make fun of himself endeared him to the American people. Bush's approach was direct and his language was blunt. This especially hit home with voters who felt they were duped by Clinton on the Lewinski scandal. The Republican themes were stronger national security, immigration reform, and cutting taxes. Shoring up his weak conservative and national credentials, Bush chose as his running mate Dick

Cheney, who had been a defense secretary in the first Bush administration and chief of staff in the Ford administration.

On November 7, the nation went to the polls and voted. On November 8, the nation still didn't know who would be the next president. The race was tight, very tight, and it came down to three states that still were too close to call: New Mexico, Oregon, and Florida. Due to Florida's large population and therefore the large number of electoral votes it garnered, a candidate winning Florida would win the election. Recount, here we come!

Market Reaction

So what did all this upheaval mean for the financial markets? Let's first consider what Alan Greenspan and the Federal Reserve had been up to doing this time.

The Fed had pump-primed the U.S. financial system leading up to the Y2K panic and had gradually begun to take it away. Figure 11.1 shows that the Fed had started to raise rates in July 1999 from 4.75 percent to 6.50 percent in May 2000. The pattern underscored the political acuity of the Greenspan Fed policy makers, as they were raising rates at a rate of 25 basis points until May 2000 and then did 50 basis points. They then went on

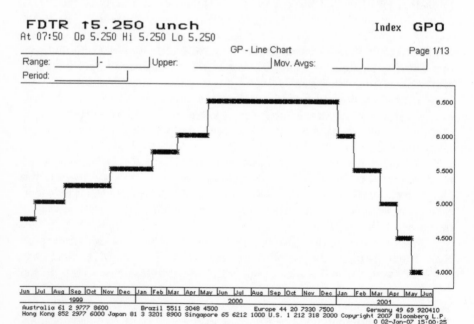

FIGURE 11.1 U.S. Federal Funds Rate
Source: Used with permission from Bloomberg L.P.

USGG10YR ↑4.682 −.020 4.686/4.682 Index **GPO**
At 15:00 Op 4.702 Hi 4.706 Lo 4.666

GPO - Bar Chart Page 1/36

Range: _____|-_____| Upper: _____| Mov. Avgs: _____|_____|_____|
Period: _____|

6.5000
6.0000
5.5000
5.0000

J |J |A |S |O |N |D |J |F |M |A |M |J |J |A |S |O |N |D |J |F |M |A |M |J
1999   2000   2001
Australia 61 2 9777 8600   Brazil 5511 3048 4500   Europe 44 20 7330 7500   Germany 49 69 920410
Hong Kong 852 2977 6000 Japan 81 3 3201 8900 Singapore 65 6212 1000 U.S. 1 212 318 2000 Copyright 2007 Bloomberg L.P.
0 02-Jan-07 15:01:16

FIGURE 11.2 U.S. Generic 10-Year Government Bond
Source: Used with permission from Bloomberg L.P.

hold until after January. They did this to finish their monetary tightening as far in advance of the election as possible to avoid any possibility of being seen as favoring one side over the other.

Whenever the Fed drains liquidity from the system, the markets are affected in several ways. In this case, the Fed acted aggressively to boost rates and had signaled to the markets that it was done. For bonds (Figure 11.2) this was a favorable situation and they proceeded to rally up to the election as the market liked the Fed aggressively fighting inflation, but the market also liked the Fed signaling that it was done. As we have seen, the Fed raising interest rates raises the cost of money, squeezes out inflation, and acts as a dampener on economic activity (and therefore earnings). For stocks (Figure 11.3), this was not a good thing and they went sideways leading up to the election. For the U.S. dollar (Figure 11.4), this was a good thing and it rallied in the lead-up to the election.

Bush held a small lead in the voter opinion surveys for most of the fall, but as the voting date drew near most surveys fell within the statistical sampling error and were too close to call. The outcome of the election would be an anticipated unknown. But the markets couldn't anticipate that the election would be won not in the election booth, but in the nation's highest court.

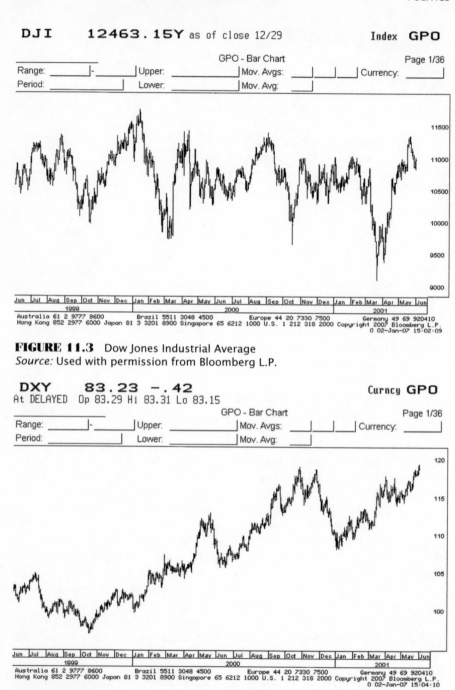

FIGURE 11.3 Dow Jones Industrial Average
Source: Used with permission from Bloomberg L.P.

FIGURE 11.4 U.S. Dollar Index
Source: Used with permission from Bloomberg L.P.

Gore Wins ... the Popular Vote

This was the first time since 1888 that a candidate who received the most popular (actual) votes lost the election. Gore/Lieberman garnered 50,999,897 votes versus the 50,456,002 votes that Bush/Cheney received. This is the unusual case where it didn't look like every vote counted, but it did ... in Florida.

On November 8, Florida began a manual recount at the prompting of the Gore campaign, which sued to get several Florida counties going on a recount, but not all Florida counties. On November 12, the Bush campaign made its court appearance to get the hand count stopped. This went back and forth in the state courts, then made it to the Florida Supreme Court, and finally to the U.S. Supreme Court. The nation's highest court ruled in favor of Bush to stop the recounts and allow the certified Florida election result to stand: that Bush won the state by 536 votes.

Although there is a popular vote for individual candidates on the ballots, what actually happens is the election of presidential electors, who in turn cast the official electoral votes for president and vice president. In other words, the United States has an indirect system. These presidential electors are allocated to each state according to the number of federal senators and representatives they have in Congress. By definition, it means that the states with the largest populations get the most electoral votes. This is why candidates spend most of their time and money in these states. It is a winner-take-all system by which if you win the state by one vote, you still get all of the electoral votes. On November 8, there were three states that were undecided: Florida, New Mexico, and Oregon. Bush had 246 electoral votes and Gore had 254. New Mexico had only 5 electoral votes and Oregon only 7, so neither would decide the election. Florida had 25 electoral votes, and therefore whoever won Florida won the election with a total over 270.

The U.S. Supreme Court ruled in favor of Bush by a 5–4 decision, the slimmest of margins. This left open the question of whether the Gore campaign would continue to fight the ruling and prolong the process. From November 8 until early December, the markets had to price in a risk premium that this election would continue to be fought in the Florida courts or even the U.S. Supreme Court. This could have led to demonstrations, akin to what has happened recently in Mexico. It also could've led to bloodshed and riots, like what happened during the 1960s.

What *did* happen was the Dow Industrials dropped almost 700 points from the election to the end of the month. When things are uncertain, investors tend to go to safe-haven plays or at the minimum cut back on their equity exposures. This activity certainly means they buy the safest security out there, and that's U.S. Treasury bills, notes, and bonds. The yield on the generic U.S. 10-year note dropped almost 50 basis points from the election to the end of the month. The U.S. dollar behaved erratically as it initially rallied with the election of a Republican and then tanked with the drop in the yields in the U.S. bond market. Essentially, we got two out of three instruments to move in the fashion that we thought would happen given the uncertainty principle and the recent end to the tightening cycle by the U.S. Federal Reserve.

In a historic show of statesmanship, Al Gore conceded the election to Bush the day after the U.S. Supreme Court decision on December 13. At the very next Federal Reserve meeting, Alan Greenspan and company cut interest rates in early January by 50 basis points, essentially taking back the rate hike they had done in May. It was like the Fed was waiting to give the next president a gift to get started on his new job. The Fed would continue this gifting by eventually cutting rates some 250 basis points by June. The nation would need all of it by September.

Last, I realize that many will be saying the real scandal to the election was related to George Bush's brother Jeb being the governor of Florida and that there was skulduggery involved in voting due to this. There was the U.S. Supreme Court connection with more conservative judges voting for the end of the recount. Then there were all the legal shenanigans and public relations involved in Florida. Studies after the elections showed various outcomes depending on how broad or how narrow were the standards used to determine voter intent. Yes, the hanging chad syndrome! One study showed that if the recount had persisted in the counties where the Gore campaign had sued for the count to be challenged, Bush would've won with a narrow majority. However, if the entire state had been done along with a broad standard, then Gore would've won. This is one of the mistakes that the Gore campaign made that I still don't understand. Why didn't they ask for the entire state? I think the biggest mistake that Gore made, though, was not getting third party candidate Ralph Nader on his side. Nader drew 97,488 votes in Florida and effectively cost Gore the election, as most of those votes would likely have gone to Gore.

2006 CANADIAN FEDERAL ELECTIONS

The U.S. neighbor to the north is a nation that became sovereign only in 1982. It is a political hybrid. The system is a representative government that has a combination of a constitutional monarchy and a federal structure. It is similar to the British parliamentary system in that it is bicameral. The House of Commons is in charge of running the day-to-day issues of the government and formulates legislation. The members are elected by a popular vote. The members of the Senate are appointed for life by the incumbent prime minister. The Senate has veto power over constitutional change and reserves itself the role of reconciling legal inconsistencies in House of Commons legislation. The smaller provinces and states were originally supposed to be protected by the Senate.

The executive side of the government is generally formed by the political party that is the majority in the House of Commons. The leader of this party becomes the prime minister and is elected by this party to that role. The party that forms the government doesn't always have to be in the majority, though. There are times when the elections split members in such a way that no majority can be formed without two parties linking up. In this case, the party with the largest number of seats can form the government as long as it can produce enough votes through its coalition of parties to pass major legislation like a budget.

One of the major differences between the United States and Canada is that the party in power in Canada produces major pieces of legislation all on its own without necessarily asking members of its party for input. It would be like the U.S. president working up a bill and then presenting it for an up or down vote by Congress without the members of Congress working on it in committee. This is one of the reasons that this form of government can be unstable—party members may end up voting for some legislation that may not be good for their riding or district. This also encourages members to leave and form third parties to get away from the one-size-fits-all type of legislation. This means that unless the majority party takes into consideration these interests, there will be more third parties and more instability that ultimately results in a failed government. On the flip side, it can mean that the people or voters don't have to suffer through lame-duck presidents like we do in the United States.

Sins from the Past

The seeds of destruction of the party in power were sown in the 38th general election. They were evident on June 28, 2004, when the 39th general election resulted in a Liberal Party victory with a minority government. The average shelf life of a minority government in Canada is about 18 months. This coalition government of Prime Minister Paul Martin was particularly unstable, with four parties—Liberal Party, Conservative Party, New Democratic Party (NDP), and Bloc Québeçois (BQ)—involved. They shared too few common views on budget or legislative matters. There were threats of no-confidence votes to bring down the government almost from day one (the Throne Speech where the ruling party lays out its priorities for the coming legislative session).

This Liberal minority government lasted until November 28, 2005, when a vote of no confidence passed. Why did this happen? But of course, scandal! Let's take a look at the explanation that Wikipedia gives for the famous (Canadian) body that was charged with investigating a potential kickback program by the majority Liberal Party. Wikipedia should be viewed like an old uncle who's very knowledgeable but sometimes doesn't remember all the facts. "The Gomery Commission, formally the Commission of Inquiry into the Sponsorship Program and Advertising Activities, was a federal Canadian commission headed by the retired justice John Gomery for the purpose of investigating the sponsorship scandal, which involved allegations of corruption within the Canadian government. The Commission was called by former Canadian Prime Minister Paul Martin in February 2004 soon after a report by the Auditor General of Canada found unexplainable irregularities in the Sponsorship Program. The Commission was part of Martin's active campaign to be seen as working to solve the problem." Note that the timing of the call for the commission was in February 2004 and there was an election held that year in June, meaning this was an issue that was unresolved and would dog the Liberals throughout their time at the helm.

It also meant that the government would be unsettled easily whenever a major item of news on the inquiry leaked out or when there was a major piece of legislation brought up in the House. The government was always teetering on the edge. In April 2005, the Liberal Party encountered such a problem when it brought the budget up for a vote. Watch the progression of problems that were going on for the government from April 21 to April 27. From the Busch Update:

> And speaking of out of control, how 'bout Canada? Not sure when a vote of no confidence will happen and not sure whether the Liberal government will enact a budget or call for elections. Here's just a microcosm of why that's bad: Deals are being attempted to stay in power and that means everything is on that table. The latest is that Prime Minister Paul Martin said yesterday he is open to changing the federal budget in an effort to win the support of the NDP as he prepared for a private meeting with New Democratic Party leader Jack Layton, according to the Globe and Mail. "Mr. Martin capped off a frenzied week of political maneuvering yesterday by praising Mr. Layton's attempt to get the budget through Parliament and 'see if we can make it work.' 'I'm going to have discussions [with Mr. Layton]. I don't think I want to preclude any conclusion on those discussions,' Mr. Martin said as he faced angry callers on CBC Radio's Cross Country Checkup. The NDP wants the Liberals to remove corporate tax cuts and replace them with increased social spending. Mr. Layton and Mr. Martin were scheduled to meet late last night." I think equity market

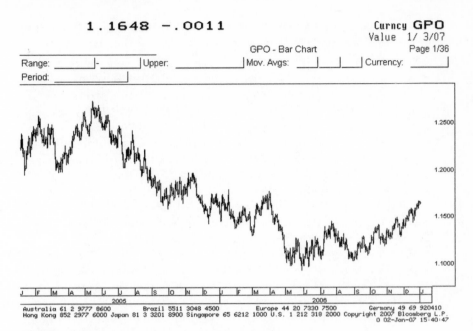

FIGURE 11.5 U.S. Dollar versus Canadian Dollar
Source: Used with permission from Bloomberg L.P.

players who had factored in tax cuts for business in Canada are going to be reassessing and revising downward their expectations should such a deal with the NDP happen. None of this is good for the currency. [See Figure 11.5 of the Canadian dollar versus the American dollar.] By the way, in case you didn't know, the NDP is the socialist party in Canada....

April 22
Okay, keep on eye on the developments in Canada as the politics continue to hurt the currency.... Adding to the uncertainty, here's this headline in the Toronto Post: *"Canadians want to wait for Gomery Report: A majority of Canadians support Prime Minister Martin's view that an election should not occur until after the Gomery inquiry into the sponsorship scandal releases its report in December, a new poll has found." It's bad enough that the government could fall at any time; now that time could appear to be put off until the end of the year. This is the last thing that the financial markets want: extended uncertainty over the resolution of the political mess. Contemplation*

of dropping corporate tax cuts to appease would-be political partner is just one example of the slippery slope....

April 27
The news out of the Canadian political morass is adding to the swamplike feeling of the loonie. Canadian Prime Minister Paul Martin inked a $4.6 billion deal with socialist party NDP's Jack Layton that is aimed at salvaging the federal budget yesterday, a move that will force the Conservatives (opposition party) to rely on the separatist Bloc Québeçois if the party wishes to bring down the government in the coming weeks, according to the Globe and Mail. *"In exchange for agreeing to the New Democratic Party's demands for more spending on the environment, social housing, foreign aid, and tuition reduction, the Liberals have secured a commitment of support on all no-confidence motions until the budget receives royal assent." Unfortunately, they haven't secured a government, as the deal doesn't mean Martin's party has the votes to defeat a no-confidence motion supported by the other two opposition parties. It only means they will get a budget void of tax cuts this year. "I guess my first response is Mr. Martin and Mr. Layton think $4.6 billion worth of taxpayers' money is the price to make corruption go away," Conservative leader Stephen Harper said during a break from a late-afternoon fundraiser. "I wonder if the taxpayers of Canada are going to think the same thing" (G&M). The financial markets aren't wondering at all; they are reducing exposure.*

The Canadian dollar was losing ground during this process, which began in March (Figure 11.5). The U.S. dollar strengthened against the Canadian dollar from a low of 1.20 in mid-March to a high of around 1.27 in mid-May. The generic 10-year Canadian bond rallied during this uncertainty, with yields dropping from around 4.50 percent down to around 3.80 percent (Figure 11.6). The Toronto Stock Exchange (TSE) sank over 500 points during the same time frame (Figure 11.7). Eventually, the budget did pass and the Liberals staved off a government collapse. This occurred with the understanding that elections would be called after the Gomery Commission issued its report.

Then the Gomery Commission did something really amusing: It held open meetings that were closed to the media. In other words, anyone could attend, but you just couldn't be reported on in the press. This meant that a little-known blogger in Minnesota could report the daily goings-on without much fear of legal reprisal. This also meant that most of the information from the testimony to the commission was out well before the commission made its first report.

FIGURE 11.6 Canadian Generic 10-Year Government Bond
Source: Used with permission from Bloomberg L.P.

FIGURE 11.7 Toronto Stock Exchange
Source: Used with permission from Bloomberg L.P.

The Change/No Change Election

On November 1, 2005, Justice Gomery released his first phase report. Again, Wikipedia:

> *Gomery criticized [Jean] Chrétien and his chief of staff Jean Pelletier but cleared them of direct involvement in kickback schemes. While people such as [Alfonso] Gagliano, Chuck Guité, and Jacques Corriveau took advantage of the programme, Gomery observed that such abuses would not have been possible had Chrétien not set the programme up without safeguards in the first place. Gomery said that Pelletier "failed to take the most elementary precautions against mismanagement—and Mr. Chrétien was responsible for him."*
>
> *Gomery also exonerated prime minister Paul Martin, the former minister of finance during most of the sponsorship programme. Gomery specifically said that Martin "is entitled, like other ministers from the Quebec caucus, to be exonerated from any blame for carelessness or misconduct," as the Department of Finance's role was not oversight, but setting the "fiscal framework."*
>
> *November 8, Busch Update:*
> *Canadian NDP Leader Jack Layton said his party will no longer prop up the Liberals because they won't support a crackdown on private health care. November 15th is the next time a no-confidence vote can be brought during an "opposition" day in parliament. But don't be so sure this will happen, as the latest polling shows that the incumbent Liberal party has rallied back from a virtual tie with the Tories. The latest polling data shows the Liberals enjoy the support of 35 percent of voters, up seven points according to the* Globe and Mail. *"The Tories garnered 28 percent compared to 31 percent, while the NDP dropped to 16 percent, from 20 percent, on the weekend." Remember, this type of political situation caused the Canadian dollar to get crushed back in May. After Layton's announcement yesterday, the Canadian dollar rallied. Huh? But of course today it has lost about 100 points.*

A vote of no confidence against the government passed on November 28; the next day Prime Minister Paul Martin dissolved the minority government and called for elections to take place on January 23, 2006. One important point to keep in mind when it comes to bringing down the government: The opposition doesn't do this unless it feels there is a strong possibility it can form the new government itself. Otherwise, the opposition won't do it if it would give the ruling government a chance to add to the number of seats it already has. Therefore, the Conservatives were confident that they could win the election and form a ruling government when they helped bring Paul Martin's down.

At the end of November, the Liberals had almost a 13-point lead in the opinion polls and were just 1.5 points away from the key 40 percent threshold generally thought necessary to form the government. The Liberals were ahead in the polling until late December and then the Conservatives went ahead and never looked back. There was very little difference between the platforms of the Liberals and the Conservatives in regard to economic policy. Therefore, the Conservatives ran against the "culture of entitlement" that they said was characteristic of the Liberals. After 12 years of Liberal Party rule, the Canadian voters, like the German voters in 2005, were probably tired of the party in power (something the 2006 House Republicans in the United States should've been worried about). The Conservatives won the most seats, but not enough to rule with a majority. They took 124 seats, the Liberals took 103, the BQ took 51, and the NDP took 29 (140 seats were needed to rule with a majority). In percentage of seats held by the governing party, the Conservative Party became the smallest minority government since confederation. Stephen Harper became the 22nd prime minister of Canada.

Market Much Ado about Nothing?

In January 2006, the markets didn't really do a whole lot, because the election didn't change very much as far as stability and economic policies were concerned. Had the election resulted in a majority status for the Conservatives, the market impact would've been larger, especially if they had run on a significantly different platform. The election turned out to be the equivalent of shifting the deck chairs on the political *Titanic* from one side of the boat to the other. There was an initial relief rally in the TSE, but this was the direction the market was already going. It was the same for the Canadian dollar and the generic Canadian 10-year bonds. Similar to most other elections, all the action occurred well before the vote took place. For the trader, this means you have to stay on top of the developing political situations and not sit back for the actual vote. The event takes place as the dynamics shift from the party in power to the party out of power. The election is merely the verification that the change that took place months/years before was valid. The phrase "It's all over but the shouting" suits the situation quite well.

A GENTLE REMINDER

Event trading for politics is then similar to other event type trading like hurricanes where the action takes place well before the actual event occurs.

Hey, if it was easy, any idiot could do this—and that's the point. No quant jockey (QJ) can model this stuff, which is why they can't make money from it or incorporate it into their trading systems. This is precisely why you should follow event trading and take advantage of these opportunities. One doesn't need a PhD in mathematics or quantum physics. No, all one needs is diligence in keeping up on current events and an imagination to perceive all the potential outcomes. This is one of the reasons you bought this book. Let this desire spill over into researching what has happened in the past. I highly recommend doing something you probably never did in high school or college: read history books. It's through understanding the event and its sequence that one truly understands the outcome and the opportunity.

CHAPTER 12

Modern, Short-Term War

The one enduring aspect of human existence over time is conflict. I think ever since humans could communicate, they would communicate that they didn't like other humans. Whether it was food, territory, riches, or religion, there has always been something to argue about and fight over. Wars are just our special way of organizing this activity on a large scale and therefore causing the most destruction.

Wars are expensive, from the human cost to the cost of machinery and arms. This is one of the reasons the United Nations was formed in an attempt to limit the number and scale of conflicts. Wars can be a boon to defense suppliers and a bane to consumers as materials get scarce for goods. They are disruptive to the culture and to the financial markets. Most important, they provide an amazing environment for making money.

If we were to review wars in just the twentieth century, it would take several books to cover them properly. Also, the nature of large, armed conflict has changed dramatically since the end of the cold war. We have gone from large, worldwide conflicts involving many countries to more regionalized conflicts involving many internal groups. Also, we have gone from many superpowers to one—and that may be changing soon. The point is that war is constantly evolving, and therefore we should spend our time focusing on the most recent wars as paradigms for the future.

U.S. GULF WAR, PART I

Amidst a rapidly changing geopolitical landscape, 1990 was a year that was dominated by events in the Soviet Union and the Middle East. Mikhail Gorbachev was still head of the Soviet Union and the Soviet Union was still the Soviet Union, but not for long. What was unheard-of and unthinkable less than two years earlier, before the fall of the Berlin Wall, was now occurring almost daily as the union began to break apart and republics within the union began to vote for change. The Soviet Republic of Lithuania became the first republic to have the Communist Party come in second to reformers and those opposed to continued Soviet rule. Georgia, Estonia, and Latvia began to demand similar change. Change also came in the form of relations between the Soviet Union and the United States. Gorbachev and U.S. President George H.W. Bush signed an agreement to ban the production of chemical weapons and to destroy most of their stockpiles.

Rapid technological changes were occurring within the United States. Computers and software improved dramatically as Microsoft shipped Windows 3.0 and the CD-ROM compact disk exploded in popularity. The stock market was performing well, with a new record high of 2,900.09 reached on June 1. McDonald's opened its first restaurant in Pushkin Square, Moscow. The year 1990 also had its business scandals as Drexel Burnham Lambert declared bankruptcy in the largest securities company failure ever and Michael R. Milken was sentenced to 10 years in jail for securities violations. George H.W. Bush began his presidency when the nation was enjoying the country's longest postwar expansion. The Council of Economic Advisers for the Bush administration boldly stated that the chances of a recession did not increase as the period of expansion ran on. By the end of the year, though, they would be proven dramatically wrong. They projected a 2.6 percent GDP growth rate for the year along with an inflation rate of 4.1 percent, which is high by today's standards. At midyear, they would revise their estimates downward to just 2.2 percent for GDP growth, but up to 4.8 percent for inflation. The combination of slowing growth and higher inflation was the stagflation disease from the late 1970s that looked likely by the end of the year.

In 1988, then vice president Bush made a campaign promise of not raising taxes. In his acceptance speech at the Republican National Convention, Bush uttered these famous words: "The Congress will push me to raise taxes, and I'll say no, and they'll push again, and I'll say to them: 'Read my lips: No new taxes.'" It was a phrase that would define his presidency and the major reason why he was not reelected in 1992. The irony is that Bush would eventually lose to someone who also could not maintain a vow and eventually would be impeached for it.

Unfortunately, it was also the fall of the first event dominoes that would lead to the Gulf War in the Middle East. Just like World War II, the seeds of this war were sown in another war. The Iran-Iraq War had ended in the summer of 1988 after Iran accepted the United Nations' call for a ceasefire. However, the cost of prosecuting the war had been tremendous and Iraq owed billions to Kuwait ($14 billion) and Saudi Arabia ($26 billion). Iraq and Saddam Hussein had hoped to export enough oil to make payments on the debt. However, a disagreement arose between Kuwait and Iraq over OPEC policy: Iraq wanted to keep the price of crude high by limiting oil production, while Kuwait did not. After supporting Iraq during the Iran-Iraq War, Kuwait was eventually accused by Iraq of slant drilling into Iraqi oil fields. On July 24, Iraq was reported to have massed 30,000 troops on the border with Kuwait. The number was increased to 100,000 with a week. Iraq invaded Kuwait on August 2, 1990.

Political Foreplay

On August 2, 1990, the United Nations Security Council met and passed a resolution condemning the invasion and demanding an immediate pullout of Iraqi troops. Resolution 660 stated that the United Nations:

> *Alarmed by the invasion of Kuwait on 2 August 1990 by the military forces of Iraq,*
> *Determining that there exists a breach of international peace and security as regards the Iraqi invasion of Kuwait,*
> *Acting under Articles 39 and 40 of the Charter of the United Nations,*

> *1. Condemns the Iraqi invasion of Kuwait;*
> *2. Demands that Iraq withdraw immediately and unconditionally all of its forces to the positions in which they were located on 1 August 1990;*
> *3. Calls upon Iraq and Kuwait to begin immediately intensive negotiations for the resolution of their differences and supports all efforts in this regard, and especially those of the League of Arab States;*
> *4. Decides to meet again as necessary to consider further steps with which to ensure compliance with the present resolution.*

Thus began a sequence of UN resolutions that were groundbreaking and established a precedent for future dealings with Iraq. It was also significant in that it marked a level of cooperation between the United States and the Soviet Union that had not happened before and enabled the UN Security Council to take action against Iraq. Remember, Iraq was supported by the Kremlin in its war with Iran and was considered a "client" state of the Soviet Union.

After Saddam Hussein rejected UN Resolution 660, the Security Council on August 6 invoked economic sanctions against Iraq with UN Resolution 661. This was also significant in that it was only the third time in the UN's 45-year history that it had done this. This was a signal to the world and the markets that the UN was serious and acting decisively toward the Iraqi aggression. It foreshadowed more aggressive action, and the markets quickly woke up to this fact. The United States moved troops into Saudi Arabia on August 7, 1990, on a "wholly defensive" mission named Operation Desert Shield. On August 25, the UN Security Council ordered a naval blockade to enforce the economic sanctions and trade ban. Another milestone was reached, as it had never sanctioned a military action without linking it to a specific UN command or resolution. Before the end of August, UN Resolutions 662, 664, and 665 quickly followed, condemning Iraq's actions on the Kuwaiti annexation and demanding the release of foreign prisoners.

The unanimity on the Security Council was stunning, with not one vote against any of the resolutions. What was also stunning was the cooperation between Mikhail Gorbachev and George H.W. Bush. In September, they met in Helsinki and issued a joint statement on the 9th that said they were "united in the belief that Iraq's aggression must not be tolerated." On September 11, Bush returned from that meeting to address a joint session of Congress and the nation on the situation. Here's an excerpt that foreshadows military action and delineates what was at risk for the United States.

America and the world must defend common vital interests, and we will.

America and the world must support the rule of law, and we will.

America and the world must stand up to aggression. And we will.

And one thing more—in the pursuit of these goals, America will not be intimidated.

Vital issues of principle are at stake. Saddam Hussein is literally trying to wipe a country off the face of the Earth. We do not exaggerate. Nor do we exaggerate when we say Saddam Hussein will fail.

Vital economic interests are at risk as well. Iraq itself controls some 10 percent of the world's proven oil reserves. Iraq plus Kuwait controls twice that.

An Iraq permitted to swallow Kuwait would have the economic and military power, as well as the arrogance, to intimidate and coerce its neighbors, neighbors who control the lion's share of the world's remaining oil reserves. We cannot permit a resource so vital to be dominated by one so ruthless—and we won't.

For the markets, this is why we care about what happens in the Middle East. Until there is discovered or invented an alternative, renewable energy source, wars in this area of the world mean danger for economic growth. The threat of Iraq taking over Kuwait and then Saudi Arabia was a possibility and a major threat to stability in not only the Middle East, but the rest of the world as well.

Market Reaction

The financial markets convulsed over this threat, with crude oil being the primary shaker and mover. Its move was simply stunning (Figure 12.1). Prior to the invasion, it was on a downward trend due to declining demand from a slowing U.S. economy. It bottomed as the Iraqi troops massed and then skyrocketed from $16 a barrel to over $40 a barrel by October.

Natural gas had a similar insane ride and collapse (Figure 12.2). Note the time frames; this occurred well in advance of when the actual invasion

FIGURE 12.1 Crude Oil
Source: Used with permission from Bloomberg L.P.

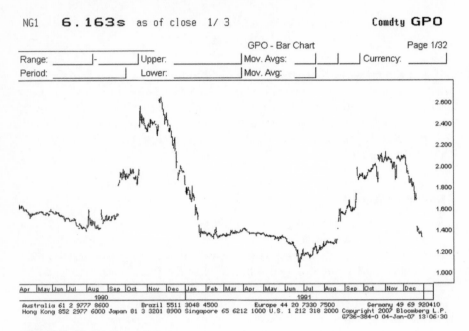

FIGURE 12.2 Natural Gas
Source: Used with permission from Bloomberg L.P.

of coalition troops into Iraq occurred on January 17, 1991! This is consistent with the patterns we have seen across many of the events covered in this book.

Getting back to the markets, you can see that the price of crude started falling and stabilized in December. It had one more spike up from $25 to around $33 as the invasion occurred and then dropped precipitously back to the levels from whence it came in July. Now that's what I call a spectacular reversal and return to the trend that was in place prior to the event. I would also add that the spike in crude oil helped cause the U.S. economy to slide into a recession and exacerbated the savings and loan crisis that was occurring at the time.

Looking at stocks, the Dow Jones Industrial Average went down about as fast as oil went up, and over the same time frames. Figure 12.3 shows the Dow hitting a peak right before the July 24 massing of Iraqi troops. Then it plunged to hit its low in October. Now, equities were clearly on unstable ground, as the U.S. Federal Reserve had raised rates to 9.75 percent by March 1989 and were just in the process of cutting rates down to 8.25 percent in December 1989, where they would stay until July 1990 (Figure 12.4). How telling was it that the Fed cut rates in July and the Dow still fell 20 percent by October?

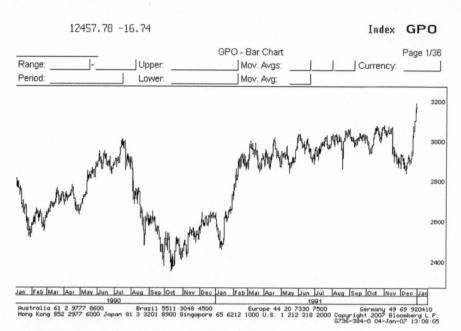

FIGURE 12.3 Dow Jones Industrial Average
Source: Used with permission from Bloomberg L.P.

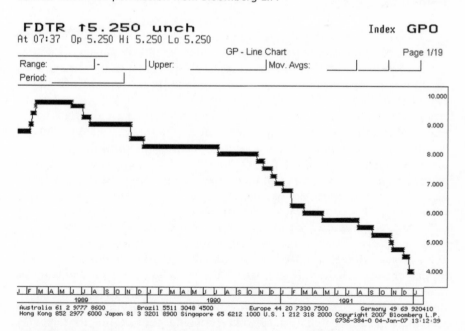

FIGURE 12.4 U.S. Federal Funds Rate
Source: Used with permission from Bloomberg L.P.

FIGURE 12.5 Russell 2000
Source: Used with permission from Bloomberg L.P.

The smaller U.S. stocks got hammered worse. Let's look at the Russell 2000 index, which is comprised of the smallest 2,000 companies in the Russell 3000 index and represents approximately 8 percent of the Russell 3000 total market capitalization. This index dropped from 170 in July to 120 by mid-October, a hefty 33 percent (Figure 12.5). This underscores that the riskier investment gets hurt the most when the market encounters events that increase the uncertainty of future returns. On this consistent front, we see that the U.S. Dollar Index was already declining before July 24 and then dropped like equities until October (Figure 12.6). However, this index made a new low in February 1991 and then rebounded in March through July. It's as though currency traders wanted to make sure the war was won before returning the U.S. dollar back to its previous levels.

Now, as we know, the markets don't always fit into nice, consistent patterns across all instruments. The generic U.S. 10-year note yields did some strange things that need some explaining. Figure 12.7 shows the yield dipped briefly in late July and early August. Then the yield went up 50 basis points from 8.5 percent to 9.0 percent and stayed around those levels until November! This is not what we would expect given the uncertainty of war and a declining economy. However, consider the consumer price index (CPI) at the time and remember what the Council of Economic Advisers

DXY   84.30 +.38   Curncy **GPO**
At DELAYED   Op 83.91 Hi 84.39 Lo 83.84

GPO - Bar Chart   Page 1/36

Range: _____ |- _____ | Upper: _____ | Mov. Avgs: __|__|__| Currency: _____ |
Period: _____ | Lower: _____ | Mov. Avg: __|

FIGURE 12.6 U.S. Dollar Index
Source: Used with permission from Bloomberg L.P.

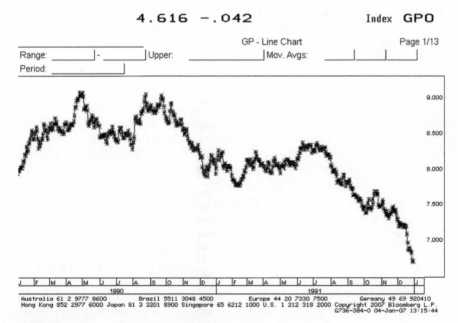

4.616 -.042   Index **GPO**

GP - Line Chart   Page 1/13

Range: _____ |- _____ | Upper: _____ | Mov. Avgs: __|__|__|
Period: _____ |

FIGURE 12.7 U.S. Generic 10-Year Government Note Yield
Source: Used with permission from Bloomberg L.P.

forecasted in the summer. CPI started the year spiking in January and then had another spike in August, with September and October still very high. This meant that fears of stagflation were abounding, and that's not good for bonds. Also, the spike in crude oil was making inflation spike as well and jacked up fears into the run-for-the-medications stage. When oil collapsed, inflation fears subsided and bond prices rallied. However, due to this bipolar nature of the bond market, bond yields never dropped in dramatic fashion like crude oil.

In summary, there were plenty of opportunities to take advantage of and trade. As a trader at the time, I was able to sell U.S. dollars for consistent profits as the buildup to attack was progressing and the U.S. economy was experiencing a mild form of stagflation. Most in the market at the time felt that oil was moving too fast to an unsustainable level given the weak U.S. economy. Granted this is in hindsight, but the best trade was to fade this move up, especially after Bush's speech to Congress. Something was going to be done; we just didn't know when. There was even a nice pattern between the end of October and the beginning of November. Oil had already seen a high and then a big drop to below 30. There were two attempts to get above 36 again that failed. You could've sold and left a stop-loss order above 36 that would've minted some very nice profits.

This is a great example for event trading. You don't have to catch the initial movement, but you have to pay attention to the overall pattern that is developing. The event puts in motion the market and creates the opportunities. Sometimes the best trades or the easiest ways to make money are not from the first move, but from the subsequent moves and retracements to the initial moves.

Aren't We Missing Something?

Oh yeah, the actual war. The United States ended up massing some 540,000 U.S. troops in Saudi Arabia following General Colin Powell's doctrine of superior strength of overwhelming force before attacking. The United States built a coalition of 34 countries that contributed money and troops totaling 120,000 of the 660,000 that were finally gathered. Ironically, Syria joined the coalition and sent 16,000 troops whereas Israel didn't join at all. The Israelis were persuaded by the United States to remain neutral to reduce friction from the Arabs in the region. However , the Palestine Liberation Organization (PLO), under Yasir Arafat, openly supported Saddam Hussein. Arafat's choice proved to be the wrong one, and would set back the Palestinians in the eyes of Kuwait and Saudi Arabia.

On January 12, 1991, Congress authorized the use of military force to drive Iraq out of Kuwait, but not to overthrow Saddam Hussein. The invasion started on January 17 with a massive air campaign. The most sophisticated weaponry the world had ever seen was put into action against Saddam Hussein's Soviet-style army. To state the obvious, it was a mismatch of epic proportions. After a month of bombing, the ground campaign started on February 24. On February 26, the Iraqi forces retreated out of Kuwait. By March 10, Operation Desert Storm was over and the United States started moving troops out of the region.

The war was interesting from another aspect as well: the media. We had all these CNN reporters on the rooftops in Baghdad reporting when air sirens were going off and when bombs were exploding. ABC was there as well, and I particularly remember making money from one unique information sequence at the time. I decided that since the trading room I was in had no TV, I would make an investment of $100 and buy a handheld mini-Sony TV for my desk. This way I could watch the news and then make trades if something occurred. We were awaiting the start of the air campaign, and every time the newswires reported the sirens going off or Iraqi antiaircraft fire, the market would start buying U.S. dollars, thinking that the war had begun.

With the live coverage, I could see what was happening real-time as opposed to the delay that the newswires would report. This meant that I had between 30 and 45 seconds to execute a trade before the news broke and the rest of the market would begin buying U.S. dollars. This was an eternity and a profitable news arbitrage. The Gulf War changed media coverage forever and also changed trading rooms around the world as well. Thereafter, every dealing room adapted by installing televisions and increasing the news services they had. Quite simply, faster information meant bigger profits.

GULF WAR, PART II

One of the fascinating decisions made in the first Gulf War was to not oust Saddam Hussein from power. This will be endlessly debated, with compelling pros and cons. Bush must have felt that taking him out would create a power vacuum in Iraq and civil war. Since the Shiites were the dominant group in Iran and were the majority in Iraq, it was not illogical to assume that Iran would easily step into that vacuum and create an Islamist government aligned with Iran. This would then create a dynamic similar to what happened when Saddam Hussein invaded Kuwait: a concentration of control over oil and perhaps a threat to Saudi Arabia. Also, Bush believed that the mandate by Congress and the UN didn't give him the right to take Saddam Hussein out and would've fractured the coalition. Along with the political costs, it would've forced the coalition forces to go into urban areas to oust the Baathist leaders and to enter Baghdad to get Saddam Hussein.

In 1992, then United States Secretary of Defense Dick Cheney put it this way:

So I think we got it right, both when we decided to expel him from Kuwait, but also when the president made the decision that we'd achieved our objectives and we were not going to go get bogged down in the problems of trying to take over and govern Iraq.

All of a sudden you've got a battle you're fighting in a major built-up city, a lot of civilians are around, significant limitations on our ability to use our most effective technologies and techniques.

Once we had rounded him up and gotten rid of his government, then the question is what do you put in its place? You know, you then have accepted the responsibility for governing Iraq.

In all fairness, he couldn't have foreseen that the United States would be attacked by terrorists who were trained in nearby Afghanistan. Also, Cheney didn't know that the problems with Iraq would persist and that the United States and its allies would have to create no-fly zones to protect the Kurds in the north. After the first Gulf War, the UN passed a resolution that required Saddam Hussein to destroy his ballistic missiles, stockpiles of biological and chemical weapons, and components for nuclear weapons. From the moment that resolution passed until the invasion in 2003, he would dodge and hide all of these from UN inspectors. In 1998, he kicked out all the UN inspectors. Under Clinton, this was tolerated as there was no reason to believe that the policy of Iraqi containment was not working.

After 9/11, all bets were off. President George W. Bush made it clear that the United States would go after terrorist groups wherever they were and the countries that harbored them. On November 26, 2001, President Bush at a press conference stated this policy emphatically:

Q: Sir, what is your thinking right now about taking the war to Iraq? You suggested that on Wednesday, when you said Afghanistan was just the beginning.

President Bush: I stand by those words. Afghanistan is still just the beginning. If anybody harbors a terrorist, they're a terrorist. If they fund a terrorist, they're a terrorist. If they house terrorists, they're terrorists. I mean, I can't make it any more clearly to other nations around the world. If they develop weapons of mass destruction that will be used to terrorize nations, they will be held accountable. And as for Mr. Saddam Hussein, he needs to let inspectors back into his country, to show us that he is not developing weapons of mass destruction.

Here's what I wrote on January 10, 2002, prior to President Bush's State of the Union (SOTU) address.

Political points of interest as we get into 2002 from last night's "Politics and Money" show:

1. *State of the Union probably won't include many specifics, unlike most of Clinton's past speeches. Look for broad themes of unity and patriotism and not much else.*

2. *Fiscal stimulus package: good chance that Bush will stick to his position of corporate-friendly legislation with a willingness to let Tom Daschle take the fall if this legislation doesn't get passed. Good political ammunition for midterm elections and cover if the economy stalls in the summer/early fall. Battle of core ideological differences shouldn't be resolved.*

3. *Midterm elections: in 32 out of the last 34 midterm elections since the Civil War, the party holding power in the White House lost seats. And the House and the Senate have never been this evenly divided before, which would lead one to believe this loss of seats is going to occur. However, latest polls show Bush's approval rating exceptionally high and Americans like the direction the country is heading in. So it's going to be a question of how long Bush's coattails are for other Republicans.*

4. *Stealing thunder: Bush is again demonstrating his political astuteness by stealing issues that normally would fall to the Democrats. Food stamp eligibility for legal immigrants is the first salvo on this agenda.*

5. *Quagmires for the administration:*
   - *Another domestic terrorist attack.*
   - *Iraq.*
   - *Iran in Afghanistan.*
   - *Israel/Palestine.*
   - *Enron and Cheney (Lieberman is staking out his political ambitions on this one).*
   - *Deficit and a jobless recovery.*

Remember that gridlock and lack of legislative action from Washington during a midterm election period aren't necessarily a bad thing.

I got a few things right, but was definitely wrong on the SOTU address. On January 29, I remember watching it in a hotel bar in Boston before I had to give a speech the next day. The SOTU laid the political groundwork for the invasion of Iraq by stating this:

States like these (North Korea, Iran, and Iraq), and their terrorist allies, constitute an axis of evil, arming to threaten the peace of the world. By seeking weapons of mass destruction, these regimes pose a grave and growing danger. They could provide these arms to terrorists, giving them the means to match their hatred. They could attack our allies or attempt to blackmail the United States. In any of these cases, the price of indifference would be catastrophic.

I had to double-check with the group I was with to make sure I heard him say this correctly: the axis of evil. This coupled with the new philosophy of "preemptive intervention" set the course for the Bush administration in its policy toward Iraq. The United States had been attacked, and the president was going to do everything possible to ensure that it didn't happen again on his watch.

The rhetoric was turned up full blast in the fall of 2002 as the United States came back from vacation and the midterm elections were right around the corner. One of the more candid comments about why the Bush administration had waited until September to press its case to the UN came from then White House Chief of Staff Andrew Card, who said, "From a marketing point of view, you don't introduce new products in August." First, on September 12, President Bush spoke before the UN General Assembly and called for the UN to address the "grave and gathering danger" of Iraq. On September 26, U.S. Secretary of Defense Donald Rumsfeld accused Iraq of harboring members of al-Qaeda and helping them acquire weapons of mass destruction (WMD). Next, on October 7 in Cincinnati, Bush gave a nationally televised address in which he argued that Iraq "on any given day" could attack the United States or its allies with WMD and could give those weapons to other terrorist groups as well. On October 10, the House of Representatives passed a resolution that declared Iraq to be in material and unacceptable breach of UN Security Council resolutions and provided Bush with almost unlimited authorization to use military force to deal with the threat posed by Iraq. On October 11, the Senate passed the resolution. On October 16, President Bush signed it.

While this was going on, U.S. Secretary of State Colin Powell was pressing the UN Security Council on Iraq. Most of the 14 members of the council wanted UN inspectors to return to Iraq. However, it was a question of what to do to Iraq if Iraq did not comply. The key group was made up of the permanent members of the Security Council, or P5, who had veto over any resolution. The United States had the backing of Great Britain, but had to convince China, Russia, and France of the need to back up inspections with force. Powell created a diplomatic masterpiece with UN Resolution 1441 and it passed unanimously. Essentially, it stated that Iraq had to immediately and completely disarm. Iraq had to declare all of its weapons of mass destruction and account for its known chemical weapons material stockpiles or "face serious consequences." To France and others on the Security Council, this meant that if Iraq didn't comply, then the United States would have to come back to the UN and get approval for force. To the United States, the resolution gave it what it wanted on Iraq and meant that it wasn't necessary to go back to the group for further discussions. However, Powell did go back on February 5 to provide a PowerPoint presentation on the WMD that the United States believed Saddam Hussein was hiding. Powell had convinced Bush to draft another resolution to specifically provide the authorization of force against Iraq for noncompliance, but it never made it to the Security Council as it was clear that one of the P5 would veto it.

From Powell's presentation on February 5, the debate on Iraq raged across the world. In the financial markets, we breathlessly awaited the reports and appearances of UN inspector Hans Blix. France, Russia, Germany, and China all would eventually be opposed to the use of force. Demonstrations were held in Rome, London, and Berlin. Pope John Paul II sent a special envoy to President Bush to urge him not to go to war. On March 20, the invasion began despite these objections. On March 22, President Bush discussed the invasion on his radio address:

> *Good morning. American and coalition forces have begun a concerted campaign against the regime of Saddam Hussein. In this war, our coalition is broad, more than 40 countries from across the globe. Our cause is just: the security of the nations we serve and the peace of the world. And our mission is clear, to disarm Iraq of weapons of mass destruction, to end Saddam Hussein's support for terrorism, and to free the Iraqi people.*

Market Reaction

Unlike the first Gulf War, this war didn't have a single event that triggered the world into action. This meant that the response by the markets would be more diffuse and occur over a longer period of time. There was also this feeling among traders of "been there, done that" in the attitudes or worries over what could happen. We all knew what the outcome would be; it was just a question of when it would begin. As mentioned in Chapter 4, the further complication to the 2003 Iraq invasion was that SARS was breaking out in the Far East. This is about as messy as it can get.

Let's take a look at the time frame from September 2002 through the invasion of March 2003. As the momentum began to roll forward with Iraq, we can see the prices of crude oil and natural gas begin to climb (Figures 12.8 and 12.9). After UN Resolution 1441 was adopted on November 13, the price graphs show both energy products start to move higher from their

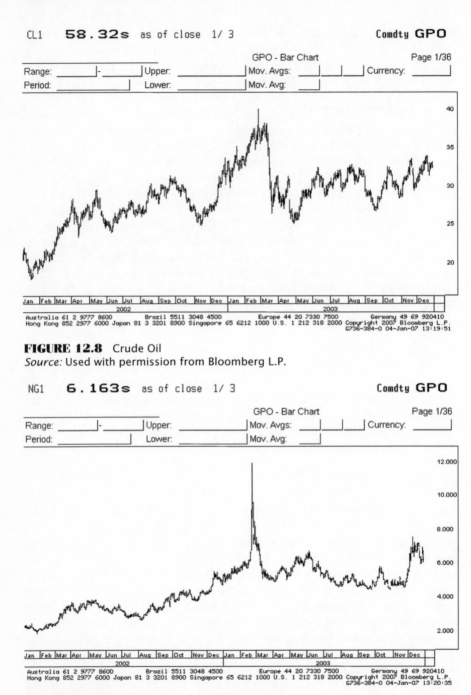

FIGURE 12.8 Crude Oil
Source: Used with permission from Bloomberg L.P.

FIGURE 12.9 Natural Gas
Source: Used with permission from Bloomberg L.P.

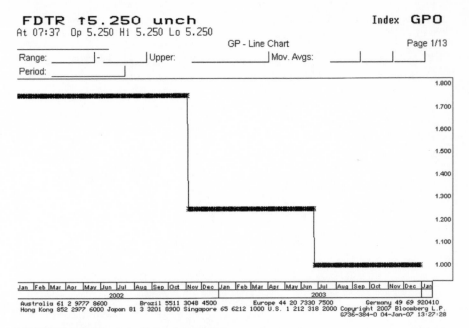

FDTR ↑5.250 unch
At 07:37 Op 5.250 Hi 5.250 Lo 5.250

Index **GPO**

GP - Line Chart

Page 1/13

Range: _____ - _____ | Upper: _____ | Mov. Avgs: ____|____|____|

Period: _____

FIGURE 12.10 U.S. Federal Funds Rate
Source: Used with permission from Bloomberg L.P.

lows. On December 7, Iraq filed bogus documentation that was panned by the U.S. and UN weapons inspectors as a rehash of information from 1997. This was when the energy markets really jumped into high gear and rallied hard as the prospect of war became more likely. Note, these rallied until the invasion and then fell precipitously, just like what happened during Gulf War I. This was the simplest way to play this event. Again, the risk of the event was thoroughly priced into the market before the event occurred. Then once the event occurred, the market reacted by taking off those bets.

The Federal Reserve at this time had been cutting rates from prior to September 11, 2001, and had taken the fed funds rate down to 1.75 percent (Figure 12.10). During the fall and the push to get the UN behind an attack on Iraq, the U.S. economy continued to slide from a GDP growth rate of 4 percent in the third quarter to a paltry 1.4 percent in Q4. Corporate accounting scandals, fears of another terrorist attack, and preparations for a war in Iraq all contributed to making investors nervous and the U.S. consumer cautious. This prompted the Fed to cut rates aggressively by 50 basis points to 1.25 percent at the beginning of November as evidence mounted that the economy was slowing rapidly. The yield on the generic 10-year U.S. government note (Figure 12.11) was declining from around 5.50 percent in March to a low in mid-October of around 3.50 percent. The Dow Industrials

USGG10YR ↓4.614 −.044 4.618/4.614   Index **GPO**
At 13:24 Op 4.658 Hi 4.666 Lo 4.602

FIGURE 12.11 U.S. Generic 10-Year Government Note
Source: Used with permission from Bloomberg L.P.

(Figure 12.12) and the Russell 2000 (Figure 12.13) fell in tandem with the bond yields as fears of deflation were beginning to grip the markets.

From those lows, all three began to move in the opposite direction in anticipation of the Fed move that would come in November. The equities would continue to rally up to December, when the certainty of war began to negatively impact investors' views, along with the higher energy costs. Equities would then sink until the start of the war in March. They would then begin a massive rally that would last the rest of the year. This was the old "Buy when there's blood in the streets" mentality. And it worked brilliantly. Think about it: We had the Federal Reserve cutting rates, the U.S. government spending billions on the war economy, and energy prices dropping after the invasion.

Let's take a look at one more piece of the puzzle: the VIX Index (Figure 12.14). The Chicago Board Options Exchange SPX Volatility Index reflects a market estimate of future volatility, based on the weighted average of the implied volatilities for the S&P 500 index. It had spiked during 9/11, it had spiked in the July/August time frame, but had stabilized going into the October/November/December time frame. Yes it spiked up to 35 percent when the equity indexes were dropping, but it began to fall almost as soon as the invasion began and collapsed in April. This was a crystal "all clear" for investors to go back into equities and buy.

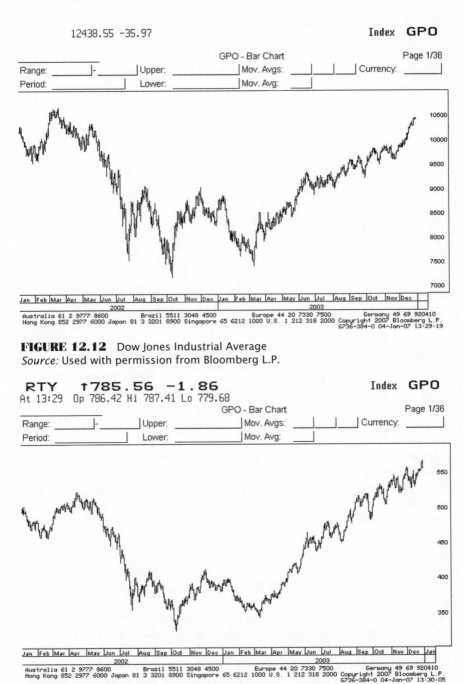

FIGURE 12.12 Dow Jones Industrial Average
Source: Used with permission from Bloomberg L.P.

FIGURE 12.13 Russell 2000
Source: Used with permission from Bloomberg L.P.

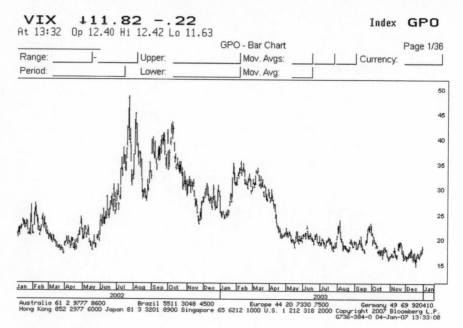

FIGURE 12.14 VIX Index
Source: Used with permission from Bloomberg L.P.

Again, Aren't We Missing Something?

Oh yeah, the war again. The invasion began on March 20, Baghdad fell on April 9, and President Bush made his ill-fated announcement on an aircraft carrier of the end of major combat on May 1. Mission accomplished! Oops. It is beyond the scope of this book to explain why the United States is still in Iraq sustaining casualties and hasn't been able to stabilize the country. Suffice it to say, the American voter heading into the 2006 midterm elections wasn't happy. Here's what I wrote on election day:

> *I'm traveling in D.C. today meeting with a few concerned Republicans and Democrats. I don't think either party is going to be happy with the outcome and neither will the voters. But this is U.S. politics at its best.*
>
> *As you know, I believe that the U.S. House will turn over to the Democrats along with the Senate. However, the Senate will be very difficult, as Democrats have to win six seats and maintain all the seats that they currently have. The magic number for the House is 15.*
>
> *Should the Democrats not take the House, this could be the beginning of the end of (effectively) two-party politics in the United States.*

Given the economy, the Kerry gaffe, the Hussein verdict, and lots o' 24-hour campaigning, the Republicans have pulled closer in the latest polls. If this election was about the economy, we would be discussing how much bigger the Republican take would be. It's not. It's about 75 percent foreign policy (Iraq) and the remaining 25 percent stuff like stem cell research, deficit spending, tax cuts, etc.

At about 8 PM ET, we'll know whether this election will be a wave of support for the Democrats on Iraq; 24 close House races will have concluded by then and therefore the split will be telling. For the Senate, Virginia, Missouri, and Rhode Island will be our benchmarks. If all three go to Democrats, then we could see a mega shift in who runs Congress.

The interesting scenario no one is talking about is this: a House or Senate that is won by only the slimmest margins by either side. This would present a situation of the ultimate gridlock that would be good for bonds, bad for small caps, good for large caps, and initially a negative for the U.S. dollar. It would be good for deficit reduction, but bad for things like the Farm Bill (coming up in 2007) and making permanent President Bush's tax cuts.

FYI, the Wall Street Journal carries a nice scorecard for the election and will help the time frames for all the different races. So get some popcorn, sit back, and enjoy the histrionics. Remember, 2008 is right around the corner.

And the day after the elections, I wrote:

The New Sheriff in Town: *As of this writing, the U.S. House has gone solidly blue as Democrats sweep to a large victory with at least 28 seats switching from Republicans. It's likely that the current Republican Speaker of the House, Dennis Hastert, will resign his seat after winning it. During the campaign, Democratic Speaker-to-be Nancy Pelosi was asked why it was important to have a Democratic majority in the U.S. House and she said subpoena power. Actually, I'm surprised she didn't say there's a new sheriff in town. Last night on CNN, now Democratic Senate Majority Leader-to-be Harry Reid tempered that by calling for "oversight" and specifically mentioned Halliburton. For the markets, it's this activity more than anything else that could have the biggest negative impact from a shift in government.*

The quickest action from the Democrats will come on raising the minimum wage and changes to House ethics rules. The real fun will be that the Democrats will have to actually present a budget. Watch Democratic Representative John Spratt from South Carolina, as he *is the ranking Democrat on the House budget committee. Remember, Dems want to reform the prescription drug benefit (PDB) by allowing direct negotiation with drug companies to gain volume discounts similar to what is being done at the VA hospitals. Just keep in mind, the original Democratic PDB was three times the size of the Republican giveaway and came in at $1 trillion. House Ways and Means controls the budget for Social Security and Medicare, and that ranking Democrat is Charles Rangel from New York. Can't wait to see the math.*

Senate Goes to ... Warren Zevon: *As it stands early this AM, the scorecard shows that Democrats have taken four of the six seats they need to retake the Senate, with two races (Virginia and Montana) that have Democrats in the lead but are too close to call official. If those two go to the Democrats, they will take control of the U.S. Senate. Unfortunately, this could go on a lot longer than most anticipate as Virginia law stipulates a recount for the loser if the race is decided by less than 1 percent. In a 2000 redux, lawyers, guns, and money are gearing up to fight any perceived improprieties that occurred during voting. (Okay, not the guns, but who knows?) This should also be the case for Montana. Remember, the power shift in the Senate is important, as the majority party sets the agenda and schedules the vote.*

For both houses of U.S. Congress, the majority party gets the chairmanships of all the committees, gets to have double (sometimes triple) the staffing levels, and of course sets the course for legislation. This is why it's important who controls, even with a small majority. However, as Republicans remember all too well, you can have a change in membership that can shift who is in the majority without an election. Jim Jeffords is a great example of this behavior. Certainly with the Senate this tight, it could happen again. Another interesting question is whether Joe Lieberman will always caucus with the Democrats, as he was abandoned by them in the primary.

President Bush: *Today, he will give a speech at 1 PM ET that I assume will outline his strategy for how he will deal with the new shape of Congress. I believe he will attempt to reach across the aisle to Pelosi to see if they can work together to enact legislation, and I would bet he will invite her to come to the White House. There may be room for issues like reducing costs for college and immigration reform. For Bush, it's going to be a question of what he's willing to give to get what he wants. Does he agree to environmental or labor provisions on trade to get fast-tracked? Does he give in to something* *more onerous for Republicans just to get something done and then upset conservatives going into 2008? How closely will John McCain be involved?*

The President's desire to compromise may be severely limited by something like an investigation into Iraq and the administration's National Intelligence Estimate. Remember, Michigan Democrat John Conyers Jr. takes over the chairmanship of the U.S. House Judiciary Committee. As an indication of his view of Bush, Conyers released a report entitled, "The Constitution in Crisis: The Downing Street Minutes and Deception, Manipulation, Torture, Retributions, and Cover-ups in the Iraq War." This is an edited collection of information intending to serve as evidence that the Bush administration altered intelligence to justify the invasion of Iraq. The conclusion of the report: President Bush and Vice President Cheney should be censured. I wonder if House Democrats now feel they have the mandate of the U.S. electorate to do this?

It's a brave new world for U.S. politics and it won't be pretty. *For the markets, this should be good for bonds, okay for large caps, bad for small caps, and bad for the U.S. dollar. U.S. stocks are going to open lower, bonds higher, and the buck lower in the immediate response to the outcome. It's hard to be positive for the markets if there are subpoenas, investigations, and acrimony between the legislative and executive branches of government.*

PARTING SHOT

It is not a stretch to understand that modern war is more compact in its time frame. It's unlikely that we will have another conflict that lasts as long as the Iran-Iraq war or the Soviet Union–Afghanistan war (both around nine years). This means the "shock and awe" effect is not limited to the battlefield, but also operates in the financial markets. Price movements are severe, but short-lived. Yet, the financial instruments that are impacted are consistent across the last two major conflicts. This shouldn't be surprising given that both occurred in the Middle East and in the same country. However, it's instructive to understand that conflict disrupts whatever goods are being traded out of that area. When the disruption hits a key commodity like energy, the fallout cascades across many economic areas and financial markets. This is one of the major reasons the world focuses so intently on the Middle East and not on other areas of the world that have conflicts.

Conclusion

Prior to 1996, most in the agricultural markets didn't spend too much time worrying about what farmers fed their cattle. Prior to 2001, most in the financial markets didn't spend much time analyzing U.S. foreign policy. Prior to 2005, most in the financial markets didn't spend much time analyzing weather patterns. Suffice it to say, things have changed as infectious diseases, terrorist activities, and hurricanes have all made their presence felt in ways that shocked the world and financial markets. The impact from these events has been concentrated into a shorter time frame due to vastly improved means of communication across the planet. Therefore, the effect is more pronounced and sharp.

The goal of this book was to show that there are consistent characteristics that events have over time. You can begin to build a strategy or portfolio and be ready to take advantage of these events should they start to appear. Of course, no new event will be exactly the same as the previous event, nor will the exact timing be the same. This means that the trader needs to be flexible and creative in figuring out what area will be impacted and when.

This book is somewhat the antithesis of program or model trading. World event trading (WET) requires an intimate knowledge of numbers and statistics, but not as the sole determinant for making money. This is more nuanced, more difficult, and more exciting. The results can be spectacular, as the events that we've covered generate extreme price movement and opportunities. These are the famous "three-tailed" or three standard deviation events that can destroy model traders who don't have strong risk management programs. To the uneducated, they seem to appear out of nowhere to disrupt trading.

As an example, look what happened to Pacific Ethanol, Inc. (PEIX) after President Bush mentioned cellulosic ethanol in his State of the Union address in 2006. At first, everyone thought he just mispronounced something about energy. Figure C.1 shows the jump in price and the sustained upward movement for this ethanol producer. This seemed to be a total surprise until one considered the desire by politicians to reduce the U.S. dependence on foreign oil and the impact of hurricanes on oil and gas production. What

```
PEIX US $                      14.53/14.54   7x8        Equity GPO
DELAY          987,381    14.38    14.66        14.38        14281995
                                        GPO - Bar Chart              Page 1/36
```

FIGURE C.1   Pacific Ethanol, Inc. (PEIX)

better way than to encourage the corn belt to become the Saudi Arabia of
ethanol? It's interesting to note that Bill Gates' Cascade Investment LLC said
in November 2005 that it planned to boost its stake in the Fresno, California,
company to 27 percent.

This is one of the many reasons why we in the financial markets monitor
what the president says in the State of the Union address, whether it's
"cellulosic ethanol" or the "axis of evil." These are pieces of the political
puzzle for the WET trader.

Having traded the foreign exchange markets for over 20 years, I can tell
you that making money is not easy. You need to take advantage of every
opportunity, every edge you can to gain advantage over the market. Inefficiencies in the financial markets don't occur with regularity. Model trading
quickly eliminates many of these. There are so many PhDs of statistics and
math from Beijing to Bucharest analyzing different quantitative angles to
trading that inefficiencies exist for only a short period of time. However, it's
almost impossible to mathematically represent SARS or Hurricane Katrina.
This is why you need an understanding of how an event develops and how
to capitalize on the situation when it occurs. WET requires broader knowledge of the planet and how it has functioned during these events over time
to generate outsized profits.

With this book, you have begun the process to do just that.

Bibliography

"Antiterror Effort Up: Even as Threat Wanes U.S. to Spend $7 Billion Next Year, While Number of Attacks Has Fallen by Nearly Two-Thirds since 1987." *Christian Science Monitor*, May 14, 1998.

Baker, Nick. "Pacific Ethanol Rises as Bush Touts Alternative Fuels." Bloomberg, January 30, 2006.

Banham, Cynthia. "Time Running Out for Pacific Climate Change Strategy." *Sydney Morning Herald*, February 13, 2006. www.smh.com.au/news/national/time-running-out-for-pacific-climate-change-strategy/2006/02/12/1139679480802.html.

Barry, John M. *The Great Influenza: The Epic Story of the Deadliest Plague in History*. New York: Viking Penguin Group, 2004.

Berkeley Seismological Laboratory. "Where Can I Learn More about the 1989 Earthquake?" http://seismo.berkeley.edu/faq/1989_0.html.

Blake, Eric S., et al. "The Deadliest, Costliest, and Most Intense United States Tropical Cyclones from 1851 to 2004." National Oceanic and Atmospheric Administration (NOAA), 2005. www.nhc.noaa.gov/pastcost.shtml.

Campbell, Ballard C., and William G. Shade, eds. *American Presidential Campaigns and Elections*. Vol. 1. Armonk, NY: Sharpe Reference, 2003.

CNN. "Pakistan Puts Quake Toll at 18,000: Emergency Workers Toil through the Night; Deaths High in Kashmir." Satinder Bindra, Syed Mohsin Naqvi and John Raedler as well as journalists Mukhtar Ahmed and Tom Coghlan contributed to this report (October 9, 2005). http://edition.cnn.com/2005/WORLD/asiapcf/10/08/quake.pakistan/.

Coll, Steve. *Ghost Wars: The Secret History of the CIA, Afghanistan, and Bin Laden, from the Soviet Invasion to September 10, 2001*. New York: Penguin Press, 2004.

Commission of Inquiry into the Sponsorship Program and Advertising Activities, http://gomery.ca/ and http://epe.lac-bac.gc.ca/100/206/301/pco-bcp/commissions/sponsorship-ef/06-03-06/www.gomery.ca/en/default.htm.

Commonwealth Scientific and Industrial Research Organisation. www.its.csiro.au/.

Council on Foreign Relations. "Energy, Resources, and Environment—Research Links." www.cfr.org/publication/4918/energy_resources_and_environment_research_links.html.

Crosby, Alfred W. *America's Forgotten Pandemic: The Influenza of 1918*. New York: Cambridge University Press, 1989, 2003.

Darlington, Richard B. "The Electoral College: Bulwark Against Fraud." Cornell University, n.d. www.psych.cornell.edu/Darlington/electorl.htm.

de Boer, Jelle Zeilinga, and Donald Theodore Sanders. *Earthquakes in Human History: The Far Reaching Effects of Seismic Disruptions*. Princeton, NJ: Princeton University Press, 2005.

Deutsch, Claudia H., "'Carbon Leaders' and 'Carbon Dogs' Join Gauges for Climate Investment (*NYT* 05/31/06)." www.iht.com/articles/2006/05/24/business/green.php.

Diamond, Jared. *Guns, Germs, and Steel: The Fates of Human Societies*. New York: W. W. Norton & Company, 1997, 1999.

Douglas, Paul. *Restless Skies: The Ultimate Weather Book*. New York: Sterling Publishing Company, 2005.

Dreazen, Yochi J. "White House Reflects on Steps Taken since Sept. 11 Attacks." *Wall Street Journal*, September 11, 2006. http://online.wsj.com/article_print/SB115792351278958822.html.

Ellsworth, W. L. "Earthquake History, 1769–1989." Chap. 6 of R. E. Wallace, ed., *The San Andreas Fault System, California*. U.S. Geological Survey Professional Paper 1515, 1990, 152–187.

Emanuel, Kerry. *Divine Wind: The History and Science of Hurricanes*. New York: Oxford University Press, 2005.

Environmental Protection Agency. "Climate Change." http://epa.gov/climatechange/index.html.

Fischer, David Hackett. *The Great Wave: Price Revolutions and the Rhythm of History*. New York: Oxford University Press, 1996.

Flannery, Tim. *The Weather Makers: How Man Is Changing the Climate and What It Means for Life on Earth*. New York: Grove/Atlantic, 2005.

Food and Agriculture Organization of the United Nations. "Animal Health: Avian Influenza." www.fao.org/ag/againfo/subjects/en/health/diseases-cards/special_avian.html.

Food and Agriculture Organization of the United Nations. "Economics: The Vietnam Perspective." www.fao.org/ag/againfo/subjects/en/economics/facts/vietnam.html.

Franken, Bob, and John King. "Lewinsky Has Spoken." www.cnn.com/ALLPOLITICS/1998/01/26/clinton.main/.

Gale, Jason. "Bird Flu Infects 3 People a Week; Spreads to Egypt." Bloomberg, March 22, 2006.

Garrett, Laurie. "The Next Pandemic?" *Foreign Affairs*, July/August 2005. http://foreignaffairs.org/20050701faessay84401/laurie-garrett/the-next-pandemic.html.

Gilbert, Martin. *A History of the Twentieth Century*. Vol. 1, *1900–1913*. New York: HarperCollins, 1997.

Gilbert, Martin. *A History of the Twentieth Century*. Vol. 3, *1952–1999*. New York: HarperCollins, 1999.

Global Security.org. "Khalid Sheikh Mohammed." www.globalsecurity.org/military/world/para/ksm.htm.

Greenfeld, Karl Taro. *China Syndrome: The True Story of the 21st Century's First Great Epidemic*. New York: HarperCollins, 2006.

Hansen, Gladys, and Emmet Condon. *Denial of Disaster: The Untold Story and Photographs of the San Francisco Earthquake and Fire of 1906*. San Francisco: Cameron & Company, 1989.

Harris, Paul, and Mark Townsend. "Now the Pentagon Tells Bush: Climate Change Will Destroy Us." *UK Observer International*, February 22, 2004. http://observer.guardian.co.uk/international/story/0,6903,1153513,00.html.

Homeland Security Council. "National Strategy for Pandemic Influenza." www.whitehouse.gov/homeland/pandemic-influenza.html.

Homer, Sidney, and Richard Sylla. *A History of Interest Rates*. New Brunswick, NJ: Rutgers University Press, 1996.

HowStuffWorks. "How the Electoral College Works." http://people.howstuffworks.com/electoral-college6.htm.

John, T. Jacob. "Learning from Plague in India." *Lancet* 344, no. 8928 (October 8, 1994).

Kimberling, William C. "The Electoral College." Federal Election Commission, n.d.

Knutson, Thomas R., and Robert E. Tuleya. "Impact of CO_2-Induced Warming on Simulated Hurricane Intensity and Precipitation: Sensitivity to the Choice of Climate Model and Convective Parameterization." *Journal of Climate* (September 15, 2004). www.gfdl.noaa.gov/reference/bibliography/2004/tk0401.pdf.

LeVay, Simon, and Kerry Sieh. *The Earth in Turmoil: Earthquakes, Volcanoes, and Their Impact on Humankind*. New York: W. H. Freeman & Company, 1998.

Marland, G., T. A. Boden, and R. J. Andres. "Global, Regional, and National CO_2 Emissions." In *Trends: A Compendium of Data on Global Change*. Oak Ridge, TN: Carbon Dioxide Information Analysis Center, Oak Ridge National Laboratory, U.S. Department of Energy, 2006.

Martin, Mark. "A Global Warming Moment: Governor Signs Measure Capping Greenhouse Gas Emissions That Could Lead to Big Changes in Industries and Life in Cities." *San Francisco Chronicle*, September 28, 2006. http://sfgate.com/cgi-bin/article.cgi?f=/c/a/2006/09/28/WARMING.TMP.

Mayer, Martin. *The Fed: The Inside Story of How the World's Most Powerful Financial Institution Drives the Markets*. New York: Free Press, 2001.

Meade, Melinda, et al. "Human Health in the Balance, Unit 4: Putting It All Together; A Case Study Analysis." www.aag.org/HDGC?www/health/units/unit4/html/4bkground.html.

Michaels, Patrick J. "Is the Sky Really Falling? A Review of Recent Global Warming Scare Stories." Policy Analysis no. 576, Cato Institute, August 23, 2006. www.cfr.org/publication/11453/cato_institute.html.

Moore, John L. *Elections A to Z*. Washington, DC: CQ Press, 2003.

Moore, Molly. "Plague Turns India into Region's Pariah: Outbreak of Disease Hurts Tourism, Trade," *Washington Post*, October 2, 1994, A29, A33.

Multi-Community Environmental Storm Observatory. www.mcwar.org.

National Commission on Terrorist Attacks Upon the United States. www.9-11commission.gov.

National Oceanic and Atmospheric Administration (NOAA). http://hurricanes.noaa.gov.

National Oceanic and Atmospheric Administration (NOAA). *A Study of Earthquake Losses in the San Francisco Bay Area—Data and Analysis: A Report Prepared for the Office of Emergency Preparedness*. Washington, DC: U.S. Department of Commerce, 1972.

Nature Conservancy. "Climate Change: What's New." www.nature.org/initiatives/climatechange/strategies/art16919.html.

New York Magazine. "9/11 by the Numbers." www.newyorkmetro.com/news/articles/wtc/1year/numbers.htm

Nezavisimaya Gazeta, Moscow. "Who Is to Blame?" www.gateway2russia.com/art/Current%20Topics/Who%20is%20to%20blame_252029.html.

NOAA National Weather Service. *NOAA Reviews Record-Setting 2005 Atlantic Hurricane Season*. www.noaanews.noaa.gov/stories2005/s2540.htm.

Overpeck, Jonathan T. "Paleoclimatic Evidence for Future Ice Sheet Instability and Rapid Sea-Level Rise." *Science* 311 (2006): 1747–1750.

Pallipparambil-Robert, Godshen. "The Surat Plague and Its Aftermath." http://scarab.msu.montana.edu/historybug/YersiniaEssays/Godshen.htm.

Pape, Robert A. *Dying to Win: The Strategic Logic of Suicide Terrorism*. New York: Random House, 2005.

Posner, Richard A. *Breaking the Deadlock: The 2000 Election, the Constitution and the Courts*. Princeton, NJ: Princeton University Press, 2001.

Prager, Ellen. *Furious Earth: The Science and Nature of Earthquakes, Volcanoes, and Tsunamis*. New York: McGraw-Hill, 2000.

Qayum, Khalid. "Pakistani Stocks Decline on Concern 'Badla' Financing to End." Bloomberg, April 19, 2005.

Reier, Sharon. "Weathering the Storm of Climate Change." *International Herald Tribune*, September 29, 2006. www.iht.com/articles/2006/09/29/yourmoney/mweather.php.

Revkin, A. C. "Global Warming Is Expected to Raise Hurricane Intensity." *New York Times*, September 30, 2004, A20.

Schlager, Neil, and Jayne Weisblatt, eds. *World Encyclopedia of Political Systems and Parties*, 4th ed. New York: Facts on File/Infobase Publishing, 2006.

Schlosser, Eric. *Fast Food Nation: The Dark Side of the All-American Meal*. Boston: Houghton Mifflin Company, 2001.

Secrest, Alan, David Walker, and Grover G. Norquist. "Direct Democracy: Good or Bad?" www.findarticles.com/p/articles/mi_m2519/is_n8_v16/ai_17379223. August 1995.

Sheen, Barbara. *Mad Cow Disease*. San Diego, CA: Lucent Books, 1995.

Stewart, Gail B. *Catastrophe in Southern Asia: The Tsunami of 2004*. San Diego, CA: Lucent Books, 2005.

Sunstein, Cass, and Richard Epstein, eds. *The Vote: Bush, Gore, and the Supreme Court*. Chicago: University of Chicago Press, 2001.

Tadaki, Joy. "Japan Stocks Fall as Quake Shakes Insurers, Railways." Bloomberg News, January 17, 1995.

Teunissen, Jan Josst, and Age Akkerman, eds. *The Crisis That Was Not Prevented: Lessons for Argentina, the IMF, and Globalisation*. The Hague: Forum on Debt and Development (FONDAD), 2003.

Thomas, Evan. "The New Age of Terror: Soldiers in the War on Terror Have Learned Much since 9/11. So, Too, Has the Enemy. How the London Plot Was Foiled—and Where We Are in the Five-Year Struggle." *Newsweek*, August 21, 2006, 38.

Thompson, Dick. "Why U.S. Environmentalists Pin Hopes on Europe." *Time*, March 26, 2001. www.time.com/time/world/article/0,8599,103985,00.html.

Time Magazine Editors. *Hurricane Katrina: The Storm That Changed America*. New York: Time Books, 2005.

Toobin, Jeffery. *Too Close to Call: The Thirty-Six-Day Battle to Decide the 2000 Election*. New York: Random House, 2001.

Tysmans, Judith B. "Plague in India 1994—Conditions, Containment, Goals." University of North Carolina at Chapel Hill, School of Public Health, Health Policy and Administration. http://ucis.unc.edu/resources/pubs/Carolina/Plague.html.

UNESCO. "Tsunami: The Great Waves." http://ioc3.unesco.org/itic/files/great_waves_en_2006_small.pdf.

U.S. Department of Health and Human Services. "A Guide for Individuals and Families." www.pandemicflu.gov/planguide/checklist.html.

U.S. Geological Survey. "Historic Earthquakes: 1906 San Francisco." http://earthquake.usgs.gov/regional/states/events/1906_04_18_pics_1.php.

U.S. Geological Survey. "Largest and Deadliest Earthquakes by Year." http://earthquake.usgs.gov/regional/world/byyear.php.

U.S. Geological Survey. "Top 10 Lists and Maps of Earthquakes." http://earthquake.usgs.gov/eqcenter/top10.php.

Wald, D. J., H. Kanamori, D. V. Helmbeger, and T. H. Heaton."Source Study of the 1906 San Francisco Earthquake." *Bulletin of the Seismological Society of America* 83 (1993): 981–1019.

Wattenberg, Martin P. "The Democrats' Decline in the House during the Clinton Presidency: An Analysis of Partisan Swings." *Presidential Studies Quarterly* 29, 1999.

Whitelaw, Kevin. "Remembering, and Wondering What's Next (Anniversary of London Terrorist Bombings)." *U.S. News & World Report* 141, no. 2 (July 17, 2006): 14–15.

Wood, Daniel B. "California Tackles Greenhouse Emissions." *Christian Science Monitor*, April 18, 2006. www.csmonitor.com/2006/0418/p03s03-sten.html.

World Health Organization. "H5N1: Avian Influenza: A Timeline." www.who.int/csr/disease/avian_influenza/timeline.pdf.

World Health Organization. *SARS: How a Global Epidemic Was Stopped*. Manila: WHO Regional Office for the Western Pacific, 2006.

Zelizer, Julian E. *On Capitol Hill: The Struggle to Reform Congress and Its Consequences 1948–2000*. New York: Cambridge University Press, 2004.

Index

237